W9-BDE-992

CRITICAL PRAISE FOR
BAD COMPANY!

"A thorough, smart book like this is the only way to get the whole story . . . fascinating reading . . . riveting."

—*Cosmopolitan*

"A quintessential story of the cocaine-driven eighties, a fast-paced tale of spoiled traffickers, greedy parasites on ill-gotten gains, and murder most foul."

—John H. Davis, author of
Mafia Kingfish

"The best kind of investigative journalism because it examines motives as well as deeds."

—John Hubner, co-author of
Monkey on a Stick

"So gripping it leaves you wired."

—*Kirkus Reviews*

"Reads like a Hollywood murder mystery à la Elmore Leonard. . . . Not only stranger than fiction, but as grisly as Stephen King's darkest fantasies."

—Bud Schulberg,
author of *What Makes Sammy Run?*

St. Martin's Paperbacks titles are available at quantity discounts for sales promotions, premiums or fund raising. Special books or book excerpts can also be created to fit specific needs.

For information write to special sales manager, St. Martin's Press, 175 Fifth Avenue, New York, N.Y. 10010.

BAD COMPANY

DRUGS,
HOLLYWOOD,
AND THE
COTTON CLUB
MURDER

STEVE WICK

ST. MARTIN'S PAPERBACKS

NOTE: If you purchased this book without a cover you should be aware that this book is stolen property. It was reported as 'unsold and destroyed' to the publisher, and neither the author nor the publisher has received any payment for this 'stripped book.'

to Debbie

"I Want It all" by Freddie Mercury, John Deacon, Roger Taylor & Brian May © 1989 QUEEN MUSIC LTD. All rights controlled and administered by SCREEN GEMS-EMI MUSIC INC. All rights reserved. International copyright secured. Used by permission.

Excerpt from "The Hollow Men" in *Collected Poems 1909-1962*, copyright 1936 by Harcourt Brace Jovanovich, Inc., and copyright © 1964, 1963 by T. S. Eliot. Reprinted by permission of Harcourt Brace Jovanovich, Inc., and Faber and Faber Ltd.

Published by arrangement with Harcourt Brace Jovanovich

BAD COMPANY

Copyright © 1990 by Steve Wick.
Postscript to the Paperback Edition copyright © 1991 by Steve Wick.
Unanswered Cries excerpt copyright © 1991 by Thomas French.
Photographs of Bob Evans and Roy Radin courtesy of Ron Galella Ltd. Photograph of Laney Greenberger courtesy of *The Okeechobee News*.

All rights reserved. No part of this book may be used or reproduced in any manner whatsoever without written permission except in the case of brief quotations embodied in critical articles or reviews. For information address Permissions, Harcourt Brace Jovanovich, Publishers, Orlando, Florida 32887.

Library of Congress Catalog Card Number: 90-33215

ISBN: 0-312-92517-4

Printed in the United States of America

Harcourt Brace Jovanovich edition published 1990
St. Martin's Paperbacks edition/November 1991

10 9 8 7 6 5 4 3 2 1

Author's Note

A WORD ON METHODOLOGY IS IN ORder. The material in this book was based on interviews conducted over a period of several years. In addition to interviews, I also used court records, in Florida, New York, and California, as the basis for parts of the narrative.

The record of criminal proceedings in Los Angeles is particularly detailed and voluminous, for which I am grateful. The proceedings arising out of the events recounted in the chapters of this book and the epilogue are still pending. All the accused have pleaded not guilty.

The dialogue that appears throughout the text is derived mostly from the versions of events provided to me in my interviews. In addition, I have based dialogue on the testimony of witnesses at criminal proceedings, and on the statements of persons interviewed by the authorities.

These statements are contained in investigators' reports, a kind of diary kept by Los Angeles County detectives of people they interviewed and what they were told. Mostly, the comments of persons interviewed by detectives were written down in these reports in a long narrative. For sty-

listic reasons, I have taken some of these statements and put them in the form of quotes.

S. W.
New York
March 1990

PROLOGUE

IN SOUTHERN CALIFORNIA, THE COUN-
try near the town of Gorman is remarkably
rugged. There are ravines and gullies where the
terrain is steep and irregular, rising and falling
sharply. The soil is alternately rocky and sandy,
covered with thin grasses, scrub oaks, and desert
bushes. In the summer, the temperature can be
fiercely hot; at night, it can drop sharply. The
landscape seems almost primitive.

On the morning of June 10, 1983, Glen Fischer
was headed toward Gorman in his Ford pickup.
The alarm had gone off at six o'clock, and by
seven Fischer was moving east along Route 126.
He was feeling good, and even the heat could not
dampen his enthusiasm. He poked at the controls
on the air conditioner, the cool air barely filling
the cab.

Owner and operator of a company called
Fischer Apiaries, he was looking for a remote
canyon where he could store his one hundred
twenty beehives. His mission was to find a place
rich with sage and buckwheat, where his bees
could forage unmolested and produce gallons of

golden honey, which he hoped to sell at a considerable profit.

With temperatures rising into the high nine-
ties, it was important that he get his day's work
done quickly. His shirt already lacquered to his
back by sweat, Fischer was uncomfortable from
the heat, and it was barely two hours after sunrise. He tried to coax more cool air from the air
conditioner as he passed through the sleepy
towns of Fillmore and Piru. At the Saugus junc-
tion, he turned north on Interstate 5, and now he
was heading toward Gorman.

Fischer called this section of the interstate the
ridge road. It rose sharply from Saugus to an ele-
vation of more than four thousand feet, and there
it continued on toward Bakersfield. Fortunately
for him, Fischer was not headed that far. All he
had to do was drive partway up the ridge road,
where he was to pull off and wait at a designated
wide spot in the frontage road. There, at eight-
thirty, he was to meet a park ranger, get into her
truck, and scout out possible bee sites.

The ranger, a pretty, well-spoken woman
named Lynn, arrived, and Fischer proceeded
north on the interstate in her truck. They were in
what was called lower chaparral country, an
area of small, low-lying scrub oaks, greasewood,
and manzanita, a chaparral plant with distinc-
tive red bark and a lovely grayish leaf. This was
not forest; on the contrary, it looked more like
desert than anything else.

At the Hungry Valley exit, they turned off, continuing north on a frontage road, then east into a
narrow canyon on a poorly maintained dirt road,
called, on some older maps, Caswell Canyon
Road. A quarter mile east of the frontage road, it
abruptly ended. It was ten-thirty when the

ranger stopped the truck and Fischer jumped out.

"This looks very good," he said. All he could hear was the faint hum of freight trucks rumbling along the interstate.

Stepping out of the truck, Lynn said she thought it would be perfect for the bees; and, of the half-dozen sites Fischer had looked at on the topographical map, this one was not used by any other beekeepers.

"You'll be alone here," Lynn said.

With its steep washed-out sides, the narrow pass where the road ended was like a box canyon. There appeared to be only one way into the canyon, and Fischer could not imagine anyone else following the same road to this exact spot. He figured his bees would be safe here.

"I really think this is perfect," Fischer said, wiping the sweat off his forehead with a handkerchief. But as he headed away from the truck, his feet crunched on something, and he noticed a number of broken beer bottles and smashed cans. Stepping back, he saw piles of spent bullet casings littering the ground.

"Looks like someone's idea of a target range," he said, kicking at one of the shells with the point of his boot. It seemed like a long way to go just to fire off a gun.

The ranger said she agreed, noting that target shooters had trampled through a lot of the valleys in the area. She said she wanted to see if she could go farther up into the canyon, and she turned and moved away from the truck. As she left him, Fischer began walking back down along the edge of the road, toward a narrow, rocky gully. What he was looking for was a flat, open area of perhaps a half acre in size.

He was about a hundred yards from the truck when he smelled something truly horrible. Something's dead, he thought.

This alarmed him, not because he was afraid of coming across a dead animal, but because he needed to be certain there was nothing living in this canyon that would upset his hives. Like a bear, for instance.

Jesus, it really smells, he thought, thinking maybe a cow had wandered into the box canyon and been eaten by coyotes.

He walked in fifteen or twenty feet, toward the far side of the dry wash, and when he came around a greasewood bush he saw a hand sticking up toward the sky, with two fingers extended and partially separated, in the manner of a sixties peace sign. The flesh was yellow, the color of skin stained by nicotine.

Momentarily stunned, he stood and stared. It was clearly a human hand; there was no getting around that.

He slowly approached the hand, and as he got closer, he could see it was attached to some blue cloth. He could make out legs, or rather the shape of legs under more blue cloth, and the other arm and a portion of the top of a head, with a shock of brownish hair. He stopped again, staring at the ground in front of him.

Fischer stood trying to answer all the questions popping into his head. He did not know whose body he was looking at, but he was certain it did not belong here. This was no hiker who fell off a cliff, he thought. Or a hunter who had somehow shot himself. The blue cloth—a suit, perhaps— seemed to indicate that these fetid remains were those of a businessman. The rank odor indicated they had been here a long time, baking in this sun, picked at by predators. It seemed upon closer inspection that only a fraction of the original body was still there and the rest had melted away into the earth, the hand protruding as the body receded.

This was the first such body he had ever seen. He tried very hard to remain calm. At least the chance of confronting whoever it was that had left the body here was remote.

He inched a bit closer, his eyes focused on what was left of the head. One side of the face was mostly gone, leaving a portion of the skull on top and the jawline at the bottom. There was nothing in between but stained earth.

Jesus Christ, he thought, deliberately averting his eyes. The head had been destroyed, blown away. The body seemed to have crash-landed against the bush. Suddenly, Fischer pulled back. Overcome by the stench and the grotesque condition of the body, he turned quickly and went to find the ranger.

"There's a body in there," he said, out of breath.

Lynn was stunned. "What should we do?"

"There's no hurry. It won't do him any good. He's been dead a long time."

They left and went to the nearest ranger station, about two miles south at Pyramid Lake. There, the sheriff's office in nearby Gorman was called, and Fischer was told to wait so that he could escort a detective to the scene.

By early afternoon, the box canyon was crawling with Los Angeles County sheriff's deputies. This was a crime scene, so nothing was touched, not the corpse nor the ground around it, while the deputies waited for homicide detectives from Los Angeles to show up. Those who went over to examine the remains did so with handkerchiefs across their mouths.

Toward the middle of the afternoon, two homicide detectives arrived, Willi Ahn and Carlos Avila. Stout and muscular, with a calm, contemplative disposition, Avila had seen enough crime scenes in his career not to be sickened by this one. He stood over the remains and stared, and immediately noticed that buttons had been pulled off the front of the suit coat.

Must have been a struggle, Avila thought. Probably more than one shooter. Then they blasted him in the head, maybe six or eight times, a goddamn free-for-all. The whole side of his face, from the temple to the jaw, was sheared off, as if by a buzz saw. Considering the condition of the skull, it was certainly possible that a shotgun had been fired at point-blank range, sending the body reeling backward into the greasewood bush.

God, that hand, someone said. Just sticking up like that.

Like he'd been praying, someone else said.

Late in the afternoon, the sun retreated, casting long shadows into the box canyon. After Avila and Ahn were satisfied they had taken note of every detail, the Los Angeles County Medical Examiner's office removed the remains. Later, they were found to weigh only seventy pounds, confirming the theory that the victim had been dead a long time.

A check by Avila of the Los Angeles Police Department's computer records of missing persons cases revealed a month-old case concerning the disappearance of a New York theatrical producer named Roy Alexander Radin. The suit found in the canyon matched the one Radin had worn on the night he disappeared. Avila needed dental records to make a positive identification, and that would take several days. There was not much in the police department file to go on. Some names, some addresses—that was about it.

On the evening of May 13, twenty-eight days earlier, Roy Radin had been seen getting into a limousine in front of the Regency Hotel in Los Angeles with a beautiful woman from Miami named Karen DeLayne Jacobs. They were going to dinner in Beverly Hills. He was never seen alive again.

Listen all you people, come gather round
I gotta get me a game plan, gotta shake you to
   the ground
Just give me what I know is mine,
People do you hear me, just give me the sign,
It ain't much I'm asking, if you want the truth
Here's to the future for the dreams of youth,
I want it all, I want it all, I want it all, and I
   want it now
I want it all, I want it all, I want it all, and I
   want it now

—"I Want It All"
Queen

Between the idea
And the reality
Between the motion
And the act
Falls the Shadow

—"The Hollow Men"
T. S. Eliot

PART ONE

"LA RUBIA"

ONE

ON A SPRING AFTERNOON IN 1981 ON the outskirts of Miami, a thirty-year-old Honduran immigrant named Joe Amer loaded boxes of cocaine into the trunk of his Fiord Blue BMW. When he was finished, he locked the trunk, pulled on it just to be sure, and drove out of the parking lot of his modern apartment complex. His destination was an address south of the city.

He had played racquetball all morning, showered, and dressed in a designer jogging suit. The game had relaxed him, but he was still anxious. He had read a story in the *Miami Herald*: two Latin men, their bodies shot through with automatic-rifle fire, had been found on a street in South Miami. This worried Amer, although he was comforted by the belief that he had treated people fairly and had no enemies. There had been so much violence in the past year and so many murders. Now there were two more bullet-ridden bodies for the new refrigerated trailer the city was using to store corpses because the morgue was full.

Until recently, selling marijuana and cocaine had been a less bloody business. Now, with the murder rate escalating, the stakes were higher. Amer, who considered himself a gentleman, blamed Miami's violence on the Cubans, particularly the most recent arrivals, who had come in the Mariel boatlift in 1980. The drug dealers all had guns; many had automatics that could spray bullets. Amer owned a pistol, too, a Walther PPK, the kind James Bond carried. But he had not bought it with the idea that he might actually have to use it. Rather, it made him feel like a character in one of Ian Fleming's novels.

Today, Amer would have preferred to stay in his lavishly furnished apartment watching movies, but there was a reliable customer to meet, business to transact, and money to be deposited. A block from his destination, he saw a woman seated at the wheel of a red-and-white Cadillac. She was waiting for the light to change. He had seen her once before. He only knew her nickname—*"La Rubia,"* the blonde.

He stopped the car to study her. She did not notice him. He waited for as long as the light held, and when it changed he watched her car until it was lost in traffic. He continued on to an apartment complex and parked behind one of the tall buildings. The client was waiting by his car.

"Hey, *sēnor*," Amer said, getting out of the BMW. He opened the trunk, and quickly the boxes were transferred to the other car.

Then the man handed over an envelope. Amer opened it, running his thumb across the bills.

"Okay, *sēnor*." Amer nodded. With that, each man headed to his car and drove off.

Four months later, Amer guided his BMW through the light traffic in Coconut Grove, the tinted windows rolled up, the radio tuned to a rock-and-roll station.

He turned off the radio as he dropped down into the underground garage, the car's antenna retracting with a slightly audible hum. Amer liked that. He loved things that worked well, like fine watches and fine cars. On his wrist was a watch he had purchased for ten thousand dollars cash from a Colombian who owned a jewelry store along the Miracle Mile. Amer liked to run the tip of his index finger in circles over the glass face. He owned several expensive watches, and sometimes just thinking about which one to put on seemed like a challenge.

His watches, custom-made suits, and luxury cars—he owned a Mercedes, a Chevy Blazer, and the BMW—fit his style in this prosperous city. There were many rich enclaves in Miami, but his favorite was Coconut Grove, with its shaded streets and Spanish-style mansions surrounded by hedges and iron fences, fences that opened with the press of a button from a waiting car. For a man like Amer, there was nothing better than real money and, to go along with it, real class.

He slowed to a halt at the curb. The uniformed valet opened the door and handed Amer his ticket, which he slipped into the inside pocket of his custom-tailored Brioni suit jacket. Vain about his handsome, boyish looks, he lingered for a moment, preening himself in the rearview mirror. He ran his hands over his slicked-back, wavy black hair, straightened his shirt collar, and cinched up his Italian silk tie.

Stepping out of the car, he reached for the wad of bills in his pants pocket and peeled off a few, handing them to the valet. More cars were pulling up to the curb—Porsches, Jaguars,

Mercedeses, BMWs. A playboy who loved Miami's nightlife, Amer went out almost every evening. There were members-only clubs in the city he preferred for their elitist clientele, but more and more he found himself drawn to Faces in the Grove. He stepped inside the glass elevator for the ride to the third floor. On the way up, he saw the lights of Coconut Grove glittering at his feet.

There was a long line at the door to the club, but Amer did not stand and wait. He walked up to the bouncer, whom he knew well, went right past everyone, and strolled in. On this night, Faces in the Grove was filled past capacity. Here, the up-and-coming millionaire cocaine smugglers, pioneers in the biggest growth business America had ever known, gathered around the tables that encircled the dance floor. They talked in their broken English about their boats, their cars, their watches, their clothes, their houses, their bank accounts, and what their old friends were doing back in South America in their dusty hometowns.

Amer looked around for familiar faces. The disco was decorated with glass and mirrored walls, red leather furnishings, circular tables, and private booths in which guests laid out lines of cocaine and chased them with expensive champagne. These were Amer's friends. They were like him: young and rich and Latin, immigrants to the promised land. A number of heads turned toward him, and Amer nodded. He walked to the bar and ordered a Scotch on the rocks. Sipping his drink, he leaned against the long bar and looked around the room. He felt as if he was on top of the world.

Amer ordered a second Scotch. Scanning the

room, he noticed a beautiful dark-haired Cuban-American woman, Sylvia Diaz Verson. She was a close friend of one of Amer's oldest friends, Joe Rodriguez. Like Amer, Rodriguez was a Honduran who had found great riches in Miami.

Sylvia was sitting in a private booth with a striking blond woman. Amer walked through the crowd to get to their table.

"Hello, Sylvia," Joe said, bending down to kiss her on the cheek.

"*Muñeco*," Sylvia replied.

"How are you?" he asked, his eyes on her friend. "How's Joe Rodriguez treating you?"

"*Muñeco*," Sylvia said, "this is Laney . . . Laney Jacobs."

Laney's platinum hair, cut short and brushed away from her face, accented her high cheekbones and fair skin. Her eyes were dark brown. Her dress was a pale pink, so light it was almost white. She wore dangling silver earrings, and on her wrist was a gold-and-diamond Rolex watch. A large diamond on the ring finger of her left hand caught Amer's eye. Her nails were long and manicured and painted a deep red. Amer watched as she took a drag from her cigarette, exhaling the smoke slowly through her lips, which were painted the same deep red as her nails.

"Hello, gorgeous," he said, finally. "I'm Joe."

"How are you?" Laney said.

For a moment, they stared at each other. Then he laughed and said, "I'm much better now. How's by you?"

He sat down next to Laney and poured from a bottle of champagne the two women had cooling in a silver bucket. It was 1976 Taittinger, pink.

She continued to chat with Sylvia, speaking in a soft Southern accent.

Amer now realized he had seen her before. She was the wife of Adolfo Ferreira, Alfie to his friends, who was one of Amer's clients. He recalled seeing her behind the wheel of her red-and-white Cadillac. Alfie had moved to Key West, Amer had heard, and he wondered whether they had split up.

Her real name was Karen Jacobs, but the Colombians who brought cocaine into South Florida had given her the nickname *"La Rubia,"* a reference to the pale color of her hair. Very few of her acquaintances ever heard her called this; to them, she was Laney, a derivative of her middle name, DeLayne. She was the only American woman Amer knew of who worked in the upper levels of the Latin-dominated drug underworld in Miami. Amer had heard through various contacts that she was distributing twenty kilos of cocaine a week—perhaps close to one million dollars' worth.

They chatted and watched the dancing while sipping their champagne.

"What are you doing tomorrow?" Laney asked Amer. "I have a yacht in the morning. We're going for a cruise. Would you like to come?"

"Sure," he replied.

When they finished the champagne, Amer and Laney left the club. They rode back down in the glass elevator, her arm hooked through his, and into the underground garage. She listened intently while he talked. Amer liked that. When the valet came, she asked for her car—a white 911 Porsche Targa. Then he brought around Amer's BMW, sliding it up to the curb and holding the door open for him.

Certain she was looking, he handed the valet a new one-hundred-dollar bill. "For both," he said.

"Follow me," she said as she got into her car.

Amer followed her Porsche through the empty streets to a house at 6660 Southwest 125th Avenue. She drove in through the gate, down the drive, and into the garage. Amer left his BMW out front and followed her into the house through the kitchen door.

The interior of the house was all white, except for black Oriental furniture. Amer walked into the sunken living room. There was a formal dining room to the right of the living room, with a glass table and six black chairs. Spotlights in the backyard illuminated a swimming pool.

Amer, who considered himself a connoisseur, could see that, like himself, Laney had expensive tastes. In the living room, there was a long black couch by a fireplace. On the couch were black silk pillows, each with an Oriental-looking *L* painted on it. Over the fireplace, a Japanese kimono hung from a cross. Laney went into the kitchen and came out with a bottle of champagne and some glasses. She put on a record, Gino Vannelli.

They sat on the living room rug, drinking the champagne rather quickly. When they had emptied one bottle, Laney went and got a second. She handed Amer the bottle, and he opened it carefully so that the cork did not fly out. While he filled their glasses, she went to the kitchen. She returned with a hand-painted porcelain bowl filled with cocaine, which had been ground to a fine white powder. In the bowl was a tiny silver spoon.

Laney asked Amer where he was from, and he spoke about his hometown of San Pedro Sula.

He explained that his father was from Jordan
and had intended to come to America, but the
freighter captain went only as far as South
America. His father made the best of a bad situation, and shortly afterward he was the owner of a
prosperous hardware business.

Laney asked if Amer's father had wanted his
son to stay in Honduras. Of course, he answered,
but there was nothing there for him. America,
particularly Miami, was a lure he could not re-
sist.

He asked where she was from, and she said Alabama. That explains your accent, he told her,
and she laughed. She said she had arrived in
Miami in the mid-1970s and had immediately
loved it. And while she traveled a lot—the West
Coast, New York, and Mexico—she loved coming
back to Miami.

They sat in the living room, getting high and
talking, until the sun came up. In the morning,
Amer left to get a change of clothes. Then he
drove to a marina at Seventy-ninth Street, where
the fifty-three-foot *Temptress* was moored. Laney
was waiting, as were two attractive young
women, who she said were sisters, visiting from
La Jolla, California.

Amer was impressed with the yacht. He loved
the ocean, and so did Laney. Strung out from lack
of sleep and Laney's cocaine, Amer remarked
that he was a little wired. She offered him a
Quaalude, which she took from a small plastic
bottle in her purse. After he swallowed it, he
asked her if she had been to La Jolla. She said
she had, adding that she loved California.

The *Temptress* headed out into Biscayne Bay.
Amer and Laney and the sisters sat up on the

deck, enjoying champagne and stone crabs. Well out into the bay, the captain dropped anchor and everyone went swimming. Laney slipped off the top of her bikini, which disturbed Amer. He thought it showed lack of respect, and he told her so when she climbed on board.

"I know about you Latins." She laughed.

Back on land after sundown, the four drove to Laney's house. More cocaine was brought out, and Amer, still tired from the previous day, took a nap. When he awoke, he sat in the living room with the sisters. One of the sisters said she was married to a Mexican, and they remarked that this was a return trip for them.

Amer deduced that they were Laney's couriers, that cocaine had been taken out to California and now the sisters were back with the cash—drugs out, cash back. The next evening, the sisters left in a taxi for the airport.

TWO

JOE AMER WAS LIVING IN AN APARTMENT at 152nd and 90th Court, in the Miami suburb of Kendall. He had a maid, a pretty, long-haired Costa Rican named Myriam Plaza, whom he had met through Joe Rodriguez.

Amer had arrived, like so many young Latin Americans, on a commercial airliner when he was still a teenager. His father decided early on that his son needed an American education. So in 1966 he sent him to a private school in Louisiana run by the Christian Brothers.

When young Amer graduated from high school in 1971, he returned to San Pedro Sula. But after four years in the United States, he found his country backward, the economy stilted, the politics venal and corrupt. There was no promise there, nothing he could count on. So he turned his back on his father's plan to install his only son in his hardware business. Selling farm equipment and paintbrushes was not for Joe Amer.

In 1972, he flew to Miami, where he enrolled at Miami-Dade Community College as a marketing major—an apt choice of majors, considering

Amer's future profession. That year, Amer was twenty-one, and restless. He failed to graduate, and by the mid-1970s he was footloose and looking for something to do with his life. He found it at the private nightclubs favored by the young Latinos, clubs like Honey for the Bears, where a membership card was necessary for admission.

At these private clubs, Amer encountered the edge of the booming cocaine market. The marijuana trade that dominated the drug market until the 1970s was fading, replaced by the awesome profit potential of cocaine. Organizations were set up, distributorships sold, and the money was coming back so fast few people knew how to handle it.

Most of the principal players were Cubans, who regarded Hondurans as mixed-blood peasants—Indians, they called them. Once inside their world, Amer could not believe what he saw. It was incredible that a young Latino of no particularly important background could come to Miami, feel right at home, and within a matter of weeks, if not days, plug into the drug market. There was nothing to learn at all—no classes to attend, no degrees to earn, no hurdles to get over on the way to prosperity.

What seemed most incredible to Amer was that a distributor could buy on credit, paying back his supplier after he sold the product. And since cocaine could be sold quickly, he could repay the Cuban he had bought it from in just a matter of days, if not hours. This way, he could work up to larger and larger quantities, on up to boatloads and planeloads.

If he was particularly ambitious, Amer found, he could sell to a network of distributors—in Phoenix and Philadelphia and Boston—who would in turn retail the product. They would drive to Miami, pick up the cocaine, take it home, and return later with the cash. The market was everywhere, and it was bottomless. All Amer and his friends had to do was put their product on the street, and it would be sold.

On the night Amer rode the glass elevator and stepped out into the loud disco music at Faces in the Grove, he was a midlevel player in his own sizable network. He had well-established connections to major players such as Joe Rodriguez, who was bright, motivated, and enterprising. Rodriguez had created a hugely profitable cocaine network, which had enabled him to buy an interest in the Collection, a luxury-car dealership in Miami.

Nearly everything Amer had acquired since coming to Miami, in fact, had come through his friendship with Rodriguez. On their first incursion into cocaine marketing, they netted four hundred dollars total on a four-ounce sale, two hundred dollars each. It was an inauspicious beginning, but Amer was thrilled. Rodriguez, more ambitious than Amer, quickly connected himself with bigger traders. He wanted to move, to make a name for himself, while Amer was content to watch from the sidelines. Besides, Amer quickly learned to hate the Cubans, whom he regarded as men without honor, capable of extreme violence over the most minor of disputes.

The key to success lay in making contacts in Colombia, and Rodriguez reached out through several Miami-based dealers so that he could begin direct importations. On his first attempt, he brought in one pound of cocaine hidden inside the tires of a motorcycle he flew into Tamiami Airport, south of Miami. It was easier than he had ever imagined it would be—there were no hassles whatsoever, not even one curious bureaucrat asking questions about the motorcycle.

Soon Rodriguez began flying lessons, telling Amer he could do the flying himself so they would not have to go through the difficulty of hiring pilots for each load. Every time a smuggler hired a pilot, he was rolling the dice, and Rodriguez wanted to cut his odds down. This allowed him to get bigger, and soon he was bringing in two-hundred-kilo loads of Colombian-processed, nearly pure cocaine that could be "stepped on" numerous times to make it fantastically profitable. At fifty thousand dollars per kilo, a two-hundred-kilo load flown in from Colombia and unloaded on a cattle ranch in central Florida or at a rural airport in Georgia was worth more money than two Hondurans could possibly spend.

In the early stages of cocaine importation, Rodriguez would hire himself out as a transporter, netting four thousand dollars per kilo as a flying fee. He liked the adventure, while Amer tended to shy away from midnight flights across the Gulf of Mexico and bumpy landings on dirt strips in the Colombian jungle. Rodriguez's pattern was to fly from southern Florida to Honduras, refuel, then go back up and cross into Colombia. Near the Magdalena River, he dropped down onto a dirt strip, where the plane was loaded by Colombian army troops. Then he would fly back to Honduras, where the plane would be protected by Honduran troops, and back across the Gulf to either the Panhandle or Alabama or Georgia.

Most times, he would circle low over a prearranged drop and kick out the packages. Rodriguez did at least seven trips, with Amer marketing the product on the American side. By the summer Amer met Laney Jacobs, he was netting $750,000 a year, and spending nearly all of it on clothes, jewelry, and cars.

A few days after the excursion on the *Temptress,* Amer moved his clothes into Laney Jacobs' house. This was not an exceptional act for him, for he had had dozens of girlfriends since his arrival in Miami. Nor was it remarkable for Laney. Amer was another Latin in her life. But Amer decided to hedge his bets and keep his Kendall apartment. He knew very little about Laney.

In many ways, Amer was like Alfie Ferreira, an excitable and high-strung man. Laney had dumped Ferreira soon after their wedding in 1980, which had come on the heels of her 1979 wedding, and almost immediate divorce, to an airline employee named Guillermo Suquet. She was not at all talkative about the men she had known, and she was particularly vague about her marriages. Amer knew about Alfie, of course, but he was not immediately told about Suquet, who, like Alfie, was a Cuban.

A constant in Laney's life was cocaine. She used it at night when she relaxed in the living room. She served it in a way reminiscent of a society queen's putting out the caviar at a cocktail party. She even kept it in the kitchen. It was stored in special bowls and colorful, ornate serving dishes she had collected in her travels. She did not act as if it was a drug. Nor did she act as if the mere possession of it could send her to prison.

Just three months before Laney met Amer, she had been stopped by a Miami policeman, who found cocaine, marijuana, and thirty thousand

dollars in cash in the glove box of her car. She
hired an attorney, a former Secret Service agent
named Frank Rubino, and he beat it in court by
challenging the legality of the car search. After
the charges were dismissed, Laney boasted that
she could do whatever she wanted and never get
caught.

In spite of her past track record with men, Laney's relationship with Amer appeared to flour-
ish. They enjoyed each other's company. In
particular, they loved going out on the town and
spending their money. One night she surprised
Amer by announcing that she wanted to have a
baby. She cried, talking about it, wiping her tears
with a pink-and-white handkerchief. She had to
have one now, and more to the point, it had to be
a boy. A boy would be the center of her life and
would slow her down, maybe force her to consider alternatives in her life, like taking her drug
profits and investing them in a legitimate business somewhere.

Sitting in the living room, listening to her favorite Italian singer, drinking champagne, she
talked about opening a boutique, perhaps in Beverly Hills. Or a jewelry store, or a hotel on the
ocean. California was where she wanted to be.

The way the rich lived out there—the big
houses, the cars—all that fascinated Laney. On
trips to Los Angeles, she had seen houses she
would have loved to move into—big, hedge-en-
closed mansions with long driveways and iron
gates.

"That's how I want to live," Laney told Amer.

It was 1947, and Alwin Jerome Jacobs was working as an automobile mechanic in a suburb of
Birmingham, Alabama. His wife, Barbara, a

pretty, strong-willed woman from a lower-middle-class background, was a housewife. They owned a small, wood-shingled house on Forrest Avenue in the suburb of Tarrant, where, in the third week of June, the couple brought home their first child, a daughter, whom they named Karen DeLayne Jacobs.

Two years later, on June 2, 1949, the couple had a son. The boy was named after his father but was soon nicknamed Buddy. At the time of his son's birth, Al Jacobs was working as a salesman for the Standard Coffee Company, and the family was living on Eighteenth Street in Birmingham.

By 1951, the family had moved again, to a house on Druid Hill Road. Now Al was working as a salesman at a Nash car dealership. Whether it was the family's unstable nature, or Al's seeming inability to keep a job for very long, or—as Barbara Jacobs charged—her husband's brutal behavior, the couple divorced in January 1952. In her petition to the court, Laney's mother accused her husband of beating her up repeatedly throughout their eight-year marriage. It had been a particularly bad beating, on June 22, 1951, that caused her to take the children and move out of the Druid Hill Road house and seek a divorce.

The war between the parents did not end with the divorce. Soon it turned into a custody battle, and the couple was back in court. In June 1958, Al Jacobs accused his wife of hiding the children from him. By that time, Laney's father was living in Miami, and a court order filed the same year gave him the right to see the children once a month—provided he had the means to drive to Birmingham—and during the Christmas holidays. Laney's mother remarried, a man named Maynord. That marriage would also fail.

By the early 1960s, the chaos in the household pushed the young Laney to the Georgia home of her grandparents, John Calvin and Willie Mae Smith. At first, the three lived in a rented house on Favor Road, across the street from Osborn High School, where Laney was enrolled in 1963. Shortly after Laney entered, they moved into a bigger house, on Renee Lane in Marietta.

In high school, Laney was a member of the Pep Club, the school's most popular club, the Drama Club, and the Future Homemakers of America. She particularly enjoyed the Future Homemakers, which strove to "teach high school girls high values . . . good citizenship and civic responsibility." The club conducted charity fund drives, held tea parties for teachers, gave fashion shows, and staged an annual dance at which a club queen was chosen.

Acting as her surrogate parents, the Smiths tried to show Laney the Christian way and keep her on a straight and narrow path. They instilled in her the solid values of their church, and they believed she accepted those values. Laney showed enthusiasm for teaching Sunday school at the United Methodist Church, where her step-grandfather also taught, and this pleased the God-fearing Smiths.

The Smiths did everything for Laney. They bought her a car, a Pontiac, they accepted her friends, one of whom was married in their living room, and they loaned her money. But what they did never seemed to be enough. Perhaps because of her troubled upbringing, Laney was a spoiled and temperamental teenager, and when she did not get what she wanted, she would go off and live with her mother.

Laney ran with a fast crowd. She smoked and

drank despite arguments with her grandparents.
She even forged her grandfather's signature on
checks. The Smiths always forgave her, blaming
her behavior on her mother's influence. Whatever effect Laney's mother may or may not have
had on her, mother and daughter shared one
trait—Barbara loved Barbara, and Laney loved
Laney.

By the time Laney reached her early twenties,
contact with her grandparents had become less
and less frequent. In 1971, she married a Cuban
named Manuel Enrique Gonzales; two years
later, just after divorcing Gonzales, she married
a North Carolina man named Leon Scott Goodman.

In 1975, now divorced from Goodman, she was
living in Miami, driving a VW Beetle, and working as a legal secretary for a civil attorney named
Philip Freidin. She dressed very well and talked
a lot about going to clubs and meeting new men,
particularly Latins. She still loved a fast crowd.
She wanted glamour, fast cars, fast men, and
loud dance clubs. Her appearance meant everything to her.

Soon her friends saw her with men they knew
were marijuana and cocaine dealers. She seemed
to be intrigued by the drug scene. Shortly after
going to work for Freidin, Laney quit. She turned
up at another lawyer's office, but soon she left
there too. She was restless. Looking for ways to
make more money and, more important, to make
the kind of connections that would push her
deeper into Miami's drug underworld, she began
working at a massage parlor on Coral Way.
There, she met a Cuban marijuana dealer named
Tony, who had come with a group to celebrate a
friend's impending marriage.

When Tony left, she gave him her phone number, and soon he was seeing her regularly. Tony considered himself an important smuggler in the city's drug hierarchy. Almost immediately upon meeting him, she quit the massage parlor. She told him she did not want to be a working-class hero. Instead, she wanted to be wealthy enough to do anything she wanted with her life.

In the course of pursuing her goals, she met a number of Miami dealers, most of them Latins. One, though, was a young American named Ulysses, whom Laney had met at a club called The Mutiny. In her conversations with the dealer and his friends, she asked specific questions: How did you meet the Cuban distributor? How did he bring his loads into the country? Where was it stored? How was it distributed? Where was the money sent? She expected answers to her queries, and for the most part she was not disappointed.

With Tony and Ulysses, Laney proved she was sharp and willing to take risks by making her own connections. Her ambition surprised them. She knew how to use men to get what she wanted.

Soon after meeting her, Tony discovered that Laney was capable of making an end run around him to further her goals. She met his contacts behind his back and was making deals without him.

"She was a small fish in a very large ocean, and she wanted to be a big fish," Tony said of Laney. "By meeting me, she grew up. I was a means to an end."

Laney ran her drug business out of her house in Miami. She had a secretary to answer the phone.

Her customers, men and women who came from several parts of the country, were precise and reliable. They were the source of enormous amounts of cash, which Laney stored in a safe she'd had built into the floor in her bedroom.

One of her couriers was a polite and handsome airline steward in his early twenties named Ed Bolter.* Bolter brought cocaine out to the West Coast and returned with the cash. Laney considered him rock solid, a man unlikely to cause trouble or to get caught. He looked too conservative, too Ivy League, to draw unwanted attention.

Another courier was Jeffrey. He always drove up to the house in a different car. Once he came in an El Camino with a stick-on TV repair sign on it, as if he were there on a job. On another occasion, he delivered $300,000 in cash stuffed into a duffel bag. There were customers who would appear, stay for a party or overnight, and leave the next morning, their cars loaded with cocaine wrapped tightly and packed in cardboard boxes or designer suitcases.

A meticulous record keeper, Laney had a ledger in which she recorded all her business transactions—where and how much and from whom she made her buys, how much was sold, for what price, and to whom. She was careful about details, noting when payments had been made and when they were outstanding. Only a fool dealt with the Colombians without keeping detailed records.

When Laney asked Amer to take over the day-to-day management of her business, he felt over-

---

* Ed Bolter declined to be interviewed for this book. He has never been accused of any crime in connection with these events.

whelmed. He had his own customers to take care of, in particular his two largest, one from Boston, the other from California. Her business brought him in contact with a higher level of dealer, and this concerned him. Amer thought the savages had taken over the Miami drug trade, and the new brutality was horrible enough to make him dream about finding another line of work. But the money kept him where he was; he could not do without it.

The bloodshed did not bother Laney. She acted as if it had nothing to do with her. Her philosophy seemed to be that as long as the blood did not wash up on her doorstep, she did not care at all what happened around her. While Amer read the papers in detail, absorbing every word about drug-related murders, Laney simply ignored the whole thing.

As soon as Amer moved in, Laney wanted to renovate the house. Although it was huge—5,800 square feet—the single-story structure was not exactly to her liking. She wanted a more modern look, and if she did have a baby, she thought she would need more room. Also, the pool needed remodeling. Laney wanted new tile installed to produce the effect of a tropical lagoon.

Early one morning, Amer was awakened by the arrival of workmen. He got up, dressed, and went outside, where he found Laney talking to a Latin-looking man standing by the pool. Amer walked over, and Laney introduced him to Milan Bellechasses. He was the owner of a home-remodeling business, she said.

She explained that it was Bellechasses who had installed the safe in the bedroom; he now had some ideas about retiling the pool.

They walked around the rim, and Bellechasses talked about what he could do. Laney was relaxed and talkative. Bellechasses did not look like a workman, or for that matter the owner of a home-remodeling business. He was casually dressed in a light jacket and a silk shirt, which was partially unbuttoned in the front, revealing a thin gold chain. His hair was cut precisely and parted on the right side of his head and combed back. Handsome and rugged-looking, he spoke with a slight lisp, the result of a harelip.

When they were finished, Laney invited Bellechasses inside for coffee, and Amer followed them to the kitchen. She made a fresh pot and offered to make breakfast for both men. Bellechasses had the casual air of someone who was on familiar ground. When the coffee was brewed, Bellechasses took a cup from the cupboard and filled it. He sat down at the table and leafed through a travel magazine.

Bellechasses stayed for the afternoon, talking to the men who worked for him. Soon he became a fixture around the house, stopping by during the day to talk with his workers. At night, he would come back in his four-door Cadillac Seville, dressed in clothes Amer, the clotheshorse, considered cheap and unworthy of the well-to-do Latino. He also wore too much jewelry.

One afternoon, Amer told Laney, "That man could buy a two-thousand-dollar Italian-made suit and on him it would look like he bought it at Sears."

She accused him of being jealous, but he shrugged it off.

"He has no class, Laney. Can't you see? You can't buy class. He thinks you can, but you can't. Jesus, Laney, the man doesn't project himself. He wears Giorgio Brutini shoes—two hundred dollars! Very tacky. If you gave me a pair of those, I'd throw them out."

Laney laughed at him.

Amer, angry that Laney was not taking his objections seriously, told her that he believed Milan was after her.

"He's after your ass, my dear," he said.

She advised him to forget about Bellechasses.

"He wants your connections," Amer added.

She stood by the kitchen door and said, sternly, "He has lots of money, Joe. He is very big."

"Christ," Amer replied in disgust, unimpressed. "He looks mulatto."

Nearly every morning, Bellechasses arrived to talk to his work crew. Standing by the pool under a blazing sun, Bellechasses and Laney acted like old friends. Amer would look at them through the sliding glass doors, fuming. Bellechasses was around too much for a mere workman. Amer did not like the way he talked, with a faggy lisp. He was overly secretive with Laney, whispering in her ear, touching her arm during conversations, telling private stories that made them both laugh. The more Amer saw him whispering privately with Laney, the more Amer detested him.

THREE

AUGUST 1980. LOS ANGELES.

Fred McKnight pulled his car into the driveway of his home. It was nearly midnight, and the houses along his street were dark. A thin, wiry man, McKnight looked like a marathon runner. His body was lean and taut. He had been running for several years, up and down the steep, treeless hills that surrounded his home, but his lifestyle was so hectic, so fast-paced, so crazy, that it alone would have been sufficient to burn any fat off his body.

His neighborhood, south of the city of Los Angeles, was more like a small town situated at the edge of a great metropolis. Here, people lived quieter, more orderly lives. It was a strikingly clean place, where people took care of their homes and yards. McKnight preferred that. In light of the chaotic and dangerous nature of his work, his home and surroundings represented calm and order.

McKnight had been a narcotics cop for the City of Los Angeles for almost twenty years. He was nearing the time when many cops bail out and take their pensions. McKnight would do that, too.

It was understandable that he would want to, considering the life he had led for the past few years. He was lucky to be alive.

Like any number of narcotics cops in cities across America, McKnight felt as if he was waging a futile fight against the wave of drugs that were pouring into Los Angeles. The city was a huge sponge, soaking up fantastic amounts of dope. By the beginning of the 1980s, the demand for cocaine appeared to be bottomless. The narcotics squad at the Los Angeles Police Department, the finest in the country, was overwhelmed trying to make even a small dent in the illicit trade.

That summer, McKnight's task was to investigate the drug world's major violators—the dealers at the top of the pyramid as well as the brokers who oversaw distribution once the drug had entered the country. These were the people who acted like generals in a secret underground railroad; their role was to divide up the loads and direct them to the right distributors in the principal marketplaces. This was a task comparable to running a nationwide multibillion-dollar industry, one in which all power was concentrated at the top. It was a dictatorship, pure and simple. Blood was often spilled.

Known as an aggressive investigator, McKnight displayed in his work courage that often bordered on the reckless. He had hidden on drug transports, flown secretly to tiny airstrips in rural Mexico, where he had seen troops loading marijuana onto planes bound for California. He was passionate about his work, whatever the dangers. He accepted the risks. If there was a secret to his success, it was his ability to develop informants, people close to the inner workings of the machine that brought cocaine into America.

On this night, shortly after he arrived home, the phone rang. McKnight picked it up in the kitchen. He was quick about it, since his wife, Jackie, was asleep upstairs. She knew about his phone calls and had developed a rapport with many of her husband's best sources. When her husband was not home, Jackie knew what questions to ask, what facts to pass on. Tonight, the caller was one of McKnight's best informants.

"Hey, buddy, how you doing?" McKnight asked.

The caller, Ned Ramone, as he will be named here, said he was fine. He had not talked to McKnight in a while, so he brought him up-to-date. Then he explained the reason for the call: he had met a businessman from Beverly Hills who was bringing cocaine into Los Angeles.

"What's his name?" asked McKnight.

"Fogel," Ramone said.

"What do you know about him?"

"He owns a business in Beverly Hills. Not much else."

"What kind of business?" McKnight asked.

"Rental cars. Mercedes, limousines, the high-priced stuff."

"No kidding? Shit, that's interesting. Where's the dope coming from?"

"He has a Florida connection," Ramone said, and the word "Florida" hung in the air for a moment before McKnight responded.

"What's his name?" McKnight finally asked.

"Don't know yet, Freddie. From the sound of it, he's big. Really big."

"Cuban, no doubt," McKnight commented.

"I would guess. But big loads, Freddie. Lots of cocaine. They're moving a lot of dope in."

The Florida connection was significant, particularly to McKnight, because in 1980, the cocaine consumed in Los Angeles came almost entirely from distributors in that state. There was virtually no cocaine entering California from Mexico. Later, this situation would be reversed. But now the brokers who oversaw the smuggling routes were all in Florida, Cubans and Colombians for the most part, and they represented the kind of violators McKnight's squad was out to get.

No one knew at the time how big the Los Angeles drug market was, but the consensus among cops with good informants was that it was huge as well as enormously lucrative. Drug profits ran into the billions, and while much of the money flowed back to Florida, and from there to Caribbean bank accounts and then to Colombia, a lot of it stayed in southern California. This money bought homes, built shopping centers, and flowed through the cash registers of the fashionable stores in Beverly Hills.

At the police department's narcotics division, considerable attention was given to trying to identify the principal dealers. Who the dealers were and where they lived was as important as how the cocaine actually reached Los Angeles, although it was assumed that the bulk of it arrived on commercial airlines and was unloaded at the city's international airport. Ramone's call represented an opportunity to identify an important player in Miami. McKnight was pleased. It was what he had been looking for—if Ramone was right. He arranged to meet Ramone and thanked him for his information.

The man Ramone named was Marc Fogel, who owned a Budget Rent-a-Car Luxury Line agency across the street from the Beverly Center shopping mall. The agency specialized in exotic cars and limousines—Ferraris, Porsches, Mercedeses, and Rolls-Royces. Fogel was the sort of successful Los Angeles businessman who would be profiled on the business pages of the *Los Angeles Times* talking about his millionaire customers—Saudi princes, Hollywood moguls, rock stars. He was relatively young and, from all appearances, rich and well regarded in business circles.

It puzzled McKnight that a man like Fogel might be involved in cocaine smuggling. And the fact that he might be involved with a Florida-based smuggling ring, one with the means to bring in large amounts of the drug, separated Fogel from almost every other dealer McKnight had encountered over the years. The most pressing question was how Fogel had come to know the big dealer in the first place. More than likely, it had had something to do with his luxury-car dealership.

A few days after the phone call, at a late-night meeting in West Los Angeles, Ramone told McKnight he had learned that the Florida dealer was in fact a Cuban. Ramone said he was high up as well as a major player. He also said he had learned that the cocaine was being transported on routine commercial flights into LAX, evidently by an airline steward. That fact bothered McKnight. It was so simple.

"I want you to get close to Fogel," McKnight told Ramone. "I mean get in bed with him."

A week later, Ramone called McKnight.

"I have a problem, Freddie," he began.

"What's going on?" McKnight asked. "They bringing a load in?"

"I told Fogel I could move coke for him," Ramone responded. "Now he wants to meet."

"When?"

"Tonight. At a restaurant in Westwood."

"You have to have money?" McKnight asked.

"I have to show them something."

"That's a problem, buddy," McKnight said. He felt it was too early to start putting money out. He had to know more first, had to have names and a sense of where this investigation was leading.

"Make the meeting," McKnight said. "Go. I'm en route from home. I'll back you up."

When he reached the restaurant, McKnight parked his Mercury Cougar in the lot, away from the entrance. It was 10:00 P.M., and the parking lot was nearly empty. He walked around as if he were getting ready to meet someone for dinner. Inside, he saw Ramone seated with a young man McKnight assumed was Marc Fogel.

He went back to his car and waited. After a few minutes, he watched Ramone and Fogel step out of the restaurant and stand talking for a moment in the parking lot. Ramone proceeded to his car, which had been loaned to him by Fogel. McKnight watched as Fogel walked to a new Mercedes, unlocked the door, and climbed in. Fogel pulled up to the street and waited for Ramone to follow. Then the two cars drove off, heading for Wilshire Boulevard.

Here we go, McKnight thought as he watched the two cars pull up to a red light. He wondered if Fogel was smart enough to notice that he was being tailed.

At a condominium complex on Wilshire, Fogel turned off the road and dropped down into an underground garage. Ramone followed, and soon the two men were standing by Fogel's Mercedes. Fogel opened the trunk and took out a red box.

"How much can you move right now?" Fogel asked.

"Maybe three kilos," Ramone said. At the restaurant, Fogel had told him that ten kilos of cocaine had arrived in Los Angeles, and he needed them moved immediately. Ramone knew this was a test to see how much he could move and how quickly. If he passed, he would be given more to sell. They stepped into the elevator, and the door closed behind them.

They got off at the seventh floor and walked to Fogel's apartment. There, Ramone met a dark-haired man who spoke poor English. He assumed he was the Cuban from Miami. In the kitchen, Fogel opened the red box. Inside were three plastic packages, each containing cocaine.

"Move this," Fogel told Ramone, "and return with fifty thousand dollars."

Ramone left the apartment, riding the elevator back down to the garage. He walked quickly to his borrowed car, putting the cocaine into the trunk and locking it. As he revved up the engine, it occurred to him that what he had in the trunk of this car could land him in a state prison for years. He was grateful Freddie McKnight was with him. McKnight would protect him. McKnight could not, however, stop the Cuban from doing something irrational. Ramone knew about the business of cocaine; eventually, somewhere along the line, even in the smallest sales organizations, the guns came out.

As soon as Ramone pulled out of the garage, McKnight pulled out behind him. They drove for a mile along Wilshire before Ramone turned into a lot behind a bank building. It was now nearly

1:00 A.M. and pitch black. Only the light from a nearby streetlamp illuminated the two men as they stood and talked.

"Holy shit," said Ramone, breathless.

"What the hell did you see up there?" Mc-Knight asked.

"A box full of coke, Freddie. And the Cuban was up there, I'm sure of it."

"What's his name?" McKnight prodded.

"No one's wearing name tags," Ramone said. "He's got a Cuban accent, I can tell you that. Did you see him? He left after I got there."

"I watched someone drive out of the garage in a Mercedes. Probably one of Fogel's cars. Where was he going?"

"Who knows?" Ramone replied.

"What do you have to do?" McKnight asked.

"They expect me to sell the dope and return with fifty grand," Ramone said. "Like tonight."

There was no coming up with fifty thousand dollars now, and McKnight knew he could not deliver. "Do this," McKnight suggested. "Go park the car on the street. Leave the dope in the trunk. I'll call a black-and-white, and we'll impound the car."

"What for?" Ramone asked.

"You gotta have an excuse for these guys, buddy, and this is it. Go back and tell them you were tailed, you panicked, drove down a side street, you were followed all the way, so you parked and ran off. Can you do that?"

"Won't it make me sound like an asshole?"

"That's the least of your worries, buddy. Right now, you gotta get them to accept your credentials."

"Okay," Ramone said. "I can do it."

McKnight gave Ramone a ride home, and from

there Ramone called Fogel. As Ramone later told McKnight, Fogel went nuts as soon as he told him what had happened. Instantly, Fogel grew paranoid, evidently as frightened at the prospect of getting arrested as he was about explaining to his Cuban supplier that three kilos of his cocaine had been seized by the cops. In his favor was that the car was from his own rental company, which meant that all he would get from the police department was an impound notice. He could deny everything and swear up and down that the car had been stolen. That was just the response McKnight had figured he would get. It saved McKnight from coming up with the money and, he hoped, it would legitimize Ramone with Fogel.

McKnight was delighted later when Ramone reported back that Fogel would account for the loss himself. It was McKnight's opinion that Fogel, if he was planning on moving a lot of cocaine, would make up the monetary loss on future sales over the next few months.

After Fogel accepted Ramone as a courier, the real work of investigating the drug ring began. McKnight assigned ten agents to a round-the-clock surveillance of Fogel. Sometime afterward, Ramone reported back that there was talk of a load coming in from Florida of at least fifty pounds of cocaine.

Several weeks into the investigation, Ramone made the call McKnight had been waiting for—the Cuban was back in town and had booked a suite at the Westwood Marquis. McKnight concluded from this that the cocaine was en route, since the Cuban would not have brought it himself. It seemed obvious the Cuban must have a very reliable courier to bring the drug to Los An-

geles, someone whose chances of getting caught
were so small that he would risk transporting
large amounts of cocaine that had been, in all
likelihood, bought on credit. A bust would result
in problems all the way back up the line. At the
top, someone would have to cover the up-front
costs, and on a fifty-pound load, that would be
very expensive.

A day after the phone call, Ramone met Fogel
and they drove to the Westwood Marquis. Mc-
Knight followed with a squad of detectives. Mc-
Knight watched Ramone, who was as far out on a
limb as any police informant would want to be,
walk with Fogel into the hotel's restaurant and
sit down with the Cuban whom McKnight had
seen leaving Fogel's apartment building. Mc-
Knight waited a few minutes before strolling into
the restaurant, a newspaper under his arm. He
took a seat and ordered a cup of coffee.

At the table, Ramone talked to the Cuban for
an hour and a half, in effect selling himself, relating in detail the steps he would take and, more
important, the steps he would avoid in selling the
fifty pounds of cocaine. After several cups of coffee, McKnight got up. Briefly, he lingered in the
lobby, looking back into the restaurant. He then
walked across the street to the rectory of a Methodist church, where he sat with another cop. "We
have to follow the Cuban," McKnight said. "See if
he'll take us to the dope."

Ramone and Fogel emerged from the hotel and
got into Fogel's Mercedes. A half hour later, the
Cuban stepped into the sunlight and stood next to
the hotel's doorman.

"Bingo," McKnight muttered, watching the Cuban through his binoculars.

Evidently the Cuban had made a phone call inside the lobby, for now a stretch limousine pulled up and he got in. Several undercover cops followed the vehicle, and a helicopter hovered in the air far enough away so that it would not attract attention.

The Cuban proceeded to do what so many other visitors do when they arrive in Los Angeles—he went shopping in Beverly Hills. The limousine then took him back to the Westwood Marquis. For several days, this was his pattern: shopping, buying, and dining. McKnight concluded from this that the cocaine had not yet arrived.

Four days later, Ramone reported to McKnight that the cocaine was in town. It was now at Fogel's.

Steve Slazes, a narcotics squad intelligence officer, learned through contacts in Florida the name of the Cuban: Florencio Tezanos. Slazes began creating an organizational chart of the group, hoping to track the names back to Miami and, with luck, to Tezanos' supplier.

On the morning Fogel summoned Ramone to inspect the cocaine, McKnight climbed into the skeleton of a high-rise under construction across the street from Fogel's building. Fogel's apartment was on the seventh floor, and McKnight hoped to be able to peer inside. He found he could and still not be seen. Shortly afterward, McKnight saw Ramone enter. Inside the apartment were Fogel, Tezanos, and a fourth man, who searched Ramone. That was all McKnight needed to see. He climbed down to the street.

A half hour later, Ramone appeared at the front of the building, having made up an excuse to leave the apartment. He stood at the curb for a moment, rubbing his hand slowly over the top of his head before he walked to his car. McKnight ran to his own car, and he met up with Ramone four blocks away.

"All the dope is there," Ramone informed Mc-Knight.

Immediately, McKnight got on his radio. "If anyone comes out, bust them. We want the dope and the Cuban."

Ramone got back in his car and returned to the building. Again he parked in the garage and rode up in the elevator. Again he was searched as he entered the apartment. Across the street, Mc-Knight and the squad put on their raid jackets. Six of them climbed the stairs to the seventh floor. They waited a few minutes, and then they kicked the door in.

Inside, as the door burst open, the man in charge of security ran for a back bedroom. Fogel was in the living room, with Ramone and Teza-nos. They bolted upright, and someone yelled. There was a quantity of cocaine on the table and a razor blade to make lines for snorting. Stacked in a bedroom closet was the cocaine, packaged and ready to go.

Fogel, Tezanos, Ramone, and the fourth man, John Parrot, were arrested. It seemed likely to McKnight that Tezanos in particular would sus-pect that Ramone had assisted the police, since he had returned to the apartment immediately prior to the bust. But McKnight knew Ramone to be a savvy man who could protect himself, and he was not worried about retribution.

Scared for his life, Fogel began talking to Slazes and McKnight. No one would ever go to trial, and in December 1983 the charges would be quietly dismissed. By then, Fogel would be involved in helping the police solve a murder.

What Fogel told them helped Slazes complete the organizational chart of the drug hierarchy he had started. At the top, he wrote in the name of Tezanos' supplier—a Cuban from Miami named Milan Bellechasses. In the summer and fall of 1981, Bellechasses was a force in Miami's drug underworld, powerful enough to buy bulk amounts of marijuana and cocaine from the Colombians.

Fogel also provided Slazes with the name of another important member of the group. This was a woman, Bellechasses' girlfriend.

According to Fogel, she was distributing his cocaine in Los Angeles. Her name was Laney Jacobs.

FOUR

IT WAS ONE O'CLOCK IN THE MORNING, and Laney and Amer were in bed. He was watching television, and she was reading a book about Elizabeth Taylor. The doorbell rang.

Amer shot up out of bed. "Who the hell is that?" Laney looked at him and shrugged. He took his Walther PPK from the nightstand and stood by the bedroom door, peering down the darkened hallway. He pulled the clip out of the grip of the pistol and snapped it back in. It was loaded.

"Stay here, Princess," he said.

Amer walked slowly to the front door, and as he did, the doorbell rang again. He froze for a second. When he reached the door, he peered nervously through the peephole. Three Latin men were standing on the front step. Mother of God, he thought. His body broke out into a cold sweat. He looked through the peephole again, his hand clutching the pistol. Then he stepped back from the door.

"O my God, I am heartily sorry for having offended thee and I detest all my sins because of thy just punishment . . ." he muttered. He had not said the Act of Contrition since he was in Catholic school in Louisiana.

He ran back to the bedroom, where Laney was standing by the bed, waiting for him.

"Three guys, Laney," he whispered, still holding the pistol. "Latins. What do they want?"

Laney put on her pink bathrobe and followed Amer to the front door. Slowly, she looked through the peephole. She leaned back and whispered, "I know them."

Amer asked who they were.

"Colombians," Laney replied.

"Holy shit," he muttered.

The pistol, which felt small and inadequate, was damp in his hand. He slipped it into the pocket of his robe. He was hardly comforted by its presence, his mind racing over photographs he had seen in newspapers and magazines of murder victims who had been shot up with MAC-10s and Uzis.

Laney motioned for Amer to open the door. He opened it a crack.

"Hello," one of the men said in heavily accented English.

Laney pulled the door open. The first man to walk into the house was tall, very thin, with black hair and dark-brown eyes. He was casually dressed in jeans and a white shirt. He was followed by the two others.

"Gustavo," Laney said. She kissed him on the cheek. "Joe, this is Gustavo."

Hanging back a bit, Amer said hello.

Gustavo told Laney that he wanted to talk to her.

"Come in, *por favor*," she said.

She led them to the living room and turned on the lights. Gustavo was the leader of the group.

The other two Latins, one of whom was Gustavo's brother, stood a few feet behind him. They were silent, and from the confused looks on their faces, Amer concluded that they did not speak English.

Gustavo looked over the living room and commented on how nice it was.

Amer stepped closer to Laney. In his mind's eye, he could see the Latins having a nice chat and then pulling machine guns out from under their jackets and slaughtering them. Like dozens of other bullet-ridden bodies in Miami, Laney's and Amer's would end up in the refrigerated trailer, tags tied to their toes, with the ubiquitous police statement about a "drug-related" murder spree released to the press.

"Laney," Gustavo said, "we have to talk. Okay?" His English was bad, and it was hard to pick up his words. He stared at Amer as Laney motioned for everyone to follow her to the kitchen.

Laney sat at the head of the wicker table, Amer to her right, and gestured for the others to sit down.

"We need to talk to you, Laney," Gustavo said. "Very, very important."

She looked at him, curling her hair into tight balls with the thumb and forefinger of her right hand.

"What do you want?" Amer asked, fighting to keep down a wave of nausea.

"There's two hundred thousand missing from the last payment," Gustavo replied, his eyes peering into Amer's.

"That's nuts, Gustavo," Laney said, leaning back in her seat and shaking her head. "Can't be."

"It's true," Gustavo said. "I'm sorry to tell you this. It's true. Do you know about it?"

She did not reply. Instead, she got up and left the room, and the four men stared at each other. Amer wondered where their guns were. A long minute later, she returned and put her ledger on the table, opening it up to long lines of neat entries, numbers on top of numbers, representing a dizzying amount of income. With her left hand, she ran quickly through the pages; her right hand was busily curling her hair into balls.

"There!" she said finally. She cocked the book toward Gustavo. "There's the signature."

Gustavo bent and looked closely where her finger was pointing. He then raised his head and turned to his brother, whose face suddenly changed expression from the blank look of a man who could not understand what anyone was saying to one who understood all too well.

Amer sensed that Laney had won her point. He got up and pulled five Heinekens out of the refrigerator.

"Here we go," he said, handing out the bottles.

"I don't understand this," Gustavo said. "I haven't got my payment."

"Someone got it," Amer said. He twisted off a top and handed a beer to Laney. Then he opened one for himself and took a long swallow.

"No way in hell I got that payment," Gustavo said. "I tell you now—*I never got it.*"

"I don't think that's our problem," Amer said confidently. "That's *your* problem, *señor.*"

"But I don't have it!" Gustavo replied.

"Calm down, *por favor*," Amer said.

Laney pointed to Gustavo's brother. "He signed for it," she said. "Joe, tell him. Tell him, Joe. Talk to him. His brother signed for it. He's been here. He was the collector."

For the benefit of the brother and the third man, Amer translated Laney's remarks into Spanish. He made no bones about pointing the finger at the brother. While he spoke, Laney held her finger to the signature in her ledger. For all Laney and Amer knew, they could have been signing the man's death order.

Laney got up and paced the kitchen, again twirling her hair around the forefinger of her right hand. She sat down, she got up again, as Amer and Gustavo talked back and forth in Spanish.

"I am not going to pay you more than I owe you," she finally said. "Do you understand me?"

"No one gets paid twice, *señor*," Amer said. "There are rules, and she has followed them. She is a very careful lady."

Gustavo stood up to leave, and the other two men silently followed. Amer opened the door for them and stood on the front step and watched as they got into their car and drove off. Laney stood behind him. When she was sure they were gone, she covered her face with her hands and let out a deep sigh of relief.

By late fall of 1981, Laney and Amer were together selling fifty kilos of cocaine a month. The incident with the three Colombians, like her arrest the year before, had no lingering effect on Laney. Her enthusiasm for the drug business remained undaunted.

Amer was still managing Laney's day-to-day business. He had to make deals and, if need be, pick up product. Since much of Laney's cocaine

came from Milan Bellechasses, it meant Amer
had to see the Cuban frequently.

At Laney's insistence, Amer went to Bellechasses' villa on two occasions. The first time was after Laney discovered that a scale used to weigh
cocaine had been stolen from the hollowed-out
air conditioner where she sometimes kept it. She
thought one of Bellechasses' workers might have
taken it, and she directed Amer to go find it. On
the second occasion, Laney needed cocaine for a
buyer, and she told Amer to go to Bellechasses to
see how soon she could get a delivery.

The inside of Bellechasses' large house looked
like a bar at the airport. There were glass fixtures
and mirrors on nearly every wall. In the living
room were huge tree trunks cut down and lacquered and used as coffee tables. Photographs of
famous boxers adorned the walls.

Amer stood in the living room, admiring the
photographs. Outside by the swimming pool, a
Doberman pinscher barked.

"What's the dog's name?" Amer asked.

"Gator," Bellechasses replied.

"Oh, Jesus," Amer said. "Milán, I'll kill that
fucking dog if he ever comes near me."

For Amer, the principal mystery in Laney's life
was her relationship with Bellechasses. He did
know that Laney had met the man in 1980, when
she was married to Alfie Ferreira. By all appearances, Bellechasses had helped Laney grow in
the drug business. With the help of a Miami attorney named Frank Diaz, Laney and Bellechasses had set up a company called Jamboni
Enterprises, incorporated in the Netherlands Antilles. They used it to launder their drug profits.
This was approximately at the time they were
both shipping cocaine to Los Angeles.

Diaz was a master at setting up corporations for many of his drug clients or helping them buy into legitimate businesses in Miami. It was Diaz, in fact, who had helped Joe Rodriguez buy into the Collection.

After Jamboni Enterprises was created, suitcases stuffed with cash were flown to the islands and deposited. Once, shortly after Laney introduced Amer to Bellechasses, she flew $1.2 million to the Caribbean. The cash had to be deposited, and Laney was forced to fly it over herself because the regular couriers were not available.

Bellechasses was a secretive man, prone to using pseudonyms. One was Milo Santana; another was Mr. Miller. Over the years, a considerable legend had built up about him. Police informants said they were scared of him. Some said he boasted of committing murders. They described him as a "man who worked in the shadows." In Los Angeles, three thousand miles from Bellechasses' home base, Steve Slazes had heard there was a Cuban buried in Bellechasses' front yard.

On September 15, Laney and Amer flew first class to Las Vegas, where they met a friend of Laney's, who had arranged for front-row seats at the Sugar Ray Leonard–Thomas Hearns fight at Caesars Palace. It was a hurried trip, and a few days later they returned to Miami. There, she announced she needed to go to Los Angeles and La Jolla. There were distributors to give pep talks to and to keep supplied.

At the end of the month, they flew first class on a Pan American flight, their best clothes neatly folded in their new Louis Vuitton luggage. In Los Angeles, they were picked up in a limousine from Marc Fogel's Luxury Line agency in Bev-

erly Hills. That afternoon, as they drove past
Fogel's business, Laney said, "I know the guy
who owns this. If we ever need cars, we can go
there." The seizure of Laney and Bellechasses'
cocaine at Fogel's apartment had occurred
twelve months earlier, and she was still angry
about it.

After driving by Fogel's agency, Laney and
Amer went shopping in Beverly Hills, where Laney had a facial at Georgette Klinger.

In the early evening, they were driven to La
Jolla. Their first appointment was with Ed
Bolter. After they settled into their hotel suite,
Laney began making phone calls, telling her contacts she was in town. Her first call was to Jesse,
her main California distributor. Jesse was a tall
Mexican with long black hair. He was the husband of one of the sisters whom Amer had met on
the *Temptress* in Biscayne Bay.

Jesse, who drove a bright-yellow Porsche 911,
came to the room first, hung around for a while,
and then left, saying he had people to see in San
Diego. Shortly after, Bolter came. The day before,
the young airline steward had brought out a load
of cocaine. Laney, wary of potential trouble, had
insisted on taking two adjoining suites in the hotel.

"I don't ever want the coke in my room," she
insisted. "If it's somewhere else, we can talk our
way out of it. If it's here, we're dead."

The next day, Jesse returned to the hotel and
took the cocaine out to his car. Later that same
day, he brought back $250,000 in hundred-dollar
bills. Laney and Amer counted the cash on the
double bed in their suite, sipping California wine
and listening to music on the clock radio. When
they were finished, Jesse took them to a little café

on a hill overlooking the ocean. After dinner, they drove around among the big, expensive homes on the bluffs, and Laney said she wanted to leave Miami and buy a house on the ocean.

Back in their room, Laney said she felt the time had come to make a decision on which direction her life would take. "I have a lot of business contacts in California, and there are things I want to do here," she explained. "I've got the money."

"Like what?" Amer asked.

"Perhaps the movie business," she said.

"That's funny," he replied. "Ever since I was a kid, I wanted to be in the movies. Maybe it's something we could do together."

A week or so after their return from California, a black Jaguar pulled up to the house in Miami, and two men got out. Laney was expecting them, and at the door she told them to move the car around to the side of the house.

She invited them in, and they sat at the kitchen table drinking Scotch. One was about five feet nine inches tall, muscular like a body builder. He seemed wired, very impatient and nervous. The other was tall and dark, but much more talkative and calm.

After a few minutes of small talk, Laney said she wanted to hire them to collect a debt. A shipment of cocaine had been seized in Los Angeles the year before, she explained, and the man she blamed for the loss, Marc Fogel, owed her $350,000. It was agreed that the two men would keep 10 percent of what they collected as a fee.

Amer was surprised that Laney could react so harshly toward a man who, by no fault of his own, had been part of a cocaine seizure by Los Angeles police. He wondered if Laney was prepared to kill Fogel if he could not or would not repay the debt. Wasn't Fogel a friend of hers? Amer guessed that Laney never let friendship stand in the way of making money.

In October, Laney learned that she was pregnant; she wept with joy. So did Amer. He was convinced that the baby had been conceived on the night of August 23. He had even told her so after their lovemaking that night. It had just felt different to him; he was sure of it.

Laney wanted a boy very badly, and one night, after she spread out one of her mink coats on the rug in the living room and got some cocaine, in one of her special bowls, she said she had a name in mind for the boy.

Amer had a name, too. "Dax," he said. "It's from Harold Robbins' novel *The Adventurers*."

"My God!" Laney exclaimed, shocked that Amer had picked a name she had carried around with her for years. "That is the name I had in mind!"

"That's incredible! It is my absolute favorite book. I've read it a million times."

"It's *my* favorite book!"

"Diogenes Alejandro Xenos," he said, naming the character in the book who was called Dax. "It's fantastic. I loved the adventure in the book. I really, really did."

They, too, were adventurers. In their world, what mattered was the bottom line; there was no right or wrong, just business. He was the kid from Honduras whose friends could pay off the national debt; she was the girl who sold tea at the Future Homemakers meetings and taught Sunday school at the Methodist church. Now she was where she wanted to be.

Basking in her reflection, Amer longed to take

her to Honduras and show her off. Laney was the richest woman he had ever known. He knew enough about her finances to place her wealth at that moment in time at five million dollars, and all of it *liquid.*

For Thanksgiving, Amer and Laney went to Laney's mother's house in Miami. Over the years, she had given her mother, Barbara, cash and expensive jewelry and clothes, even a car, a chocolate-brown Buick Regal.

When Laney came to the house, she was usually in a Porsche or a Mercedes, a big step up from the Beetle she drove when she was first living in Miami and working as a legal secretary.

She seemed awash in expensive luxury items and cash. Once, a member of Laney's family came to Robert Greene, who was her mother's third husband, and said, "Don't tell Barbara. I was at Laney's house and I counted four hundred thousand dollars in hundred-dollar bills."

Greene had met several of Laney's Latin husbands and boyfriends, and all of them drove expensive cars and wore imported clothes. Amer was no different. He had a penchant for Italian-made suits and handmade shoes, which he bought at a store called Luciano's, owned by a Colombian. And tonight Amer was wearing his favorite watch—a nine-thousand-dollar Piaget Polo that Laney had given him.

At the dinner table, the Greenes asked Amer how he liked Thanksgiving. He smiled and said he loved the holiday.

"My grandfather on my mother's side was from Virginia," he explained. "His name was Von Slyke. My mother was raised in Honduras, but with all the American traditions like Thanksgiving."

Barbara sat quietly and listened, smoking one cigarette after another.

"Where were you born?" she asked.

"I was born in Honduras," Amer replied. "I am the only son in my family. My father is Jordanian."

"What was your grandfather doing in Honduras?"

"He was a civil engineer. He went there to work for United Fruit. He met my grandmother, and they had eighteen children. All but three of them died in accidents."

Everyone thought that tragic, and Amer remarked how lucky he was to be living in the United States.

"This is the greatest place," he said. "I could never go back to Honduras."

FIVE

ON THE NIGHT OF FEBRUARY 5, SIX months after they had met, Amer and Laney. and eleven of their closest friends crowded aboard the *Temptress*. It was a beautiful night on Biscayne Bay, cool and cloudless. A few minutes before midnight, a cousin of one of Amer's dealer friends, who was a notary public, married them. Amer was Laney's fifth husband in eleven years. On her marriage license, she wrote that Amer was her second husband, an act of disingenuousness she had also committed with her two previous marriages.

Laney, more than five months pregnant, was considerably heavier than when she had met Amer. She was uncomfortable, and her back ached if she stood for too long. Because of the pregnancy, she decided not to wear anything formal, and instead she was casually dressed in a loose-fitting, light-colored dress. Still, she was a striking bride. Amer, a groom for the first time, adhered more to tradition and wore a dark, Italian-made suit.

After the ceremony, Laney and Amer found a seat in a quiet corner of the yacht. She rested her head on his shoulder, watching the lights of passing boats on the bay. Laney wanted this baby very badly, but she was afraid something might go wrong. Amer tried to reassure her, but she worried anyway.

A few weeks later, Laney and Amer went to Joe Rodriguez's wedding at the Doral Hotel. He was marrying a young Cuban named Mei-Lin Echeverria. Laney and Amer went in spite of the sickness and light-headedness her pregnancy caused. Both of them felt strongly about going; after all, it was Rodriguez, Amer's best friend and mentor, who had helped launch Amer's drug-dealing career.

After the service, guests danced to the music of a local Cuban band. Later, a small group went upstairs, where suites had been rented for guests to party in privately. Some were laying out lines of cocaine, while armed guards stood in the hallway to ensure security.

In a crowded suite, Rodriguez and Amer embraced warmly, patting each other on the back. Rodriguez was living in a large Mediterranean-style house in Coral Gables. They were wealthy beyond their wildest dreams.

Laney was feeling ill, and she left the suite and found a bed in one of the rooms. While she rested, Rodriguez asked Amer if he had met Mei-Lin's friend, a woman named Jackie Silva. Amer had noticed Silva at the ceremony, an attractive blonde in a bright-red dress who seemed to be alone. He was delighted when Rodriguez called her over to say hello.

"Hello, beautiful," Amer said. "I'm Joe."

* * *

When Laney could no longer fit into her Porsche, Amer bought her a Jaguar for $32,000 cash, which he brought to the dealership in a brief-case. There were other reasons for the expensive gift, however.

By the middle of March, five weeks after the wedding, their relationship was in trouble. Laney, in the last trimester of her pregnancy, wanted more and more to be left alone.

For his part, Amer perceived that Laney was less and less interested in him. He had become a guest in her house. And there was always the lurking presence of Milan Bellechasses, speaking on the phone with Laney or pulling up to the front of the house to chat with her on the front step. Amer hoped that buying Laney gifts would, as it had in the past, endear him to her.

Once, Laney asked Amer to go to Los Angeles with her. He refused, saying he was not as inter-ested in California as she was. So she flew west with Bellechasses.

When Laney returned from California, Amer arranged for Myriam Plaza, his maid, to move into the house. He was hoping her presence would help ease the strain on Laney. When he brought her over, he introduced her as Dax's fu-ture nanny. Laney took an immediate liking to her, and because Myriam did not have a car, she bought her a Mustang. She helped her buy clothes and improve her appearance, and the guest room in the house was fixed for her.

Not long after Myriam moved in, Amer called Jackie Silva and asked her to dinner. Soon they were seeing each other regularly, meeting at his old apartment in Kendall. At first, he would stay away for several days, returning to Laney's house to get more clothes or pick up things he needed.

He took all his jewelry, including his collection of watches. One afternoon, he sat in his car in front of Laney's house, holding in his hand a gift she had given him. It was a gold chain with a rectangular plaque. On it, she had had engraved, in Japanese, "Health, Money, Love."

To find out what her husband was doing, Laney hired a private detective. Soon she had a grainy, faraway picture of Amer and Jackie Silva leaning against his Porsche in front of his apartment building. Amer returned to her house one afternoon, hoping to talk to her; he found his luggage packed and waiting for him at the front door. When he asked to speak with her, she ordered him out of the house. He started shouting at her, and she followed him into the bedroom.

"I'm going to kill you," Laney said angrily.

"Why don't you sic your friend Milan on me?" he said.

"Get out of this house!" she screamed.

After Amer had gone, Laney worried about the baby not having a father in the house. Myriam told her not to worry: it was her son; the father did not matter. Trying to cheer Laney up, Myriam prepared her favorite meals, including arroz con pollo. Laney also ate a lot of caviar, another favorite; she would sit at the table and eat as Myriam cleaned house. When the chores were finished, the two would go off on long shopping trips.

Bellechasses, the mysterious Cuban, had in many respects become the center of Laney's life. As her supplier, Bellechasses was making her wealthy. His ability to fly cocaine to a landing strip in the Bahamas and from there travel by boat to South Florida impressed Laney. She admired him, looking up to him as a model of success.

With Bellechasses, Laney was continuing her pattern. She looked for bigger and better prospects with each dealer with whom she became involved. She was working her way up into the drug hierarchy, and it was now Bellechasses who was helping her graduate to bigger things. Her rise in the past five years had been remarkable, but in spite of this, she remained relatively unknown. In the spring of 1982, the only narcotics cops who even knew her name were two members of the Los Angeles Police Department—Fred McKnight and Steve Slazes.

On the morning of May 11, Amer changed into his designer exercise clothes and put his racquetball gear into a gym bag. He kissed Jackie Silva goodbye and walked to the parking lot outside his apartment complex. He threw the gym bag into the trunk of his Mercedes.

As he was pulling out, he realized he had left a new box of balls in the apartment. He drove to the front of the building, double parked, and ran inside. As he came into the lobby, he saw two men trying to pry open his mailbox.

"Hey!" he yelled. "What are you doing?"

The two men did not answer. One continued to work on the mailbox, while the other walked threateningly toward Amer.

"Jackie!" Amer screamed, terrified he was going to be murdered on the spot. The two men grabbed him tightly by both arms, quickly patted him down, and twisted his hands behind his back. Handcuffs were clasped to his wrists.

As he was being led out of the building, Amer screamed again for Jackie. The men led him to a car, opened the back door; one of the men put his hand on the top of Amer's head and pushed him onto the back seat. The two got in the front of the car, and at that point, the driver pulled a badge from his coat pocket and said they were federal drug agents.

"Oh, my God," Amer muttered, his head falling back onto the car seat. He could only hope and pray that somehow this was a misunderstanding, a big foul-up by the feds.

When Amer arrived at Drug Enforcement Administration headquarters, he phoned Jackie. He told her to gather his collection of watches—a Piaget Polo, a Rolex Presidential, a Patek Philippe, a gold Rolex, and a Vacheron Constantin—and give them to Joe Rodriguez. They were worth almost twenty thousand dollars, and Amer figured that this way he would have at least that amount when and if he got out of prison.

He told Jackie to call Frank Rubino, the lawyer who had got Laney off the hook after her drug possession arrest.

"Find Frank," Amer yelled. "Find him *tonight.*"

In all his years dealing cocaine, Amer never thought he would be caught. He had seen some of his friends get arrested, but they were big players, certainly bigger than he was. He did not know that the investigation that had led to his arrest had begun in Arizona, with the arrest of a man who told investigators that he had come to Miami and bought cocaine from Amer.

After his arraignment in federal court, Amer broke down and called Laney's house. He was desperate to talk to her, desperate to apologize for everything that had gone wrong in their brief time together. He was looking for forgiveness,

but he did not get it. Laney, who had heard Amer
was in jail, refused to speak with him.

On May 15, 1982, a few days after Amer's arrest, at Baptist Hospital in Kendall, Laney gave
birth to a son, whom she named Dax. On the
birth certificate, she designated Amer as the father, though later she would say it was Bellechasses.

A few weeks later, while Amer was in jail
awaiting trial, Laney announced to Myriam that
they were moving. Myriam suggested Chicago as
their new home, but Laney had California on her
mind, the place she had told Amer was her
destiny. By fall, Laney, Myriam, and Dax would
be on their way to Los Angeles.

Part Two

Ocean Castle

SIX

ROY RADIN WAS SEATED BEHIND HIS massive wooden desk, scrutinizing Jonathan Lawson, a tall man with thick blond hair. It was midafternoon, but Radin was still in his bathrobe. The terry-cloth robe was wrapped loosely around his three-hundred-pound body and secured with a rope belt. His short black hair was disheveled, his face unshaven.

"We've been up most of the night," Radin said by way of explaining his appearance.

Stretched out on a couch next to Radin's desk was another man still in his bathrobe. He, too, appeared to have just gotten out of bed. His name was Joey Bishop, and he had flown in from California to help Radin organize his next vaudeville show. Bishop was to be master of ceremonies.

Radin fished for his coffee cup amid the piles of overstuffed manila envelopes and folders that littered his desk. They were filled with glossy photographs of men dressed up to look like Elvis Presley; of entertainers dressed in sequined suits, holding decks of cards; of comedians and magicians and sword swallowers. There was a color picture of a chimpanzee in a three-piece suit.

"Real family entertainment," Radin said to Lawson as he pushed everything aside. "It's the foundation of everything I have."

That morning, Radin had phoned Lawson and asked him to come to Southampton. He had gotten Lawson's name from an entertainment agent in Manhattan, who explained that Lawson, who had worked in the theater for years, was available for work. There was a sense of urgency in Radin's request, because he would shortly be opening his show in Cleveland, and he needed a manager. It was the last week of February 1982; the show was to open on April 1.

Hoping to spend the day resting, Lawson had tried to delay leaving his Manhattan apartment, but Radin had persisted. Hours before Radin's call, Lawson had stepped off an overnight flight from Spain, and he was tired. But he needed a job, so he reluctantly dressed and took a cab to the train station, arriving in Southampton at approximately 3:00 P.M. There, Lawson was met by a uniformed chauffeur, Malcolm Grigg, who took him in a limousine to Radin's mansion, which stretched over a grassy section of sand dunes overlooking the ocean.

A neat and meticulous man, Lawson could not get over the mess that was Radin's office. He had been told by his agent that Radin was a successful theatrical producer whose reputation had been made staging vaudeville revivals. But he had difficulty equating that reputation with the slovenly, obese thirty-two-year-old man who stood before him. The cluttered office looked more as if it belonged to a carnival owner than to a big-time producer.

"My next show will be big," Radin said. "Lots

of stars. I need someone to handle the lights and sound equipment."

Lawson told Radin that what he needed was a technical director, adding that his own expertise was as a road manager.

"Hey, call it what you want," Radin said. "If you take the job, it would be four hundred fifty a week. I have to fill the job."

He asked Lawson how soon he could move in.

"Move in?" Lawson asked incredulously. "I just got into town, you know. This will take time."

"There isn't any time," Radin responded. "You have to move in. All my employees live in the mansion."

"I could possibly come out next week—"

"Can't you come sooner?" Radin insisted.

"Look," Lawson said, flustered. "I have to organize my life. I just can't pick up and move out. I need a few days."

Radin stood up and walked around the desk to where Lawson was standing. The two men shook hands.

"See the place while you're here," Radin said. "It's a grand home. I call it Ocean Castle."

The mansion was built in 1929 in the style of castles in Normandy. The exterior appeared to be constructed of stone, but it was actually made of concrete blocks cast in white cement. The tiles, fabricated in Colorado, were designed to replicate the tiles on a French château. Radin liked to say the house and grounds resembled those found in fishing villages along the French seacoast.

Lawson found Ocean Castle too large, with dark, airless spaces that appeared to serve no useful purpose. The house was U-shaped, its separate buildings linked together by various entrances. In all, there were seventy-two rooms, with, at different times, perhaps half a dozen people living in them.

On the east side of the house was a turret-shaped structure with a winding staircase. Radin maintained his offices in the turret; his living quarters—a huge bedroom, with two large dressing rooms, two bathrooms, and walk-in closets—were next to it.

Opposite the front entrance was a living room and dining room, and behind them, a den, a paneled library, and a pantry and kitchen. A staircase in the living room led to a lower level, where there were more rooms, including the so-called Media Room, little more than a drably furnished space with a large television set, its screen cracked, pushed against one wall.

Also on the lower level were a game room, several small bedrooms, a dank storage room where Radin's light and sound equipment were kept, a second kitchen and pantry, and a large liquor storage area, dubbed the Wine Cellar. A door led out to the beach. Lawson found the naming of rooms pretentious and incongruous.

On the top floor of the mansion were three additional bedrooms, a bathroom, and another living room. Radin's security chief, Charlie Donchez, and his wife, Irene, occupied one of the bedrooms, and guests usually stayed in the other two.

Radin was not the sort of man people were able to say no to, and a few days later Lawson was back. He moved his clothes into one of the bedrooms on the top floor, and soon he began work on the sound and lighting system.

From the beginning, he found it strange to live

and work in the mansion. There was very little routine in the household. People came and went, and the phones rang all the time. The office in the turret was loosely organized, with employees arriving when they wanted. Sue Myers, Radin's bookkeeper, opened the office around 9:00 A.M. Then Donchez, in a suit and tie and, sometimes, a gun tucked into a belt holster, would arrive. He was usually followed by Mickey De Vinko, a former bandleader, whose function was to oversee crews of workers who solicited businesses for contributions to the small-town police departments for which Radin staged benefits. Copies of De Vinko's book, *Weep No More, My Lady*, about his brief marriage to Judy Garland, were found in several locations throughout the house.

Radin was a man who followed no apparent schedule. Some days he would work in a frenzy right through the night, calling people all over the country. Other days, he would stay in bed, sleeping, eating, and watching television on a set he had had mounted in a cabinet. He could raise and lower the set with a remote control device that operated an electric motor. Although he insisted his staff call him Mr. Radin, that was the extent of the formality.

The only other rules that seemed to be closely observed were that the household staff were not allowed in Radin's office. They were also required to wear uniforms and to take their meals in the kitchen and never the dining room, which was reserved for Radin, his guests, and his business staff.

The household staff reported to Toni Fillet, whom Radin had married the year before. Fillet, who was in her early thirties, was rail thin, with long brown hair and dark eyes. Radin adored

her, although it was apparent to everyone who
lived in the mansion that their relationship was
both odd and unstable. She behaved like a society
princess, which she was not, and had a habit of
calling downstairs to the servants' quarters to ask
someone to come to her bedroom to open a window for her. She was attractive and dressed in
expensive clothes, and Radin beamed in her
presence. Almost to a person, the staff loathed
her; the resulting tension in the house contributed to a large turnover of employees. It was not
uncommon for Fillet to hire someone who would
quit later the same day.

Ever since his childhood in Pennsylvania,
Lawson had displayed an ability to organize. He
was the perfect office manager, meticulous about
details and not shy to point out laziness and
abuse by the other employees. He found Radin's
office a disaster. Money seemed to be spent willy-
nilly, with little or no accounting of the funds
that arrived in the mail from the businesses that
supported the road shows. Radin kept too many
details in his head about how the business was
run, and Lawson needed to learn more if he was
going to get anywhere. He spent considerable
time going through the files and grilling staff
members about how everything was put together.

The core of Radin's business centered around
vaudeville-style road shows that stopped in cities
in the Midwest and Northeast and performed
benefits for police departments. Bright, ambitious, and hardworking, Radin had begun his
business when he was still a teenager. At first, he
booked rock-and-roll bands into Long Island
nightclubs, but later he hit on the novel idea of
putting has-been entertainers into buses and
sending them out to perform in Masonic temples

and high school auditoriums. The crowds loved them.

The profits, which were divided with the police departments that sponsored them, were generated by haranguing businessmen in the cities where the show stopped to take out advertisements in a program. Threats and strong-arm tactics were the norm. As a result, Radin's business was, at different times during its existence, the focus of civil investigations in states where officials found his methods improper. He managed to stay out of serious trouble.

If things were not confusing enough, Radin was eccentric about his personal habits. He ate in binges, raiding the refrigerator, leaving sandwich scraps on his unmade bed for the maid to clean up. Dinners were either phoned in to a take-out place, with every single item on the menu ordered, or Radin would take a group of friends and Southampton cops to dinner at Herb McCarthy's, a casual steak and seafood restaurant in the village.

The household method of food shopping summarized Radin perfectly. He wanted everything. On food-shopping day, he would order an employee, usually Sal Miglionico, a childhood friend who had been hired as a personal assistant, to buy every kind of lunch meat sold in the supermarket, every kind of bread, every roast available, every kind of cookie, plus potato chips and snacks by the cartload. There were cases of wine and Radin's favorite champagne, Taittinger, stored in the basement wine cellar.

Radin's bingeing also included cocaine, which he consumed in large amounts. Cocaine energized him, or at least he believed it did. The drug was so much a part of the man and his personality that he included the money for it in his household budget. It was bought for him by his driver, from dealers who lived in expensive apartments in Manhattan, or it was dropped off at Ocean Castle by a man who had a summer home in the area. Radin also consumed what he called "horse pills," which were tranquilizers he took when he was trying to cut back on his cocaine use. But inevitably he would return to the drug.

In late March, Lawson and Charlie Donchez packed Radin's troupe into a rented bus and left for Cleveland. Radin, as was his habit, flew out with Toni Fillet. Because Radin needed his limousine with him, Grigg drove the stretch Lincoln out and met Radin and Fillet at the airport. He took them to the Holiday Inn, and from there Radin went to rehearsals, at a local theater.

For the tour, Radin had signed Allan Jones, whose big hit had been a tune called "Donkey Serenade." He also had an agreement with Tessie O'Shea, who strummed a tiny banjo and sang "Two Ton Tessie from Tennessee." Jackie Vernon had joined the show, along with singer Esther Marrow; a group called the Harmonica Rascals, which included a midget who did comedy; a magician; a juggler; and a French vaudeville act called Pierre Du Pont and His Wonder Dog Sparky. Joey Bishop was master of ceremonies as well as performer. The schedule for *Roy Radin's Tribute to Vaudeville* was thirty-six shows in six weeks, with performances in Ohio, Pennsylvania, Indiana, West Virginia, Virginia, and Delaware.

Radin preferred the acts go quickly, and he timed each one with a stopwatch. He wanted his performers to follow one another without any

breaks for the ninety minutes of show time. "Do
it quick—don't let the audience think about what
they are watching," was his show business motto.

At the rehearsal, everyone but Joey Bishop
laughed at Pierre Du Pont and Sparky. "I hate
that act," he told Lawson. "I can't follow a fucking dog."

Lawson reported Bishop's objections to Radin,
who said, "You watch. It'll be the dog that gets
the applause, not Joey."

The next night, the theater was packed, and as
the show began, the orchestra went into a medley
of vaudeville tunes. Then Lawson took a microphone at the side of the stage to introduce Bishop.

"Ladies and gentlemen," he began, "welcome
to the Cleveland Police Benevolent Association's
presentation of *Roy Radin's Tribute to Vaudeville*! Now here's our star, Mr. Comedy himself—
Joey Bishop!"

Bishop came out and did a joke about Cleveland. Then he introduced Tessie O'Shea, a very
large woman in a tentlike dress, her white hair
pushed up in a bun. She was holding a banjo, and
after the applause died down she indeed sang
"Two Ton Tessie from Tennessee."

When she was finished, the lights dimmed.
"Now," she began, "I want to take you back . . .
to the Victoria Palace . . . 1952 . . . my name in
lights . . . I introduced a song that would become famous throughout the entire world . . ."

She yelled: "Hit it!" and began singing. "I've got
a lovely bunch of coconuts. There they are
a-standing in a row . . ."

Lawson, at the edge of the stage, clapped along
with the audience. When Tessie O'Shea was finished, the magician came out, and after his ten

minutes, Jackie Vernon did his "slide show" of a recent vacation.

For Vernon's skit, the projector was a spotlight that cast a circle of light on the curtain. "First slide, please," he commanded. The spotlight on the curtain would go quickly on and off, and, holding a clicker in his hand to signal for the next "slide," Vernon narrated. It took a moment for the audience to realize what Vernon's routine was, and that no pictures were to be shown.

"This is a picture of me backing out the driveway." Click. "This is me backing into my neighbor's car." Click. "Here I am having coffee at the rest stop." Click. "Here I am picking up a hitchhiker." Click.

"That's it," Vernon said a few minutes later. "I'll come back next year with more exciting slides."

Vernon was followed by the juggler, who threw Ping-Pong balls up in the air, catching them in his mouth.

"Hey," Bishop yelled into the microphone, "try that with matzoh balls."

The high point of the evening, as Radin had predicted, was Pierre Du Pont and Sparky. In his act, Du Pont tried to coax Sparky into jumping through a tiny hoop.

"Sparky—jump! Jump! Come on, boy, you can do it—jump! Jump!" The audience howled at the sight.

"Roy," Lawson whispered when Radin came toward him. "They love that dog. I can't believe it."

"Real family entertainment," Radin said to Lawson with a grin. "Just like I told you."

SEVEN

IN THE LATE 1960s, WHILE HE WAS STILL in his teens, Roy Radin discovered that there were places in the American heartland where people would pay to see a kangaroo act. He also discovered that people in out-of-the-way towns would pay to see singers who had not had hits in two decades and comedians who had long fallen out of favor.

Enterprising and imaginative, Radin rounded up singers, jugglers, fire eaters, kangaroo and chimp acts, comedians, magicians, and sword swallowers, and booked them into Masonic temples, motel banquet halls, and high school auditoriums. Admission was cheap, and the lines on opening night were long.

Fancying himself a modern-day P. T. Barnum —who began his show business career by exhibiting 160-year-old slaves, Siamese twins, and other human and animal oddities—Radin was an instant success, if an unheralded one.

Radin's enormous drive was, in the beginning, a product of his close relationship with his father, Alexander Radin. A nightclub owner in Manhattan in the 1930s, 1940s, and 1950s, Alexander Radin was known as "Broadway Al" by his many show business friends. In his circle of acquaintances, Broadway Al was a man who was much admired. And to his impressionable son, he was a legend and a giant, someone to be emulated.

In June 1971, when Radin was twenty-two years old, he walked into the Sanders recording studio, on the corner of Forty-third Street and Sixth Avenue in Manhattan. He knew that an odd-looking man named Herbert Khaury frequently recorded there. Radin had admired Khaury's career for several years, seeing in him the kind of entertainer who could draw crowds to a vaudeville tour. Khaury's career had been going steadily downhill for several years, but still Radin wanted him to come and work for him.

Baby-faced and overweight, as he had been throughout his youth, Radin was dressed in an expensive three-piece suit, custom fit to accommodate his large body. His dark hair was cut short and combed precisely. He looked like a chubby teenager dressed in his father's best suit. He walked up to Khaury and introduced himself.

"Please call me Tiny Tim, Mr. Radin," Khaury replied in a soft voice. But Radin would always call him Herbie.

Presenting himself as a hardworking, talented go-getter who made things happen, Radin talked about people in show business he had worked with, like Milton Berle and George Jessel. He was full of bluster and confidence. As Radin talked about himself, Tim was reminded of a young Flo Ziegfeld.

First, Radin explained, he would help Tim get booked into better nightclubs—no more dives in Camden or on the Jersey shore. Radin also proposed that he take over the management of Tim's career, saying it was time Tim shook off his image as a flaky weirdo with a squeaky voice.

"Herbie," Radin concluded, "you could do a lot for me. In turn, I could do a lot for you." Tim agreed.

For his 1971 tour, Radin hired Jessel, who had been a close friend of Radin's father. Jessel's glory days were long over. He was old and feeble and could do little more than stand at the front of a stage in a coat covered with military medals and tell jokes and sing patriotic songs. The tour went through Ohio, Pennsylvania, Massachusetts, Rhode Island, and Connecticut, and wound up at a theater in Hempstead, Long Island. As the headliner, Tiny Tim sang "Earth Angel," and the audience applauded.

With the help of his father's old friends, Radin wanted to succeed where his father had managed only to scratch the surface. His father ran speakeasies during Prohibition, and later managed nightclubs. "Broadway Al" was a man of the street who had drinks with Orson Welles and provided show business tips for Walter Winchell. Those who knew both Radins—Al in his older years and Roy as a bubbly, enterprising teenager —saw them as a dynamic duo.

"Al has the class, Roy's got the brass," was how they were described.

What the young Radin particularly loved about his father was that he was a "man in the know," as comedian Red Buttons would say. "Al knew everyone," said Buttons, who toured with the young Radin in the 1970s. "Roy, in turn, liked the whole idea of being the Broadway guy. His father knew important people lurking in the shadows of New York. He knew people who were 'connected,' and that meant he knew people who mattered and could pull strings. That impressed Roy, and he wanted the same thing, only bigger. He wanted what his father had, or what he thought his father had, but he wanted to go further with it."

Roy worshiped the memory of his father, so much so that years later he would sometimes take entertainers and business associates to his father's grave in Southampton. He would park his car by the gravesite, take a bottle of champagne from the trunk, pop the cork, and, while standing over the grave, toast Broadway Al's memory.

"To the greatest man who ever lived," he would say.

In the early 1960s, well after his days as a nightclub operator and friend of show business personalities were over, his father retreated to a small waterfront hotel he owned in Bay Shore, on Long Island. The Cooper's Hotel was a dozen rooms, a bar and restaurant. Al Radin would sit in the bar and tell stories about his life and do impressions.

At that time, after his parents had divorced, the young Roy lived near the hotel with his mother, Renee, who had once been a stripper in New York. Al Radin left his first wife to marry the beautiful, black-haired Renee, and they had one son, Roy Alexander Radin, who was born on November 13, 1949. He was raised a Catholic, his mother's faith, although for most of his life he was fascinated by his father's, Judaism.

Al Radin died when Roy was still in his teens. The boy was devastated, believing that the one force in his life that had motivated him to succeed was now gone. As it turned out, Radin was virtually adopted by some of his father's friends, including Orson Welles as well as a comedian named Joey Marx. They promised they would help Radin become a major producer, and they introduced him to the people in New York who could help him.

Through these connections, Radin got to know the characters his father knew—talent agents, producers, singers, tipsters, gossip columnists, press agents, and the assortment of people along the shadowy fringes of Broadway. With his new contacts, he started a business booking bands for Long Island nightclubs. He would stay up for days in a row, sleep for days, get in his car and drive all over Long Island to meet club owners. He assumed a posture, a pose, as his father had. Promotion was his skill. He helped small rock-and-roll bands get record contracts and others get booked into basement clubs in the New York suburbs. Radin sang, too. He loved Bob Dylan's music, though his real skill was not as an entertainer.

By the early 1970s, he started talking about bringing back vaudeville in the form of road shows and police department benefits. Radin had always loved vaudeville, mostly because of his father's connection to it. The idea took off. In just a few years, his income was such that he and his new wife, Loretta, were able to move into the seventy-two-room mansion he called Ocean Castle in the wealthy village of Southampton, where Wall Street and entertainment-industry tycoons maintained summer homes. To ingratiate himself with the local police, he did benefits for their unions and hired cops as drivers and assistants.

All the while, Radin was developing a new persona—the rich entrepreneur, the self-made man.

At some point, Radin even began dressing like his father. He donned fedoras and capes at some of the shows, acting the role of an impresario, the new P. T. Barnum. He told people that someday he would be big in show business. He talked of staging a huge event, something so grand everyone would know who he was.

A secretive and complicated man, Radin had another connection, which he mentioned only in whispers. Once, on a bus heading for a show in New Hampshire, Radin was seated next to Red Buttons. In his enthusiastic way, Radin talked for hours about his father and his own future plans. Then he added, almost in a whisper, as if it had something to do with the grand future he knew would be his someday, that he had a godfather.

"I got some muscle," Radin told Buttons.

His "muscle" was an aging New York gangster named Johnny Stoppelli, one of Al's friends, who had extensive show business contacts. Radin referred to him as his Uncle Johnny. Stoppelli, who lived with his wife, Sylvia, in an apartment in the Murray Hill section of Manhattan, was literally Radin's godfather, appointed to the task shortly after Roy's birth. It was an interesting choice, considering that the portly, balding man was listed in New York City Police Department files as a soldier in the Genovese crime family.

While Radin treated Stoppelli as an honored guest, bringing him out to Ocean Castle in his limousine, Stoppelli was helping Radin book acts for his tours. He also helped him financially by investing in Radin's business. But his behind-the-scenes role was a secret. In all likelihood, no police department would have hired Radin for its fund-raisers had his association with a reputed mob soldier been known.

By 1975, Radin was putting tours together that included the Shirelles, George Gobel, Donald O'Connor, Frankie Fontaine, Jack Carter, Jan Murray, and a number of animal acts. A few years later, perhaps predictably, considering the whirlwind life he was leading, Radin's marriage to Loretta broke up.

They had married when they were both very young, in their early twenties. She was pretty and headstrong, and to many of the entertainers who worked with Radin, she was the brains while Roy was the drive. After they married, they adopted two children, a son they named Julius Caesar Radin and a girl, Retta. When the marriage broke up, several years later, the children went off to live with their mother. Radin, devastated and heartbroken, made every effort to see them whenever he was in town.

In nearly all respects, Loretta was the opposite of Toni Fillet, whom Radin had met in a Southampton bar. Toni liked the lifestyle her marriage to Radin allowed—chauffeur-driven limousines, trips to Manhattan nightclubs, dinners at expensive restaurants. Together, they hoped to fulfill Radin's show business dreams.

In 1980, Radin's name began popping up in the New York tabloids' gossip pages. Sometimes the papers would print his picture, too—a smiling fat man in an expensive suit, ducking into Studio 54. He was practically a fixture at the club, where he would spend the night snorting cocaine in a private room and talking about his deals. Radin always had grand schemes. He was going to finance a Broadway show, buy a circus in Florida, bring back old-time theatrical musicals. An abundance of ideas was his trademark.

Wherever Radin went, he tried to make it an event. He needed to make an impression on people, to leave them with his name on their minds. At bars, he would buy everyone a round of drinks or dinner. He had the aura of a supercharged dynamo, a man with money to spend and places to go. Most of the time when he was out on the town in New York, he would bring along an aide, usually the stout and muscular Sal Miglionico, to act as a bodyguard.

Until the weekend of April 11, 1980, however, the name Roy Alexander Radin had not made any headlines. The event that launched him into tabloid history began innocently enough on Friday afternoon, when a young, beautiful model and sometime actress named Melonie Haller walked into Ferrara's, a busy Southampton pharmacy. She was with a date, a management consultant from New Jersey named Robert McKeage, and they were on their way to Ocean Castle. In a few minutes, she bought Topol toothpaste, Nivea skin cream, cologne, hair coloring, tampons—and three dog chains.

That night, the couple were to be Radin's dinner guests at Ocean Castle. Their visit had been arranged by a New York photographer named Ron Sisman, who was a friend of Haller's and who had told her that Radin might be able to help her. Up until then, her career had included modeling assignments, including a photo spread in *Playboy*, and several episodes on the television show "Welcome Back, Kotter."

Joining Melonie and McKeage were two Rhode Island narcotics detectives, Wellington Ray, Jr., and Joseph Vendittelli, who had also come to Ocean Castle for dinner. Ray was a friend of Radin's, and the two cops had flown to Southampton in a private plane at his suggestion to discuss a show Radin was shortly to produce for the Rhode Island State Police union.

At dinner in the dining room at Ocean Castle, the guests were joined by Fillet and Radin. McKeage, not knowing the two men were narcotics detectives, discussed cocaine purchases he had made in the past, while Melonie, who was drunk, knocked over wineglasses.

That night, after the cops had left, McKeage tried to woo Melonie and another woman houseguest into bed with him. He showed the women his impressive drug collection—cocaine, Quaaludes, amyl nitrite, and mescaline. After midnight, McKeage and Melonie dressed up in skimpy leather outfits and Nazi caps and marched into Radin's bedroom, where they began whipping each other. Both were wearing dog collars and chains.

Early Saturday morning, Melonie went back to Radin's bedroom to show him her portfolio, which contained her photo spread in *Playboy*. Radin did not wish to speak with her, however, and at his direction, Melonie was taken downstairs to her bedroom, where she began fighting with McKeage. At some later point, Melonie again went into Radin's bedroom, and in a wild thrashing about, broke the lens on his video camera, which was set up on a tripod and pointed directly at his bed.

The houseguests spent most of Saturday sleeping. Late that night, as if enough had not happened in the house, Mickey De Vinko, a moody and often depressed man, swallowed a bottleful of sleeping pills. He was rushed to Southampton Hospital, where his stomach was pumped. To his dismay, when Radin returned from the hospital at dawn Sunday morning, he found Melonie screaming hysterically and running around the house. She was cut and bruised and appeared hopelessly disoriented. Radin ordered her out of Ocean Castle.

Shortly before 8:00 A.M. on Sunday, another one of Radin's employees, Ray Wouters, was summoned to take Melonie to the train station. Wouters found her in the foyer, stumbling and staggering around and mumbling incoherently.

Wouters went and got McKeage, who, upon seeing Melonie, threw her to the floor and kicked her in the ribs, face, and chest. Wouters stopped McKeage when he threatened to smash Melonie's skull with a porcelain dog. Wouters picked her up, put her in the car, and McKeage drove her to the station, where she was dumped on a city-bound train.

That morning, just before 9:00 A.M., a railroad conductor found Melonie slumped over a seat. She was taken to a hospital, and a Suffolk County police detective, Lee Roman, was summoned. He found her in the emergency room, her long blond hair pushed straight back out of her face, which was bruised and discolored. One eye was partially shut from a swollen eyelid. There was a line of blood on her lower lip.

"I was beaten," Melonie mumbled to Roman, her voice quickly dropping off. "They dumped me on the train like I was baggage." She began to cry. "They beat me and kicked me."

"Where did this happen?" Roman asked.

"I was invited to Southampton for the weekend," she said. "To meet a producer." She pointed to a large loose-leaf book on the table next to her. "I brought my portfolio."

"What's the producer's name?" Roman asked.

She thought for a moment. "Ravin," she said.

Roman knew of a Radin house in the village, and he wondered if she meant him.

"Could it be the Radin house?" he asked. "Roy Radin?"

Melonie nodded.

Roman was called away from the bed by a nurse, who directed him to a telephone on the emergency room wall. He picked it up, and the caller identified himself as a reporter with the *Daily News*. He wanted to know what had happened to Melonie Haller.

The reporter told Roman that Haller's mother had called the newspaper and said that her daughter had been beaten at a mansion in Southampton. Roman replied that he knew nothing and abruptly hung up.

Before noon on Monday, reports that a model who had posed for *Playboy* had been beaten up in Southampton were all over the airwaves, and reporters began descending on Ocean Castle. Inside, at his desk, Radin told one of his assistants that he could not believe this was happening to him. A publicity hound at heart, Radin instructed his staff to record all the radio and television news and clip all the newspapers.

Later in the day, Roman and his partner, Detective Bob Heller, took another statement from Melonie, who now added that she had been raped at Ocean Castle. She also mentioned seeing a gun in Radin's bedroom, as well as large amounts of cocaine. In the course of describing the sexual attack, Melonie said the video camera had been on the entire time, and that she had broken it in the struggle.

Radin learned through a police friend that his house would be raided on Monday night. The

household staff was ordered to do a complete
cleanup. The sheets were stripped off his bed and
dumped in the washing machine, the carpet was
vacuumed, drawers were cleaned out, pills
flushed down the toilets, and ashtrays emptied.
Most important, the tape that had been in the
video camera was erased.

Charlie Donchez feared the publicity would
kill his boss's ability to work with police departments. When he voiced his concern, Radin said
he hoped and prayed that Donchez was wrong.

Minutes before the police arrived, a housekeeper who was going through Radin's bedroom
found a pistol under his pillow and some pills on
a side table. She flushed the pills down the toilet
and gave the pistol to Radin, who promptly hid it.
Then someone yelled out that there were fifty
cops in the driveway.

Roman was the first through the door. "We are
Suffolk County police officers," he called out.
"We're here to execute a search warrant."

Radin stood in the foyer. "What are you here
for?" he yelled.

"We have a rape and assault complaint," Roman said.

"Bullshit!" Radin said. "Absolute bullshit."

Officers spread out through the house, down
the hallway to secure Radin's bedroom and into
the living room to gather his employees together.

"Do you know who I am?" Radin inquired
loudly of Roman.

Roman, who did not care, ignored him.

"I have friends in your PBA," Radin continued.
"I know the sheriff of this county." When he saw
he was having no effect, he announced loudly
that he was calling his lawyer.

While Radin lurched toward a phone, Fillet approached the officers. "You have no right to be here!" she yelled. "We had nothing to do with Melonie Haller! *Get out of here!"*

"Shut up, or you're going to jail," Roman coolly told Fillet.

Within minutes of entering the house, the officers began carrying out Radin's belongings—sheets, pillows, pillowcases, towels, videotapes, clothes, the video camera, and a host of other things. Detective Heller found what appeared to be bloodstains on the floor in the hallway near Radin's bedroom. They were scraped up, bagged, and hauled out to waiting cars. (The stains were later determined to be red paint.)

Radin, meanwhile, continued to phone his connections. At one point, he insisted that Roman get on the phone with his friend the sheriff of Suffolk County, who wanted to talk with him. Roman told the sheriff it was none of his business and hung up. A few minutes later, another county official called, wanting to know what was happening, and Roman put him off, as well.

In Radin's big bedroom, a detective found the pistol in his walk-in closet. Heller presented it to Radin and asked him if it was his. Radin said no, adding that it belonged to a cop in Louisiana.

"You're under arrest for illegal possession of a gun," Roman asserted. Radin was handcuffed and taken away, while Fillet ranted in the doorway.

After he was booked, photographed, and released on bail, Radin found himself deluged with embarrassing publicity. At first, he tried to laugh it off, saying it would work itself out. But he knew it wouldn't. He sank into depression, complaining to his friends that he did not see how his vaudeville business could survive.

In his anger over the events of the weekend,
the person he railed against most was Ron Sisman, the photographer who had sent Melonie
Haller out to Ocean Castle for the weekend. Radin called him a pimp and accused him of being
behind some sort of setup to ruin Radin's reputation.

Reporters called Ocean Castle for information
as if the Melonie Haller story were of enormous
significance. Radin blew up one day when a copy
of the *New York Post* landed on his desk. The
headline read: MOTHER BEGS: SHUT DOWN SIN PAL-
ACE. Radin was described as a show business
huckster who produced shows in the hinterlands
that were made up of "Gong Show" rejects.

Convinced he was ruined, Radin became paranoid. He raged about being watched and about
not being able to go out to village restaurants
anymore without having people point at him. Instead of living at his usual frenzied pace, he
stayed home, sitting up all night watching television. Seeing himself on the news, catching
glimpses of his round, bearded face photographed in the back seat of his limousine as it
drove in and out of Ocean Castle, he felt as if he
were watching his own funeral.

Several weeks after his arrest, a relative of
Melonie's called Ocean Castle. According to one
of Radin's attorneys, the relative demanded
$200,000 in exchange for Melonie's dropping the
charges. Radin, on the advice of his attorneys,
did not accept the offer.

Nearly a month after filing her sensational
charges, Haller appeared at the Suffolk County
District Attorney's office, wading through a mass
of photographers. Prosecutor Barry Feldman
grilled her about the events that had occurred

during the notorious weekend she spent at Ocean Castle. Later that day, after her testimony before a grand jury, some of the star-struck jurors asked her to autograph copies of *Playboy* magazine.

The morning after Haller's testimony, Radin sat in his office at Ocean Castle and read the newspaper accounts. He reiterated his conviction that he was as good as dead in his business.

He wondered whether people on the West Coast were reading about him. Perhaps it was time to think about leaving New York and setting up business in California. He had produced records there in the past, as well as managed several actors, including his close friend Demond Wilson. And he had always wanted to produce movies, seeing it as a natural extension of his road show business.

Radin was in Los Angeles a few weeks later when he heard that he had been indicted on misdemeanor charges of gun possession. He broke down and wept. When he returned to Southampton, he sat forlornly in his office.

"What about Roy Radin Enterprises?" an office worker asked.

"We'll make it," Radin assured her. "I talked to Joey Bishop about doing a show. We'll make it."

Six months after the Melonie Haller weekend, a person or persons broke into Ron Sisman's apartment in the Chelsea section of Manhattan. He was pushed to the floor and executed, a single shot to the head.

Radin read about the murder in the New York tabloids. Several of the stories mentioned Sisman's connection to Haller and Radin. Radin laughed off the suggestions of his friends that he had arranged the murder in retribution for the shame and publicity he had suffered. There was no evidence to connect Radin to the crime, which would remain unsolved.

EIGHT

BY THE SPRING OF 1982, TWO YEARS after the Melonie Haller incident, Radin's business was near collapse. Radin had struggled to keep his business going, but he had found it nearly impossible.

Not ready to give up, he put all his hope for the future of his vaudeville revival business into a new tour, which was to open on April 1 in Cleveland and finish at the end of the summer in Atlantic City. He was desperate for the tour to succeed. This was one of the reasons he had hired Lawson.

Hopeful, but not optimistic, he wanted to prove to himself that he could still produce moneymaking road tours. But the reality was that he was in deep financial trouble, and he began finalizing plans to move to the West Coast.

Before Haller, Radin's business had generated up to six million dollars a year in revenues. But after all the fallout over Haller's charges, suspicious police department officials Radin had worked with for years were no longer returning his calls. Several promised contracts were canceled. To make matters worse, departments he had worked with in the past were demanding a greater share of the profits before agreeing to new contracts.

Over the years, Radin had become remarkably adept at manipulating the profits of his shows so that the police departments received the smallest share possible. One of his schemes was to deduct from the police share of the profits all his business costs—phones, salaries, even the overhead for Ocean Castle. After his name had been dragged into the newspapers, many police groups he had worked with caught on to what he was doing.

Many friends deserted him, too. He became an outcast, shunned by his professional peers, who now viewed him as sleazy and amoral. In addition, his marriage to Toni Fillet was collapsing.

Radin and Fillet fought wildly and frequently. He accused her of having affairs while he was away on business trips, and of running up large bills at posh Manhattan department stores.

She accused him of possessing a violent temper, of making frequent threats to have unnamed parties beat her up. Several times he had had her removed from Ocean Castle and bolted the doors behind her. She also claimed he tapped the phones in the mansion to see if she had boyfriends. Finally, she also had come to loathe her husband's cocaine binges, although she had used the drug herself.

Once, Radin tried to intimidate a trusted secretary, Christine Broderick, into admitting that Fillet was having an affair with another employee. Radin maneuvered Broderick into the front seat of his car, next to his bodyguard. Radin got in the back. When the doors were shut, the bodyguard put his gun on the dashboard.

Broderick deftly talked her way out of trouble, denying any knowledge of Fillet's personal life.

The Cleveland tour had to work, financially as well as professionally, or Radin would have to find another line of business.

On the second night of the show, however, there was trouble. Joey Bishop informed Radin he would not perform. Bishop's decision to boycott had to do with his pay. He was getting ten thousand dollars a week, and he had spoken to Radin about receiving most of it up front.

In his dressing room at the Holiday Inn, Bishop was sitting with his manager, Larry Fox, when Lawson walked by.

"Five minutes," Lawson said.

"I'll tell you when you call five minutes," Bishop said angrily, rocketing out of his seat.

"The show *will* start in five minutes, Joey," Lawson repeated.

"There may not be a show tonight," Fox said. "Tell your boss that one."

Lawson sought out Charlie Donchez. "I'm holding the orchestra," Lawson said. "You'd better work something out. Fast."

Lawson repeated Bishop's demands to Radin, who was infuriated.

"That man will not tell me what to do," Radin said. "Who does Bishop think he is? The man would not be working if it weren't for me."

Radin stormed off to talk with Donchez. He was given the authority to do whatever he had to do to control Bishop.

The comedian could not be roughed up, since he was supposed to perform. But Larry Fox was another matter. He—and, by extension, Bishop—could be taught a lesson.

As the orchestra waited to begin the show, two men assaulted Fox. The beating was severe enough to send him to a local hospital. Bishop, horrified at the violence inflicted on his manager, complained angrily to Radin, threatening retaliation. Fearing the arrival of the local police, Radin hurriedly packed up his belongings and headed for the airport.

Bishop nonetheless continued with the tour. Whether he would stay for its entire run was another matter. Frankly, Radin told staffers, he was waiting for the next confrontation with the comedian. He laughed off Bishop's angry claims that he had muscle in Philadelphia, who would exact revenge.

Not one to take chances, though, Radin hired an armed bodyguard to stay with him twenty-four hours a day.

In late June, the tour arrived in Atlantic City. They were to play at Bally's for the entire summer, ending in mid-September. When the tour was over, Radin was hoping to take the show to a theater on Broadway, or possibly to Las Vegas.

A flood of publicity prepared by Radin's New York publicist, Richard Gersh, had preceded the show to Atlantic City. For the first time in months, Radin was buoyant. Most of the cast moved into a seedy motel outside the casino area, and Radin moved into a suite at Bally's.

Not long after his arrival, Radin's appendix ruptured, and he had to be taken to Philadelphia for emergency surgery. Lawson was immediately promoted to run the company, and Bishop, still smarting over the events in Ohio, went on the attack again. With Radin out of commission, he evidently did not fear for his safety.

One night, shortly after Radin had returned

from Philadelphia, Lawson was told that two performers were not at rehearsal. Bishop immediately seized on that fact and used it to confront Lawson.

"I want a meeting," he said. "This cannot happen."

Lawson told him the show would go on, with or without the performers. When Bishop continued to scream, Lawson warned him to calm down. Minutes before show time, as the orchestra was beginning the overture, the two performers appeared. Bishop demanded they be kept in their dressing rooms, but Lawson ignored him.

"I am not going to have them onstage," Bishop said. "You remember who the star is."

"I'm the fucking star, asshole," Lawson shot back. "And I'm going to walk out of here if you don't stop this."

"You remember," Bishop warned, jabbing his fist toward Lawson's face, "this is my territory."

"Your 'territory'?" Lawson asked, dumbfounded. "What sort of crap is that, Joey?"

"You will never set foot in this theater again," Bishop said. "All I have to do is snap my fingers, and you are done."

Lawson yelled back that at least he was not a broken-down has-been, and then he went to talk to Radin in his room. He repeated what Bishop had said about his "territory."

Astounded, Radin said, "He doesn't know what he's talking about. This is no one's territory. It's an open city."

Unwilling to run the show with Bishop around, Lawson told Radin he would stay in the office. Meanwhile, Bishop named his own stage manager and informed Lawson he was never to set foot on the stage again. Bishop made it clear that he had friends in Philadelphia who could play hard ball.

Shortly afterward, however, Bishop dropped out and was replaced as master of ceremonies by Jackie Vernon. But there were still financial problems to be worked out between Bishop and Radin, and a meeting was set up at a restaurant in New York's Little Italy.

On a rainy morning in Manhattan, Grigg drove Radin and Johnny Stoppelli to the rendezvous. They waited at the curb, and shortly a Cadillac pulled up. Bishop and a couple of Philadelphia gangsters got out. Everyone went inside the restaurant, emerging four hours later after an agreement had been reached. Bishop's and Radin's relationship was over.

Several times over the summer, Stoppelli, in fedora and trench coat, showed up at Bally's. His wife, Sylvia, had taken a job in the box office, selling tickets to Radin's show. Some nights, Radin and Stoppelli would spend the evening in the casino, gambling and talking.

Directed by Radin to examine closely the company's accounting records, Lawson found odd, conflicting numbers. The show was losing money, yet one set of books showed the company was making a nine-thousand-dollar weekly profit.

Radin's fervent hope that the show would restore him as a producer foundered in late August. He had believed he had a sure deal to take the show to Las Vegas, but it fell through. He did not know whether it was the lingering effects of the Haller mess or whether someone—perhaps Bishop—was sabotaging him.

In addition, Radin found he no longer had the clout to take the show to a Broadway theater. It was now clear that this show would be Radin's last tour.

"I want to start concentrating all my energies on the West Coast," Radin told Lawson. "I've always wanted to get into movies. That's what I really want to do."

He told Lawson that whatever happened, he wanted him there with him.

Over the summer, Lawson had closely examined the household bills. He determined that it was costing between $12,000 and $15,000 a month to keep Ocean Castle, more than $150,000 a year. Radin's only option was to sell it.

By going through canceled checks and old checkbooks, Lawson also calculated that Radin was spending upwards of $1,500 a week on cocaine. He wondered how long that habit could continue.

In early fall, Radin made plans to sell Ocean Castle, the Xanadu he had bought when he was only in his twenties. He spoke with some real estate brokers around Southampton and put out the word that the house—which he had paid under $300,000 for in 1978—was for sale.

In mid-October, Radin and Lawson boarded a TWA flight to Los Angeles. Lawson had arranged for two apartments at the Regency Hotel, on Hollywood Boulevard. A Mercedes convertible was rented through an agency in Beverly Hills.

In the days before they left, Lawson had added up some other numbers, and he learned that Demond Wilson, whom Radin managed, owed $60,636.50 in back payments. The financially strapped Radin hoped to work out some sort of agreement whereby at least some of the money could be paid.

He also wanted to tell Wilson of his plans to relocate to the West Coast. Radin had stacks of screenplays that had been sent him over the years, and now he hoped to find financing to produce at least one of them.

His favorite was a musical about the old Harlem nightclub, the Cotton Club. Radin hoped to find investors who would back either a Broadway show or a feature film, and he wanted Wilson to have a part in it.

On the night Radin and Lawson arrived in Los Angeles, Wilson came to their hotel suite shortly after dark. Wilson and Radin talked for a few minutes about the actor's role in "The New Odd Couple," a weekly television show (which would shortly be canceled), while Lawson set out a mirror and some cocaine in lacquered Chinese bowls.

When Radin returned to Southampton, he concentrated on unburdening himself of Ocean Castle. Though emotional about selling the house, he knew he had to make a killing on the sale to provide the nest egg necessary for him to start over in California. He was delighted when a New York investor named Barry Trupin agreed to pay more than eight million dollars for the estate.

Lawson secured a duplex at the Mayflower Hotel in Manhattan as their base before they moved west. The plan was to bring along part of the staff, including Grigg and Miglionico, both of whom Radin said he needed with him.

Holidays in the oceanfront mansion had always been grand occasions. So for his last Christmas at Ocean Castle, Radin wanted to stage an extravaganza, even though he was living on his last dollars before the house money came through. It was to be staged like a Broadway musical, an unforgettable send-off.

Renee, Radin's adoring mother, and Lawson were put in charge of the celebration. Lawson had to scour the place in search of serving platters, since a lot of household items had been taken during the packing. He asked Loretta, who had been invited along with Radin's two children, Julius and Retta, to bring china and serving platters and tablecloths. An eighteen-foot Christmas tree was erected in the living room and decorated with live roses and baby's breath. Seventy-five poinsettia plants filled the staircases and flowed down the hallways.

The day before Christmas, Malcolm Grigg brought Johnny and Sylvia Stoppelli out from Manhattan. Radin greeted them in the driveway, hugging them both. It was a brilliant, cold morning, and the sea air was bracing. Radin remarked how nice it was that they could all be together.

Stoppelli and Radin stood quietly by the limousine. For a moment, they surveyed the house, perhaps thinking about the years they had spent there. And about the remarkable rise—and now the fall—of Radin's business fortunes, which had made it all possible.

PART THREE

HOLLYWOOD

NINE

IN OCTOBER 1982, LANEY, MYRIAM, AND Dax arrived in Los Angeles. Laney contacted an acquaintance, Carol Johnston, whom she had met through a hairdresser in Miami. Johnston worked at the travel agency Laney had frequently used on her trips to Los Angeles. When she mentioned she needed a place to live, Johnston said her father's home in Benedict Canyon was for rent. Shortly after their arrival, Laney, her son, and her maid moved into the big house.

Laney was in Los Angeles to be the West Coast end of Milan Bellechasses' multimillion-dollar cocaine-smuggling operation. Her plan was to buy a house as quickly as possible. A rental was not a good investment, nor was living in someone else's home a good idea for her, since the owner might drop in unexpectedly.

She decided to buy a large house at 3862 Sherwood Place, in Sherman Oaks. It was set back from the street and situated on a quiet cul-de-sac reachable only by twisting roads through the hills. There was a garage, which she required for her cars and as a place to store large amounts of cocaine and money. It suited her needs perfectly.

When finally she closed on the Sherman Oaks property, putting down one hundred thousand dollars in cash, Frank Diaz, who had helped set up Jamboni Enterprises, flew out to handle the legal work.

Laney decorated the house with expensive Chinese antiques and artwork. She liked vases and glass pieces, and placed them on the shelves in the living room. She bought a large glass dining room table, installed new carpeting in all the rooms, and put up new wallpaper.

Dax was eight months old when Laney moved into the house in January of 1983. She showered him with toys, and the nursery was well equipped with stuffed animals and mobiles that hung from the ceiling. Although Laney's involvement with Dax was minimal, since Myriam essentially did the work, Laney wanted everything to be perfect for her son.

That fall, she began telling friends that Bellechasses was Dax's father. Bellechasses' picture was displayed prominently in the living room of the Sherman Oaks house. On a number of occasions, she referred to Bellechasses as her husband. Joe Amer had apparently been forgotten.

When Laney first moved into the house, she lived quietly. Myriam did not cook, and they would order in fried chicken or go out to dinner. Soon, though, Laney got into the swing of the city, and she began frequenting restaurants and nightclubs.

During the day, she and Myriam would take Dax to the beach or to Marina Del Rey, or they would park on Rodeo Drive and window-shop. Laney, with her love of expensive things, felt right at home in Beverly Hills. Once, they took Dax to Sears and had baby pictures taken.

Occasionally, Bellechasses would fly in from Miami, and he and Laney would go out on the town. They had become lovers, although when he was gone, Laney dated other men.

It took almost no time to get their business in order. Selling cocaine in Los Angeles through a network of distributors was simple. To transport the product to Los Angeles, Bellechasses hired a courier named Tally Rogers. An affable man of modest build, Rogers dressed in work shirts, jeans, and designer sneakers. A Tennessean, Rogers spoke in a deep Southern drawl; he had a quick wit and a finely developed instinct for protecting his interests.

Every six weeks or so, Rogers would drive from Miami to Los Angeles, the trunk of his car stuffed with ten to twelve kilos of cocaine in packages wrapped with duct tape. He would pick up the drugs at Bellechasses', where on one trip he saw 2,200 kilos of cocaine stacked in his basement, floor to ceiling. At the Los Angeles end, Rogers was also a money courier. As cash accumulated in the storage closet in the back of Laney's garage, he would box it or pack it in suitcases and drive it to San Francisco. There, he would hand it over to two Latinos, whose job was to deposit it in local banks so that it could be wired to bank accounts in the Caribbean.

With her cocaine business operating smoothly, Laney turned her attention to the dream she had been talking about for years—moviemaking. A friend in Palm Beach had referred her to a limousine driver named Gary Keys. He had picked Dax, Myriam, and herself up at the airport, and she had used him on several occasions thereafter. Keys was an employee of Ascot Limousine, which was partially owned by Robert Evans, the former head of production at Paramount Pictures.

On one of her trips about town, Laney casually mentioned to Keys that she wanted to be a movie producer. She told him that she had a considerable amount of money she wished to invest. For years, Keys had heard people in the back of his limousine talking about movies. His passengers talked about deals at studios and movies in various stages of production. Evans, he knew, was looking for funds for a number of pictures he hoped to make as an independent producer.

When Keys mentioned to Laney that he could introduce her to Evans, she screamed with delight. She gave Keys her phone number, which he promised to pass on to Evans.

A few days later, Evans called her, and they arranged to meet. Laney was beside herself with excitement. She told her friend Anna Montenegro, a Cuban-American from Miami who had recently relocated to Los Angeles, that she had made contact with a famous Hollywood producer and they were going to work closely together. That, after just a few weeks in Los Angeles, she had met a producer with a track record that included such films as *Chinatown* and *The Godfather* only fueled her belief that she was a naturally lucky person.

When Laney arrived at Evans' Beverly Hills house, she met a handsome and charming man, with a deep tan, thick black hair, and sunglasses tinted the color of raspberries. He affected an air of privilege and great wealth, which was, for the most part, a sham, but nonetheless convincing. As he gave her a tour of his French-style château, he spoke about the movies he had made and the people he knew. At one point, he told her he had

produced *The Adventurers*. Laney responded excitedly that *The Adventurers* was her favorite
book and that she had named her son after one of
its characters.

Evans was a genuine Hollywood legend, a one-
time actor who, at the age of thirty-six, had become Paramount's head of production. Under his
supervision, the studio released films such as
Love Story and *The Godfather*, which were box
office smashes. He was friends with the biggest
names in Hollywood, among them Warren Beatty
and Jack Nicholson, who was perhaps his closest
and most loyal friend. He had had brief, if well-
chronicled, marriages to Ali MacGraw and later
Phyllis George. George divorced Evans in 1978.

A fixture on the Hollywood social circuit, Evans was photographed at parties and balls and at
the events that made the film community unique.
He had it all—looks, charm, money, and the right
connections. In fan magazines and gossip col-
umns, Evans was portrayed as a shrewd producer with a Midas touch, a boy wonder.

By the late 1970s, Evans was an independent
producer. On his own, he seemed to lose his way.
In short order, he produced a string of flops,
including *Black Sunday, Players*, and *Popeye*.
While he was certainly not the only independent
producer in Hollywood to make financially un-
successful pictures, Evans, after so many big
hits, was no longer the toast of the town. To make
matters worse, he was convicted in New York in
1980 on federal charges of possessing five ounces
of cocaine.

The conviction only served to underscore what
had been whispered in Hollywood: that Evans
had a drug problem. By way of explaining the
downward slide of his filmmaking career, people

who knew him spoke of his sloppy cocaine use. Some said he was an addict. It fit the pattern of his recent life that the television special Evans produced as part of the unusual plea-bargain arrangement that kept him out of jail—the show was called "Get High on Yourself"—bombed in the ratings.

Evans was a man that few people in positions of influence wanted to work with any longer. His producing days appeared over, for he seemed powerless to raise funds through his studio contacts. For years, Evans had virtually been able to write his own checks, drawing millions of dollars from his old studio, Paramount, to make movies that, in turn, brought the studio riches. This was the Hollywood system, and Evans had been highly successful at making it work to his advantage.

For many producers, the system is more hindrance than help. Projects are pitched to production chiefs, who, if they like them, dole out the necessary resources. Even for the most talented producers, selling projects is often an exasperating process, a merry-go-round of rejections, approvals, personnel changes, and, if they are lucky, approvals again.

But after his flops and his drug conviction, Evans found that his calls were not being returned. It was said that he had not stopped using cocaine. Perhaps the worst thing said about Evans was that he was no longer in control of his own life; therefore, studio bosses were reluctant to loan him the millions necessary to make movies. Evans was now a nonplayer. He began complaining to his closest friends that he was going broke.

Then he met Laney Jacobs.

Charming, alluring, and mysterious, Laney

told him that she had five million dollars of her own in Miami, and on top of that she had friends with access to even larger amounts of disposable cash, perhaps as much as fifty million dollars. If Evans was suspicious of the source of her money, he did not immediately say so. A friend of Laney's who attended a meeting with her at Evans' house said Laney had mentioned that she had access to "narcotics money."*

It was after one of her meetings with Evans that Laney told Tally Rogers, who had just stuffed another ten kilos of cocaine into the closet in her garage, that she was working with the producer. She claimed that Evans was interested in obtaining drug money to finance his pictures and had indicated that eight or ten other producers were similarly disposed. It now seemed that Laney, after only a few weeks in Los Angeles, had hit the jackpot. Here, money was what mattered.

Evans soon became enamored of Laney. He sent flowers to the Sherman Oaks house and asked her to dinner and parties. In turn, she offered him cocaine out of her considerable stash.

Radin was a New Yorker at heart. He considered Los Angeles an ugly city with neither a center nor a soul. But he knew, now more than ever, that his new home offered him hope for reviving his business. He was an optimist, a man who wanted to do the right thing, and what drove him at this point was the absolute belief that by turning his attention to the West Coast, he would finally achieve the future he'd always dreamed he would have.

* Evans has denied any knowledge that drug money was involved.

There were still considerable details to be taken care of in New York, and Radin's plan as the new year began was to maintain his apartment at the Mayflower. Some business files would be kept there, although the bulk of his records would be moved into a building in Hampton Bays on Long Island.

The whole point of moving to Los Angeles was to make movies. He had several plans in mind, one of which was to produce musical comedy films, now a rarity. He had a file of properties he had carried around with him for years, including the Cotton Club musical. *I Love My Wife* and *Hallelujah Baby* were the titles of other projects.

Radin was also considering turning Mickey De Vinko's book about his marriage to Judy Garland into a television movie. As much as he had come to dislike De Vinko, Radin believed the project was worth doing.

Before leaving for Los Angeles, Lawson set up a system with Radin's secretary, Christine Broderick, to keep track of the revenue that continued to come in to Roy Radin Enterprises.

Lawson's view of Roy Radin Enterprises was that it was a fraud waiting to be exposed. He believed cops in the various cities where the tour stopped had been paid off in exchange for looking the other way when the profits were divided up. The business was a cash machine, but it depended on fleecing the police departments and performing accounting tricks so that Roy Radin Enterprises could keep the maximum profits.

Now, though, with Radin determined to get the most out of the income that still came in to the company, it became Lawson's responsibility to determine if any money was being taken fraudulently. Lawson told Broderick he wanted her to call him in Los Angeles every day, with the totals in all the company's bank accounts.

Radin and Lawson flew to Los Angeles in early January, with scripts, proposals, and film treatments stuffed into luggage along with their clothes. They moved back into the Regency. Not a fancy hotel—it was set up for short-term rentals—it was clean and comfortable. Their suite had a large living room and spacious bedrooms.

After getting settled, Radin called Milton Berle, an old friend, and asked him about the possibility of headlining a new spring tour on the East Coast. No police departments had committed themselves yet, but Radin believed there was a possibility for one more tour, perhaps a smaller one.

Radin also checked in with some old friends and relatives who lived in the area. One was his cousin Jimmy McQuestion, who years before had worked for Radin on a tour that Eddie Fisher headlined. McQuestion had not particularly enjoyed traveling with his cousin's troupe. The hours were long, and he had had trouble adapting to Radin's wild behavior and cocaine use. But McQuestion nevertheless liked his cousin and appreciated his calling when he was in town. Henry Fillet, soon to be his exfather-in-law, also lived nearby, and in spite of the breakup of his marriage to Toni Fillet, Radin kept in touch with him.

Because Radin did not know many people in Los Angeles, a friend of his in New York had told him about Carol Johnston, a travel agent, and suggested he meet her. She was acquainted with a lot of Hollywood people whom Radin would want to get to know. She phoned Radin a few days after his arrival. They chatted, and John-

ston offered to show him a house in Benedict
Canyon that her father owned. An acquaintance
of Johnston's—Laney Jacobs—was in the process
of moving out of the house, and Johnston said it
was available for rent, if Radin was interested.
The five-bedroom home had a pool and a tennis
court, and Radin thought it sounded ideal.

A few days later, Johnston left a message at the
Regency, inviting Radin to a party she was having for her father, who had recently retired from
a high position at one of the film studios and was
moving to Miami. Radin was excited, telling
Lawson that he hoped there would be a number
of Hollywood executives in attendance.

On the night of the party, Radin dressed in his
customary dark suit and tie, and Lawson drove
him in their rented Mercedes to the house in
Benedict Canyon. Radin asked him to come in,
but Lawson declined, informing Radin that he
had business to attend to. He would return when
Radin phoned.

An hour and a half later, Lawson's phone rang.
Radin said excitedly that he was returning to the
hotel with Johnston and another woman.

"She is not like anyone I've ever met," Radin
said. "I can't believe her. She's incredible. Would
you put something together for us to eat? Call
somewhere and get some champagne. Taittinger,
if you can find it.

"Oh, and you won't believe my new friend,"
Radin added before he got off the phone. "She's
got incredible coke."

Lawson had brought a few kitchen utensils
from Ocean Castle. He called a gourmet shop
near the hotel and ordered meat and some vege-
tables for a big salad. After putting a bottle of

champagne in the refrigerator to chill, Lawson prepared a small dinner.

An hour later, the door to the apartment burst open, and in walked Radin with the two women. Carol Johnston was attractive and well dressed. The second woman had short hair that was light in color but flecked with gray; her eyes were dark brown, almost black, behind a pair of designer glasses that had a bit of a rose tint. She had on a long evening dress that was brightly colored and tight-fitting.

She talked loudly, laughing and hanging off Radin's arm. Radin motioned for Lawson to come out of the kitchen, and holding on to his new friend, he made the introductions.

"Jonathan," Radin said, beaming, "meet Laney Jacobs."

Lawson extended his hand, and Laney stepped toward him.

"It's *so* nice to meet you, Jonathan," she said. "Roy was telling us about you."

Lawson went back into the kitchen to get the hors d'oeuvres. He talked to Johnston while Laney and Radin sat in the living room, laughing and chatting. Lawson poured champagne for all of them. Laney took cocaine from a small plastic compact she had in her purse. It opened up like two small dishes, with a little spoon that fit neatly inside. She ordered the white powder into lines on the coffee table.

For the past month, Radin had cut way back on his cocaine use. There had been none around during the holidays at Ocean Castle. Even at the New Year's Eve party, just days before Radin had to move out of Ocean Castle, Lawson, who used cocaine infrequently, and only when he was not working, had successfully kept Radin off the powder.

Lawson believed too much was at stake for Radin right now—the selling of the house, the move to Los Angeles, the meeting of new people on the West Coast who might advance his career. Radin could not afford any problems, so Lawson felt a strong responsibility to his boss to act as his policeman.

After an hour, Laney's cocaine was gone. She announced that she had more back at her house, and excitedly offered to show everyone the home she had bought.

They walked to the curb in front of the Regency and got into Laney's limousine. Driving to Sherman Oaks, they parked in front of a large, Spanish-style house on a cul-de-sac. Everyone went inside, where they were greeted by Myriam and a small, dark-haired boy whom Laney held and introduced as her son, Dax.

Lawson spoke to Myriam in Spanish. He asked about the house and how Myriam liked Los Angeles as compared to Miami. Meanwhile, Laney and Radin went off to her bedroom to talk privately. Lawson and Carol Johnston sat in the living room.

Laney and Radin soon emerged from the bedroom, and Laney said she had some marijuana. She did not have a pipe or cigarette papers, however. Lawson went into the kitchen, where Myriam was fixing drinks. He asked, in Spanish, for aluminum foil, and on his way back into the living room, he fashioned a pipe. He handed it to Laney, and for a few minutes admired the spacious, beautifully decorated living room. There were several photographs on a shelf on one wall, and he looked closely at them.

One picture showed a handsome Latin man with one arm draped around Laney. They were standing in a backyard, next to a swimming pool.

"Who is this, Laney?" Lawson asked.

"Oh," she said, "that's Dax's father. He is buying this house."

The man was Milan Bellechasses.

"Where does he live?" he asked as he examined the photograph.

Laney said he lived in Miami. She turned away and proceeded to put some marijuana in the pipe, then invited Radin back into her bedroom, where they took drugs and talked. Lawson was left in the living room with Johnston. He shrugged his shoulders and jokingly said, "Wake me when they come back, will you, please?" He lay down on a couch and closed his eyes.

Lawson awoke at dawn. Radin was standing over him, shaking his shoulder. Johnston was asleep on another couch. Lawson sat up and rubbed his face.

"Roy, this isn't for me," he said. "I didn't think we were going to sleep here. We have to leave."

Radin sat down next to him. There were dark circles under his eyes.

"We didn't do anything," Radin said. "We just talked."

Lawson said he did not care one way or the other; he just wanted to leave. He suspected they had been up all night bingeing on cocaine. He was sure that Laney and Radin were very similar in their love of partying and taking drugs.

When Laney came into the room, she offered Lawson a car, a Lincoln, so that he could return to the Regency. He got up and said goodbye, and drove back alone to the apartment.

Late in the afternoon, Radin called and asked

Lawson to come back up to Sherman Oaks in their rented Mercedes. When Lawson arrived, he honked the horn, and Radin and Laney emerged, smiling and laughing as they got into the car. He asked about their plans, and Radin directed him to drive them to the Regency. On arriving, Lawson went up to his room. Later in the evening, Laney and Radin went out for dinner.

The following morning, Radin said that they had to return to New York. There were still details to be worked out about Ocean Castle.

Lawson asked about Laney, and Radin beamed.

She had a lot of cocaine, he said, adding that he was sure he would be seeing more of her.

Lawson asked if that was all he saw in her, and Radin nodded his head. He seemed to have found the perfect Hollywood playmate.

TEN

TALLY ROGERS WAS A COURIER ON whom Laney could always count. He arrived at predictable times, unloaded his packages, and often stayed a few days, usually in a motel in Sherman Oaks, before going back to Miami. A good listener, he was talkative and high-spirited. He was good with his hands, too, and had installed a safe in Laney's bedroom for storing cash. He'd agreed with her decision to install bars on the windows of the house soon after she moved in.

Rogers had gotten his job with Bellechasses through another Southern acquaintance, Tim Whitehead, who lived in Mississippi. Rogers and Whitehead had once worked together at an asphalt plant in Tennessee. Bellechasses had promised Rogers twenty thousand dollars for a round trip, which meant that if he went back and forth twice a month, twelve months a year, he could make nearly half a million dollars tax free. Rogers intended to get very rich driving the interstates.

Rogers and Laney got along well, but he was particularly attentive to Bellechasses. The Cuban acted as if he were the toughest man in Miami, and he frequently boasted about having people bumped off. Specifically, he mentioned relatives, brothers-in-law, he had had killed. Rogers was sharp enough to realize that Bellechasses was probably trying to scare him. After all, Rogers was handling a product worth an enormous amount of money; one ten-kilo load was selling in California for more than six hundred thousand dollars. If Bellechasses was buying it for forty thousand dollars a kilo, a ten-kilo sale netted him two hundred thousand dollars profit. If he sold twenty kilos a month, he could make almost five million dollars a year tax free.

Rogers also knew one of the secrets of Bellechasses' trade: he was buying cocaine "on the come"—on credit—from his Cuban and Colombian suppliers. This meant that the suppliers were not being paid until after the cocaine was sold in California and Rogers had delivered the cash to San Francisco. The entire system, from Miami to Los Angeles, was very fragile. The glue that held it all together was the fear of bloody retribution. That simple fact more than explained Bellechasses' trying to frighten Rogers with talk that he was ruthless enough to kill his own relatives.

For Laney, this structure meant that she was the guardian of a product that had not been paid for when it was packed away in her garage for sale to a number of Los Angeles–based distributors. This put a special burden on her, and she responded by installing burglar alarms in the house, more locks on the doors, and bars on all the windows except one, the window in the nursery, where Dax slept. Her new home, though, was meant to be more than just a stash house.

She wanted to live well while she went about the task of trying to fulfill her fantasy of producing movies.

While Laney was busy with her new house, Radin was back at his apartment in the Mayflower Hotel in New York, presiding over what amounted to the end of his Southampton life. The last of his belongings in Ocean Castle were moved out, the business records forwarded to the new office in Hampton Bays. Thus ended his years of high living in the wealthy village.

But he was not sad about it, as he had been a month earlier at the Christmas party at Ocean Castle. Now he had new reasons for being optimistic, and they had to do with meeting Laney. He spoke about her all the time. She was wealthy and attractive, he said, and possessed large amounts of cocaine.

Laney's interest in Radin seemed to be for different reasons. She was intrigued by his vaudeville business, which had made him so successful at so young an age, and by his desire to become a Hollywood-based movie producer. She, too, wanted this, and knowing Radin might be of great assistance to her.

One cold afternoon in early February, Laney called Radin at Ocean Castle while he was there to make sure everything had been moved out. When he hung up, he told Lawson that Laney promised to have "stuff," meaning cocaine, for them as soon as they returned to Los Angeles.

From a conversation with Carol Johnston, Lawson had learned that Jacobs possessed large amounts of cocaine, more than she would ever need for her personal use. He could only guess why she had so much. He and Radin had been around a lot of people who sold cocaine, and they had found nothing threatening in it. But Laney was different. Her appearance and demeanor raised questions in Lawson's mind. So did the picture of Bellechasses in her house. The Cuban *looked* like a drug dealer. Lawson knew from reading the newspapers that the Latin drug dealers in Miami could be violent.

Radin, though, saw in Laney only a classy woman who affected the ways of a society queen, a rich divorcée.

Radin was determined to get to the West Coast as soon as loose ends in New York could be tied up. He intended to live on both coasts, perhaps until he had a number of projects going in Los Angeles. Then he would buy a home there and move out permanently. In mid-February, he was ready to go, but a snowstorm forced him to delay.

The third week of February, Radin and Lawson returned to Los Angeles. Lawson had set up an arrangement at the Regency whereby they could have one or perhaps two apartments on a monthly basis. A semipermanent office could be kept there, and Lawson would not have to box and ship all the files every time they returned to the East Coast.

After their arrival, Laney called and said she had cocaine for them. Lawson drove to a motel in Sherman Oaks, pulled into the parking lot, and waited for Laney. A few minutes later, she arrived in her Mercedes, and he got inside. It was the middle of the day, and the parking lot was busy. This was not the way she usually sold her cocaine. Normally, it was picked up by distributors, who parceled it out to their sellers. She was willing to sell it to Radin personally, however. He seemed like a good bet—a rich producer from

New York interested in making movies in Hollywood.

Lawson handed her $2,500 in cash, and she handed him a nicely wrapped package. He was curious about her, and her cocaine, and he decided to press her for details.

"How did this come out?" he asked.

"It came out, that's all," she said.

"I know that, but how?" Lawson persisted.

"Look," she said, not accustomed to being grilled about her cocaine. "I'm a clothes designer. I helped set up Suzie Creamcheese."

Lawson asked who Suzie Creamcheese was.

"She has boutiques in Las Vegas and Houston," Laney said. "We're great friends."

It was clear she did not want to talk about it any further, so he dropped the subject. Laney asked about Radin. Lawson told her he was busy but fine.

As he got out of Laney's car, she said, "You won't see me for a while. I'm going down to Palm Springs to get a face-lift. I'll call when I'm back in town."

After years in vaudeville and music promotion, Radin knew a number of important people in Hollywood. He set up meetings at various talent agencies and at Paramount, hoping to pitch his movie ideas. In particular, he wanted to present Paramount executives with a proposal he and Lawson had devised for a television series about a man who dressed up like a woman in order to get a job at a newspaper editing a "Miss Lonelyhearts" column. Radin hoped to interest the studio in allowing one of the actors he managed, Ben Powers, to star in it.

Radin had Powers dress up in drag and took

him to a meeting at the studio. He introduced
Powers as "Roberta," and it was not until the end
of the meeting that he asked Powers to take off
his wig. Afterward, the Paramount executives
said they were interested. Radin was buoyant
and immediately began jotting down ideas for
scripts.

When he returned to his apartment, he called
New York and told people in the office that he
was close to a deal with Paramount. He ordered
Lawson to send Godiva chocolates to his mother,
his ex-wives, Loretta and Toni, and his "Aunt"
Sylvia Stoppelli.

The day before they were to return to New
York, Laney called. She had just returned from
Palm Springs and wanted to come over. Late the
following afternoon, a few hours before their
flight was due to leave, Laney knocked on the
apartment door at the Regency. Lawson opened
it, and she walked in with a man she introduced
as Tally Rogers.

Immediately, Radin, Laney, and Rogers started
doing cocaine, while Lawson packed. Radin
found Rogers funny, and the two hit it off. At approximately seven o'clock, Laney announced she
wanted champagne. Lawson called a nearby
shop and asked that four bottles be sent up to the
apartment. Everyone contributed cash, and
shortly a delivery boy dropped off the champagne.

At nine o'clock, Lawson reminded Radin that
they had to leave. But Laney complained they
were having too much fun, and she offered to
drive them to the airport herself.

"Roy, this is the last flight," Lawson said. "We
have to make it."

Radin said it was no problem; he was sure they would get there on time.

"Then I'm going myself," Lawson said. "Laney can drive you out. I'll meet you at the gate."

Laney assured Lawson that she would get Radin there on time.

At the airport, Lawson waited nervously for Radin to arrive. When the flight was called, he debated getting on and flying east alone. Instead, he ran down to the check-in area and saw Radin step out of Laney's car. They rushed back to the gate but were too late. They stayed in the airport until morning, when they caught a flight to Chicago and then New York.

ELEVEN

WHEN HE RETURNED TO MANHATTAN, Radin announced he was going to try to quit taking drugs. It was not the first time he had said he would stop, but this time he seemed quite determined.

Since he and Lawson had moved into the apartment in the Mayflower, Radin had bought cocaine from a Russian woman whom Lawson called Svetlana. She made deliveries to the apartment. Once, she sold what Radin considered bad cocaine, and his nose bled profusely.

To help Radin refocus his priorities, Lawson told him that he had to be in his best shape if he was to make something of himself in Hollywood. Radin agreed, saying there were more sharks in the film business than he had encountered in all his years in vaudeville. As part of an effort to cut back on his cocaine use, Radin began seeing a psychiatrist, hoping to get at the root causes of his addiction.

The psychiatrist also convinced Radin that he had to lose weight. Lawson began preparing diet meals for him. But Radin would sneak out and grab a snack in the Mayflower coffee shop. De-

spite minor setbacks, however, it looked, for
those few weeks in late February and early
March, as if Radin was on the way to a new and
drug-free self.

Radin's attitude toward his divorce had also
improved. After months of agonizing over the
breakup of his marriage to Toni Fillet, he decided to hold a party when the divorce was final.
He invited a huge crowd of friends to the Underground, a Manhattan discotheque, where he announced that bad marriages and bad times were
now finally behind him. A band played loud disco
music, and hundreds of Radin's friends danced
into the early-morning hours.

Radin stayed in New York for only two weeks
before deciding to return to California. There
were only a few good reasons for him to be in the
East, all of them having to do with overseeing the
details of a crumbling Roy Radin Enterprises.

The brief stay in New York had allowed Lawson to examine more closely the thirty-five accounts that made up the business. There
appeared to be certain irregularities in the accounts, and he reported his findings to Radin. For
the most part, Radin acted as if he did not care.
He wanted to concentrate almost entirely on the
deals in California he believed were imminent.

In mid-March, Radin and Lawson flew to Los Angeles. When they arrived at the Regency, Radin
was surprised to find that Tally Rogers had
rented an apartment there. Soon Rogers was
spending most of his free time with Radin and
Lawson.

Radin and Lawson had come to believe that
Rogers was Laney's drug courier. He seemed to

go back and forth between Los Angeles and Miami every few weeks.

A few days after their arrival, Radin's rented Mercedes was stolen in Hollywood. Lawson mentioned it to Rogers, and soon Laney called to tell Lawson she could get him a deal at the Budget Rent-a-Car office in Beverly Hills. The agency was owned by Marc Fogel, and he gave her cars or rented them to her at very low rates.

At Budget, Laney filled out the rental papers, paying for the car with an American Express card. When Lawson picked up the papers, he saw the imprint of the card, and the name Karen Bellechasses. He asked who Bellechasses was, and Laney reiterated that he was Dax's father. Lawson recalled the picture he had seen at her house. He asked if Bellechasses was her husband, and Laney said he was.

Later that week, Radin invited Laney to see Ben Powers perform at the Improv, a comedy club. He also invited Jim Weller, a close friend who worked for an advertising agency, and Weller's wife.

At midnight, Laney, Radin, and the Wellers went back to the Regency. After the Wellers left, Laney sat with Radin and began talking in detail about her personal plans. For some time, she explained, she had wanted to get into show business. Her goal was to finance and produce movies. This was the first indication she had given Radin as to why she had moved to Los Angeles. Radin had assumed she was there to sell cocaine; now she introduced another reason altogether, and he was surprised, even shocked, at her announcement. Laney a movie producer? It did not seem possible.

Then she mentioned that she had met Bob Evans, whom she described as eager to raise financing for a package of movies he hoped to produce. She said she was currently in the process of helping him raise the funds. Radin knew the name, of course. He was immediately interested.

Radin asked how much Evans was looking for, and Laney said millions of dollars. "Hell, I can do that," Radin boasted confidently. "That's no problem at all."

A day or two later, Laney called the Regency and told Radin that she would be glad to introduce him to Evans. Radin excitedly jumped at the chance.

"Bob Evans!" Radin yelled out to Lawson when he got off the phone. "That's incredible!" He paced around the room. "He produced *The Godfather,* for God's sake. He's a legend."

He bounced around the small apartment, ticking off the names of potential projects he could present to Evans. One was his Cotton Club idea, and he began pulling his papers together. Radin told Lawson this could be his big break and just the connection he needed to make everything finally come together.

One morning in late March, a week after Laney's conversation with Radin, Rogers arrived in Los Angeles to drop off cocaine at her house. He then called his wife, Betty, who lived in Tennessee, and asked her to fly to the West Coast. The couple had been separated for a long time, but Rogers was hoping for a reconciliation. The next day, she flew into Los Angeles, where Rogers picked her up in Laney's Mercedes.

Later that day, Rogers came for Betty at her motel and drove her to the Sherman Oaks house, where she met Laney, Dax, and Myriam. While waiting to go out to dinner, Laney asked Betty to come into her bedroom. They chatted for a few minutes, then Laney asked Betty to get a dress from the closet. Betty walked into the closet and saw white blocks sealed with duct tape stacked from floor to ceiling. She recognized them as cocaine, enough to keep a thousand users in the drug for a month.

Later that evening, more people began arriving at the house. One was an attorney named Sol Besharat, whom Laney had met a few weeks before in Palm Springs. The others were Anna Montenegro and her date, Frank Diaz, who had flown into town.

Montenegro, with her shoulder-length black hair and dark eyes, was a strikingly beautiful woman. It had been Diaz who introduced her to Laney, and almost immediately Laney had offered her work as a drug courier. Montenegro turned her down but would frequently go out with Laney and act as her personal assistant. She knew a great deal about Laney's background and had dated Bellechasses and, before him, Alfie Ferreira, Laney's fourth husband.

After nine o'clock, the group, including Rogers and his wife, went to dinner in Hollywood. Afterward, apparently to impress Betty Rogers with her friendship with Evans, Laney drove to his house in Beverly Hills. She approached the house's security gate and announced her arrival through a speaker phone; the gate opened.

At the front door, she and Betty were greeted by Evans. Laney whispered to Betty that Evans used to be married to Ali MacGraw.

Soon after their arrival, two Latin men came to the house. As Betty listened, the two men began talking in Spanish, with Laney doing her best to translate into English. Well after midnight, this meeting ended, and Laney drove Betty back to her motel.

Not long afterward, Laney and Besharat knocked on Betty's door. Laney had a bottle of champagne, and the three of them sat in Betty's room, talking and drinking, until four o'clock in the morning. Then Laney announced that they were going in a private jet to Las Vegas. Loud and demanding, a party woman who could stay up for days, Laney was difficult to walk away from. Reluctantly, Betty agreed to go along.

The group reached Las Vegas just after sunrise. Betty had tried to sleep on the plane, but the others were wide awake. When they landed, Laney suggested they go to her friend Leslie Dekeyser's house. Dekeyser was the owner of the Suzie Creamcheese clothing boutique in a mall on the Strip. Rental cars were obtained, and Betty, Besharat, and Laney drove to the outskirts of the city.

At Dekeyser's house, the group sat by the pool and had breakfast. Later in the morning, Dekeyser fitted Laney for a dress. Dekeyser offered to show Betty the clothes in her shop, and an appointment was made for the following morning.

When they left Dekeyser's house, Laney, Sol, and Betty went to the Sands Hotel and booked a suite of rooms. At 11:00 A.M. the following morning, the phone rang in Betty's suite. It was her husband.

"Let me talk," he said. His voice was emotional, and he sounded frightened. "Get out of Las Vegas. There is a plane out of there in thirty minutes, and you have to be on it. . . . Don't carry any clothes. If you don't get out of there, you are going to be killed."

Then he added, "When you get to Memphis, take Paula out of school. Hide out until you hear from me."

Badly shaken, Betty immediately left Las Vegas.

TWELVE

TOWARD THE END OF MARCH, LANEY, Radin, and Evans met for lunch at a restaurant in Beverly Hills. Evans told Radin he wanted to make three pictures back-to-back. Radin brought up his Cotton Club idea and Evans said he had long thought of doing a movie about the club himself. Evans' idea was to make a film in the vein of *The Godfather,* not a musical, as was Radin's proposal.

After a three-year absence, Evans was determined to make his comeback. What was needed to make it happen was money, but now over lunch, with the bubbly, self-confident Radin boasting about his financial sources, this obstacle seemed about to crumble.

After Laney had dropped him off at the apartment, Radin excitedly related to Lawson the details of what had been discussed at the lunch. Radin was so thrilled he paced around the room, waving his arms wildly. He felt he had made the most important connection of his career.

A skeptic about unconsummated deals, Lawson asked about Evans' track record. "What's he done lately, Roy?" he asked. "You realize he's made a few flops—*Players, Popeye,* to name a few."

"Well, yeah," Radin replied. "But what's the difference at this point? He's talking about bringing together the *Godfather* team. Don't you see what this means? He'll be big again—and me along with him."

Lawson asked about Laney: What was in it for her? It seemed so odd to Lawson that this party woman whose main interest up to now seemed to be cocaine wanted to make films.

"She's not in the movie business," Radin said flatly. "She's nothing but a broker, that's all. She made an introduction. Big deal, right? It's Bob and I who are going to be working together."

Radin figured that Evans liked Laney and sought out her company for the same reason he did—her cocaine. She was pretty, charming, and sophisticated, which added to the pleasure of being around her. But as far as Radin was concerned, Laney was not someone he had to take seriously.

He talked to an agent at International Creative Management and to other friends in Hollywood about his meeting with Evans. Their opinion was that Radin should not get involved with him. The ICM agent said Evans was washed up.

During the previous year, Evans had approached a number of rich acquaintances, looking for money to revive his career. In January, three months before Radin walked into his life, Evans had discussed the same proposal to raise funds for his production company with two Las Vegas casino owners, Edward and Fred Doumani. The brothers, who owned the El Morocco Club, decided to invest $1.6 million toward the preproduction costs of *The Cotton Club.* They brought in another investor, a former Denver insurance broker.

The brothers' interest in Evans did not last long. Soon after signing an agreement with him, they began to quarrel with Evans over what they regarded as his excessive use of cocaine. Just about the time Gary Keys brought Laney to him, Evans was again looking for new funding to make the movie.

In spite of the warnings against Evans, Radin pressed ahead. The information that Evans was washed up meant, in Radin's view, that he could be controlled.

"Here is a guy with a big Hollywood name, the former head of a studio," he told Lawson. "He's got a huge track record, and he is down-and-out and falling a mile a minute. I can control him. Do you see that? It's perfect. *I can control him.*"

At the end of March, Radin and Lawson returned to New York to attend to Roy Radin Enterprises. Almost immediately after their arrival, Laney called, demanding to speak with Radin.

When Radin got on the phone, she yelled, "Do you know where Tally Rogers is?"

"What are you talking about?" he asked. "Why would I know where he is?"

"I want to know if you've seen him," she said. She was excited and angry. "The house has been ripped off. I'm out over a million and I think it's Tally, because he's disappeared. I want to know what you know about it."

"Jesus Christ, lady," he said. "Who are you to talk to me in that tone of voice?"

Laney referred pointedly to the fact that Rogers had been staying at the Regency, and she reiterated her demand that Radin tell her where he was.

"You think I set him up?" Radin asked.

"I want to know when you last saw him." Laney sounded as if she was about to go over the edge.

Radin was shocked that she had that much cocaine in her house in the first place, but he knew nothing about any theft, and he told her so.

"I'm out a million dollars," she yelled. *"Do you know what that means?"*

Radin reiterated that he knew nothing about it.

"You've been partying with him, Roy. He lives at the Regency."

"So what?" Radin said, raising his voice. He cupped his hand over the receiver and whispered to Lawson, "What is she talking about?"

"I don't know, Roy," Lawson said. "She's nuts."

A few minutes later, Radin angrily hung up. For a moment, he stood silently by the phone, then he told Lawson to try and find Rogers. Rogers had, in fact, been partying with Radin, and Lawson had made two cocaine purchases from him recently, paying for them with checks made out to Laney for a total of fifteen thousand dollars.

Lawson told Radin that he did not like what was happening.

"Don't worry about it," Radin said. "It'll blow over. But see if you can find him. I don't like being accused by this bitch of having something to do with a theft from her house—particularly a theft this large."

Radin's goal was to conclude a deal with Bob Evans and to begin a new career as a movie producer. A theft from Laney's house was of no concern to him.

* * *

Even as Laney was speaking with Radin, Tally Rogers was halfway across the country. Since leaving Los Angeles, he had stayed in motels along the interstates, eating in his room and watching television with the curtains drawn. Then he would have an early breakfast and get back out on the road, heading east toward a small town in South Carolina where he intended to hole up. He loved to drive long distances, ticking off the states he passed through as he crossed another border.

The week before he had summoned his wife to Los Angeles, he had had an argument with Laney. It had followed his demand for payment for two trips back and forth between Miami and Los Angeles. In Florida, Rogers and Bellechasses had agreed to thirty thousand dollars for the two trips, but Laney said she would only pay twenty thousand dollars.

It had happened once before, and Rogers was furious. He believed Laney was taking advantage of him. When he left her home the day of the argument, he decided he was going to get even, regardless of Bellechasses' comments that he had had people killed.

Aware of Laney's jet-set lifestyle, Rogers knew that if he waited long enough she would leave her house on an overnight trip. On the afternoon Laney flew to Las Vegas in the private jet, Rogers went to the Sherman Oaks house and took ten kilos of cocaine as well as $270,000 in cash from the safe in the garage and from the safe in her bedroom that he had installed himself.

After yelling at Radin over the phone, Laney went to see Marc Fogel at his rent-a-car office in Beverly Hills. He had seen her sporadically since 1980, when her cocaine was seized by Fred Mc-

Knight and Steve Slazes. Charges were still pending in that case, but the prosecution had been on hold because Fogel had become an important informant for McKnight and Slazes. Naturally, Fogel hoped he would never have to set foot in a courtroom and answer charges that he smuggled cocaine into the city. He was also scared of Laney. Once, she had brought Bellechasses to the lot, and on another occasion a man came to him and said he had been sent by Laney, who was demanding that Fogel make up for the loss of the cocaine.

One of the things Fogel had done for Laney since McKnight and Slazes had seized her cocaine was to introduce her to his former lot manager, Bill Mentzer. A body builder with thick dark-brown hair and a handsome face, Mentzer had quit working for Fogel to become a bodyguard for Larry Flynt, the pornographer, who lived in a large estate in Bel Air. Flynt was a cripple as a result of an attempt on his life, and out of fear that someone might want to finish the job, he had hired bodyguards to propel him around in his wheelchair.

At Fogel's office, Laney told him about the theft. She was frightened and emotional, pacing and shaking her head and nervously folding her arms across her chest. When she wasn't pacing, she stood curling strands of hair around the forefinger of her right hand.

Fogel asked her who had done it, and Laney said she was certain that it was her courier, Tally Rogers. Only Rogers knew where the cocaine and the money were stored, and had keys to unlock the safes. He had the means, and after the fight over the payment he was to receive, he had the motive. She explained that she was concerned enough about the theft to have hired Bill Mentzer to be her bodyguard.

"I am going to have to pay for the drugs," she said. "I have to make good on this."

A few days later, Laney returned to Fogel's office and met a man named Michael Pascal, who owned a private investigations agency. It was Mentzer who had suggested that Pascal might be able to help her.

Stealing cocaine was a death-penalty offense. With that in mind, Mentzer brought in several of his friends, most of whom hung out at a body-building center in Santa Monica. One of them was an Argentinian immigrant in his mid-twenties named Alex Marti. Short and stocky, with a round, mean face and narrow eyes, Marti had also worked as a bodyguard for Larry Flynt. Marti loved guns, had a fascination with violence, craved money, and hated lots of people, but particularly Jews. A watercolor portrait of Adolf Hitler adorned one wall of his Los Angeles home, and he was a collector of books and writings about the Third Reich. He talked a lot about killing people; his most quoted remark was that to really put someone away, you had to shoot him in the back of the head. That was the way the Nazis did it.

Together, Mentzer and Marti were a formidable pair, although it was Marti who was the more cold-blooded of the two. Mentzer, on the other hand, was the sort of gunman who had to get juiced up on wine before he pumped a round of bullets into a man's head.

The two men hung out with a group of dedicated body builders, nearly all of whom had one thing in common—they consumed large amounts of muscle-building steroids. Consequently, some

of them, men like Carl Plzak, who had moved to
Los Angeles from Stevens Point, Wisconsin, had
odd-looking bodies—big torsos and huge upper
arms with thick necks. Not quite athletes, they
were steroid junkies with bodies created more by
chemicals than by hard work.

At first, Laney requested that Pascal watch her
home. Evidently concerned that Rogers might return to steal more cocaine, she wanted the house
closely observed. Additional locks were installed,
and windows and doors were checked to make
sure they were secure. Then Laney began dating
Mentzer, and Marti and their muscular friends
would hang out at her house or sit in cars out
front on the street.

Next, Mentzer showed Pascal a photograph of
Rogers and Laney. Mentzer asked him to take the
photograph and make a number of four-by-five
copies of it. The photographs would be used to
help track Rogers down. After that, Laney asked
Pascal to trace phone numbers for her. The numbers were off her own phone bills. Specifically,
she wanted to find out whom Rogers had spoken
with in recent weeks and, more important, whom
he was likely to get in touch with now.

Pascal called another investigator, who had access to confidential phone records. Most of the
numbers Rogers had called were in the South,
but one was Anna Montenegro's. Laney had considered Anna a good friend, but now, in her de-
termination to find out who knew about the theft,
she wanted to know if she had been in secret
communication with Rogers.

As Pascal traced phone numbers and addresses, Laney was making calls, desperately trying to find Rogers. Her approach was not to sound
threatening but, rather, to put out the word that

if Rogers returned the ten kilos of cocaine, he could keep the $270,000. She was lying, of course, but she hoped Rogers was dumb enough to fall for it.

For days after the rip-off, Laney tried the phone number of every place she thought Rogers could have gone. She tried to locate Betty Rogers, who, on leaving the Sands Hotel the morning of the theft, had returned to Memphis. But instead of going home, Betty had booked a room at the Peabody Hotel, where she and her daughter, Paula, planned to stay for the next month.

Rogers managed to call his wife from South Carolina. Betty told him that some thugs had been to their daughter Clarissa's home. She was frightened.

A girfriend of Betty's began receiving calls from Laney, who begged her to get in touch with Betty as soon as possible. At her friend's urging and against her own better judgment, Betty called Laney.

Laney sounded frantic and desperate. "They're holding my baby, and they're going to kill us," she told Betty. "Tell Tally to keep the money, just return the merchandise."

In the middle of the conversation, a man got on Laney's phone. "I'll come and find you," he told Betty, "and I'll use an ax and cut you up and cut your head off."

Shocked and frightened, Betty quickly hung up the phone.

THIRTEEN

AFTER LANEY'S ABUSIVE PHONE CALL to Radin, Lawson tried to get in touch with Rogers. He called a phone number in Tennessee that Rogers had given him soon after he moved into the Regency. He hoped, at the very least, to warn Rogers that Laney was after him. But no one answered, and after a week of trying, Lawson gave up.

In New York, Radin began serious negotiations with Evans over the future of their moviemaking enterprise. Evans had rented a town house on the Upper East Side of Manhattan and planned to spend most of the spring in New York. The two men spoke to each other daily and sometimes several times a day.

Their plan was for Radin to raise the bulk of the money needed to produce three pictures. If he was successful, which he confidently predicted he would be, then he and Evans would form a movie production company and possibly even build a modern studio facility. To Radin, it all sounded too good to be true. From his perspective, everything seemed to be coming together.

The key to Radin's grandiose scheme with Evans lay in his relationship with a Puerto Rican banker, Jose Alagria, a skilled financial expert who lived in San Juan. Alagria and Radin had met at a party in Puerto Rico in 1979, and like so many people who encountered Radin, Alagria had been impressed with his zeal and energy.

The day after his lunch meeting with Evans, Radin called Alagria and told him of Evans' plan to make movies. He said the two of them were going into business together and needed money to get their idea off the ground. He threw out a figure of fifty million dollars.

Alagria offered to test the financial waters in Puerto Rico. Then, after a series of conversations with Radin, it was agreed that initially Evans and Radin would own the company, with Alagria and a San Juan attorney, Porto Paniagua, getting a broker's fee. Later, after movies had been made, the two Puerto Ricans would be given shares in the company.

Over the next few weeks, a deal was put together whereby Alagria would obtain $35 million in official Puerto Rican government bonds. He had told Radin that the proposed $50 million budget was far too large. The money would be held until Radin and Evans had raised enough collateral to guarantee the costs of making the first movie. The collateral discussed was Evans' home, which was supposedly worth eight million dollars; the funds Radin had received for the sale of Ocean Castle; and the value of movie rights that Evans promised he could sell in Europe.

The three movies Evans told Radin they would make were a sequel to *Chinatown* called *The Two Jakes*; *The Sicilian*, based on a novel by Mario Puzo; and *The Cotton Club*. The last picture was to be written by Puzo and directed by Francis

Ford Coppola, the writer and director of the *Godfather* movies. For that reason, Radin began referring to *The Cotton Club* as *Godfather III.*

In a few months, Evans had gone from Las Vegas casino money, to Laney's offer to put up five million dollars of her own money (which would most likely have come from her cocaine profits stored in the Jamboni Enterprises account in the Netherlands Antilles), to Radin and Alagria's Puerto Rican bonds.

Evans would have settled for Laney's money. However, Radin's plan was bigger—$35 million—and considerably more grand, particularly after Alagria mentioned that the Puerto Rican government was likely to help pay for the construction of film studios in San Juan.

Meanwhile, Laney remained in Los Angeles, conducting her drug business. She was not a party to the negotiations, nor did Radin consider her part of any of his plans. He told Evans that he would, at most, pay her a finder's fee for bringing the two of them together. Other than that, he intended to put her out of his mind.

The second week in April, Radin and Lawson flew back to Los Angeles. When they arrived at the hotel, Lawson called the telephone answering service and was given a number of messages from Laney Jacobs, who was demanding that Radin call her the minute he was back in town.

When Radin returned Laney's call, she immediately began to yell at him about Tally Rogers. It had been three weeks since Rogers' disappearance, and Laney was more determined than ever to find him. Radin listened to her for a minute and then began yelling back at her.

"Why are you asking me this?" he said. "You know I had nothing to do with it."

"You put him up to it!" she yelled.

Radin refused to listen to her and angrily hung up.

"Oh, my God," he said to Lawson. "She thinks I engineered the whole rip-off. She said I put Rogers up to it."

Lawson was horrified. "Are you kidding me?" he asked. "You mean she actually accused you of being behind it? When she called the last time, all she wanted to know was whether you had spoken to him."

"That's what she said," Radin said. "Goddamn bitch! How can she do that?"

Lawson knew that Rogers was acquainted with a woman named Deborah Devine. Thinking that she might lead him to Rogers, Lawson drove to her apartment in West Hollywood. He found the apartment empty; no one in the area knew anything about her.

As he had in New York, Radin immersed himself in his efforts to form the movie company. He was convinced that it would work and that he and Evans were about to become the producers of three huge hits. Before it could happen, though, there were details to be worked out with Evans. If a company was to be formed, contracts had to be drawn up, finalizing the details of the relationship between Evans and Radin. In addition, a prospectus of the joint venture had to be written.

A few days after their arrival, Lawson drove Radin to Evans' house for a meeting to discuss the prospectus. Evans appeared to live in the huge, elegant, and expensively furnished home, with only a housekeeper and a young butler.

After seeing Radin inside, Lawson asked if he wanted him to stay. Radin declined. "You may need to catch calls at the apartment," he explained.

Lawson agreed, and reminded Radin to call him when he was ready to leave.

As it turned out, Radin was not ready to leave until the following afternoon. When Lawson returned to Evans' house, he found Radin clutching a pile of yellow legal pads covered with his handwriting. He looked jittery, and Lawson could tell from past experience that Radin was wired, presumably from doing large amounts of cocaine. Radin handed Lawson his papers, and at first glance Lawson could not make any sense of them. Radin had written that he and Evans were to make three movies and that they would be equal partners. Then there were scrawled comments about the responsibilities each would have in the company. It all looked like pseudolegal gobbledygook. Nothing had been finalized, nor were the two men any closer to agreeing on the actual nature of their relationship.

"Roy," Lawson said as they stood in Evans' projection room, "this is gibberish. What did you agree to?" Lawson was convinced that Radin and Evans had been sitting around the house snorting cocaine instead of trying to negotiate a deal.

Lawson drove Radin back to the apartment and tried in vain to make some sense out of his notes. Looking for guidance, Lawson called Radin's friend Jim Weller, the advertising executive. Upon hearing what Radin had written, Weller told Lawson that as far as he could tell, the deal had to be renegotiated.

When Radin awoke from a long nap, Lawson told him that he had to start over with Evans and that the relationship could only proceed with a firm, legally binding agreement between them.

Radin agreed and asked Lawson to accompany him to Evans' house to see what he could do.

The next morning, Lawson drafted a prospectus that spelled out in detail the nature of the movie company and the responsibilities of the two principals. Early in the afternoon, he and Radin drove to Evans' house. In the projection room, Lawson handed Evans the prospectus. Evans scanned it quickly and then took a pen from his shirt pocket. He said that what Lawson had written would never do, and he began crossing out paragraphs and entire pages of the prospectus.

From Lawson's perspective, Evans was interested in being the controlling member of the company. He did not want Radin to have a voice. Now they had to start all over again. Radin and Lawson prepared to camp out in Evans' house until the document was written to everyone's satisfaction.

They would dictate drafts, which were typed by Evans' secretary. Then they each would retreat to a different part of the house, read the drafts, and meet and argue about the wording. It was a never-ending process, made even more difficult by the egos of the people involved.

After a day and a half of this, Evans handed Lawson another version of the prospectus. Lawson looked it over. "This isn't even English, Bob," he said. "It's gibberish. How do you expect anyone to take this seriously? This is crap."

Evans brushed Lawson off and said he had been doing this for years.

"No one will take this seriously," Lawson insisted. "It's crap, crap, crap."

At that point, Radin took the papers from Lawson. He told him to go watch a movie in the projection room, assuring him that it would indeed work out.

Lawson pulled Radin away from Evans and whispered, "Don't you see? You are being pushed aside. He's the superstar, and you're nothing."

Later in the day, Radin, holding yet another version of the agreement, came and found Lawson. They got their belongings and left the house. On their way back to the Regency, Lawson looked over the papers.

"You realize," Lawson said, "that you can't present this to anyone who speaks the English language. These aren't even complete sentences." Lawson reiterated his belief that Evans was trying to push Radin aside.

Radin tried to act nonchalant. He insisted it would work out, adding that he would give the document to his attorney to review.

For two days, neither Radin nor Lawson left their apartments. They were exhausted. The plan was to wait for Radin's attorney's comments before going back to Evans.

Then Laney called.

Acting as if there was no bad blood between them and the conversation of a few days before had been forgotten, she told Radin she wanted to come over. She had a friend she wanted to introduce to him. She brought Anna Montenegro to the Regency.

Both Radin and Lawson were surprised to see Laney and taken aback by her pleasant demeanor. The acrimony over the theft seemed to have totally vanished. Perhaps she now thought Radin had had nothing to do with Rogers.

They were curious, though, about her suddenly
introducing Radin to her friend. Laney's explanation was that she was just being friendly. But
in the aftermath of her bitter accusation that Radin had stolen her cocaine, the most obvious conclusion was that Laney was using Anna as a spy
to discover if either Lawson or Radin knew Rogers' whereabouts.

Laney said she and Anna were going shopping,
and it was agreed that they would meet Radin
later in the day for drinks on Sunset Boulevard.

That night, Anna returned to the Regency with
Radin. Over breakfast the next morning, she told
Lawson a little about herself, enough to make
him curious regarding her relationship with Laney and what exactly she was doing in Los Angeles. Until he knew more about her, Lawson
decided to tell her very little.

When Lawson asked where she was living,
Anna explained that she was staying in an apartment Laney rented in Beverly Hills. Lawson was
surprised to learn that Laney kept an apartment
in addition to her large and lavish house.

"The apartment is for when she sees men,"
Anna explained. "She doesn't want Myriam to
know she is having affairs. She might tell Milan."

For the next few days, Anna stayed at the
Regency with Radin and Lawson. Radin told
Lawson he thought she was in love with him.
Lawson was skeptical.

Anna asked too many questions—about Radin's
family in New York, his vaudeville business, his
relationship with Evans, his movie plans. But
since Radin enjoyed Anna's company, Lawson
kept his suspicions to himself.

When Radin's attorney finished drawing up a

new letter of agreement, Lawson sent the document to Evans for review. Almost immediately, Laney called Radin.

"I know you've been negotiating with Bob and you have a letter of agreement," she told Radin in an accusatory voice.

Radin tried to put her off, but she insisted on talking about the proposed letter of agreement, which spelled out that Radin and Evans were each to be 45 percent owners of a movie company, with the remaining 10 percent held by Jose Alagria. Presumably, Laney had learned the details through Evans, and she was not happy about the situation.

Unaware of Evans' close relationship with Laney, Radin suspected Anna of giving her the information. Laney was angry. She believed she was being cut out of any involvement in the company, even though it was she who had made the introduction to Evans. Earlier, they had argued about the missing cocaine; now it was the movie company.

"Look," Radin told her. "Bob is off in Las Vegas this week, and we're waiting for him to return. When he does, we'll talk everything over and I'll get back to you."

But Laney could not be dismissed so easily. She kept calling the apartment, though Radin would not take her calls. She left messages with the phone service and with Lawson. Radin told Lawson he did not want to socialize with her any longer, and to keep her away from him as best he could. If she came unannounced to the apartment, Lawson was to tell her Radin was away on business.

As he waited for Evans' return from Las Vegas, Radin held meetings with Milton Berle at the

Friars Club about headlining a new summer tour. Again Lawson was to manage the tour, and he began calling jugglers and magicians to see if they were available. Radin and Lawson kept busy, but the specter of Laney Jacobs haunted their lives.

The more Radin tried to avoid Laney, the more she persisted. Finally, he decided to give in and talk to her on the phone. It became immediately clear that she wanted to be considered a part of any movie company that might be formed between Evans and himself. To leave her out was to court trouble: this was her unmistakable message.

"I want to know," she told Radin, "exactly what my participation is worth."

Radin said he did not see any place for her in the company, but he added that he was willing to pay her a finder's fee for making the introduction. Laney demanded fifty thousand dollars, asking that she be paid immediately upon the finalization of the letter of agreement.

She demanded to know when she would get her money. Radin told her she would have it shortly. She asked again: When? Radin hung up, cursing her loudly.

As if their relationship was not antagonistic enough, Radin began experiencing severe nosebleeds, which he blamed on the cocaine that Laney had sold him. He called her and angrily accused her of selling him bad cocaine. Her response was that there was nothing wrong with the dope. She named a Beverly Hills physician who might be able to help him.

Radin made an appointment to see the doctor, but first he ordered Lawson to stop payment on a four-thousand-dollar check to Laney. When she discovered this, she immediately phoned Radin.

"I have to have this money," she said. "You don't know how this works. I have taken the product, and I have to make good. Do you understand? I have to have that money."

"Listen, honey," Radin said. "Bad coke, bad check."

She yelled that she had to have the money.

"Listen," Radin told her calmly. "I will get another check to you—once you replace the coke."

"You don't know whether the coke is good or bad, Roy," she responded. "You're doing too much."

He hung up.

One evening a week later, Radin's mother called and informed her son that his apartment at the Mayflower had been burglarized. Renee was not sure what had been taken. Radin told her not to touch anything; he would come back as soon as possible to see for himself.

After the call, Lawson told Radin about his suspicions that Anna had been planted by Laney to spy on them.

"Look," Lawson said. "Anna works for Laney. We have to be careful. This is getting nuts. Laney is big, and she thinks you stole her stuff. Now she wants to be included in your movie deal. Is there no end to this?"

Radin said he was convinced that Anna was not a spy. He was very fond of her, and he was certain she felt the same way about him. Anna had also, according to Radin, confided in him a lot of derogatory information about Laney.

"Let's not get crazy and paranoid about this," Radin said. "But be careful. Keep your guard up."

Lawson asked how Laney could have found out about the details of the letter of agreement with Evans. Only a few people knew those details—Radin, Lawson, Evans, and the attorney. Radin said he would talk to Anna.

Radin confronted Anna on the morning he was to leave for New York. When he asked if she was relating any conversations she might have overheard about the movie company, she cried, insisting that she would never have told Laney.

Anna warned Radin to be careful of Laney, whom she described as a dangerous woman with ties to Colombian traffickers. In Miami, Laney was very powerful.

Afterward, in a conversation with Lawson, Anna went further. She said Laney was not married to Bellechasses, who, she believed, was Dax's father. She said Laney and Bellechasses were major players among the cocaine elite in Miami. Based on what she had seen and heard at the Sherman Oaks house, Anna said Bellechasses had been putting a great deal of pressure on Laney after Rogers stole the money and cocaine.

The cocaine had been bought on consignment. It was to have been sold and then the supplier in Miami paid. People were now demanding their money, which was why Bellechasses was demanding that Laney find out what had happened.

"Milan is really on her case," Anna added. "Laney is using Roy as a scapegoat. She is blaming Roy."

FOURTEEN

BACK IN NEW YORK, RADIN INSPECTED the results of the burglary. He discovered that a filing cabinet containing business records had been pried open. Nothing seemed to be missing. After he reported the theft to the hotel management, Radin once again turned his attention to Evans. Meetings had been scheduled at Evans' rented town house.

Unbeknownst to Radin, a few days before his arrival in New York, Evans had flown into town with Laney. They had stayed one night at his town house, where they slept together for the first time since they had met in January. From New York they flew to Miami, where she wanted, among other things, to introduce Evans to Belle-chasses.

Even as Evans had agreed to meet Radin in New York, he was growing skeptical about their proposed partnership. Evans' brother, Charles, had pointed to the Melonie Haller charges as proof that Radin was some kind of oddball. His advice was to tell Radin he wanted nothing to do with him and to back off.

But it was not that simple. Evans owed the

Doumani brothers $1.6 million. He had already
spoken to Mario Puzo about writing a *Cotton
Club* script, and he had asked Francis Ford Coppola to direct the picture. Evans was out on a
limb. A man who promised he could raise $35
million could not easily be turned away.

Then there was Evans' relationship with Laney. He believed she was a rich divorcée from
Miami, whose dream was to get into movie production. He knew she possessed cocaine; they
had shared it together. But, he would later say, he
did not know she was a trafficker.

When they arrived in Miami, Laney and Evans
were met at the airport by Laney's friend Sylvia
Diaz Verson, who drove them to Laney's house.
On the way, Evans talked about his plans for his
movie company, and he asked Sylvia whether
she had any rich friends or relatives who might
be interested in investing their money in his venture.

The weather was bad in Miami, so he and Laney canceled their plans to charter a yacht to
Palm Beach. Instead, Evans met Laney's two attorneys, Frank Diaz and Jose Luis Castro, to talk
about another plan to raise money for Evans.
This one involved American Express, which
Diaz said might be interested in investing in the
movie business. The idea was to raise enough
money to pay back the Doumanis and end the
relationship with Radin.

Laney had described Diaz as a topnotch tax ac-
countant, and after meeting him Evans came
away thinking he was indeed very bright. It was
agreed that Diaz, now acting as Evans' attorney,
would set up a meeting in New York with American Express officials. It was further decided that
Diaz and Castro would be in New York for Evans'

meeting with Radin: Evans and Laney expected to sever their relationship with him.

When they finished with the lawyers, Laney drove Evans to Bellechasses' house on Ludlum Drive, near where the street dead-ended with Royal Palm Drive. Bellechasses had purchased the property the previous March, and title was registered under a Panamanian holding company, BBN Corporation. As they got out of the car, Laney told Evans she wanted him to meet her ex-husband because she wanted Bellechasses to understand and be proud of her moviemaking efforts in California.

They went inside the three-story house, and Bellechasses showed Evans his collection of boxing pictures, explaining that boxing was a favorite hobby. He invited Evans to an upcoming fight in Las Vegas; Evans declined.

"I am very happy Laney is involved with you," Bellechasses told Evans. "If I can help you, I will be glad to."

After his conversation with Radin three weeks earlier, Jose Alagria had started putting together the financing for the Radin-Evans joint venture. In a short time, he had accomplished a great deal. The Puerto Rican government was willing to finance, through the sale of industrial development bonds, the costs of forming the company as well as building a studio facility in San Juan.

It was all proceeding remarkably well. Alagria's friends in government saw the project as a means of bringing movie production to the island, thereby creating hundreds of jobs and millions in new revenues.

The Puerto Rican government was so excited about the project that there was even discussion of establishing a film institute. Evans, the Hollywood legend, was to be offered a professorship in film at the University of Puerto Rico. The governor, Carlos Romero Barcelo, found the project intriguing. His interest had been piqued by his campaign manager, Porto Paniagua, who was the attorney for the project.

From the Puerto Rican side, the deal was as good as done. Alagria had commitments to deliver the $35 million if certain requirements could be met. Evans was to bring in up to eight million dollars of his own toward the budget of the first movie. And he was to raise another eight million through the sale of foreign rights. To that end, Evans had made up a poster of Sylvester Stallone, who he had said was interested in starring in *The Cotton Club*. On the strength of his own reputation and Stallone's involvement, Evans boasted that he could easily raise the money in Europe.

Radin needed to raise eight million dollars, too. He had funds from the sale of Ocean Castle, and Uncle Johnny Stoppelli had indicated an interest in investing in the movie. Radin, who already owed Stoppelli roughly $750,000 for his investment in the Atlantic City tour, had confidently predicted that the three movies would gross at least $150 million, so paying back Uncle Johnny seemed all but a certainty.

An additional obstacle to be overcome was the posting of a performance bond, essentially an insurance policy guaranteeing the budget of the films. This was Evans' responsibility. Another sticking point, which appeared much more problematic, was the sudden and unexpected emergence of Laney Jacobs into the negotiations. Her demands had to be resolved, or a deal could never be finalized.

Of all the partners involved, Radin was the most confident. At his duplex at the Mayflower one afternoon, he told Sal Miglionico that in a couple of weeks they were going to be million-aires.

On another afternoon, as he rode around town with Malcolm Grigg, Radin asked him how he would like to live in a big mansion in California.

As if to underscore the importance of the deal to Radin, Johnny Stoppelli came to the May-flower almost every afternoon to talk. He would sit in the living room and chat, offering guidance on how the new movie company should be run. Stoppelli advised Radin to secure the upper hand in the company; otherwise, he could get pushed out.

Toward the end of April, on a bright New York afternoon, Miglionico drove Radin to Evans' town house for a meeting. Radin was dressed in a dark three-piece suit, in contrast to Evans, who was dressed casually. Standing in the downstairs area of the house, Evans shook Miglionico's hand and said, "Hey, you look like a natural for the movies, you know that? You should have been in *The Godfather.*"

Miglionico, who had always wanted to be an actor, was flattered.

"I'll put you in *Cotton Club,*" Evans added. "There are gangster parts you'd be perfect for."

Impatient for the meeting to start, Radin asked Miglionico to go and get some batteries for his tape recorder. Evans proceeded to show Radin around the comfortably furnished house. There was a garden in a courtyard in the back, and a large sitting area on the ground floor. A spiral staircase led up to bedrooms and a library.

Miglionico returned and waited outside the library for Radin to come out for the batteries. He emerged a half hour later, shaken and angry, and said they were leaving.

Outside, he said, "Evans is a real piece of work. Who the hell does he think he is?"

Miglionico asked what was going on, and Radin mentioned Laney Jacobs and the fact that she now wanted a percentage of the company. Specifically, she wanted half of Radin's 45 percent. Worse, in Radin's view, was that Evans had said he supported her demand.

"How come he's backing her?" Radin asked. He had left the town house in such haste that he had forgotten his overcoat. "Does he want this deal to go forward or not?"

"A bunch of sharks, that's all they are," Miglionico replied.

They got in the car and went to Studio 54. When Radin finally emerged, at 4:00 A.M., he was bleary-eyed and wired.

In spite of his anger toward Evans, Radin returned to his house the following night for a meeting with Alagria. Laney was there, and Radin stepped into the courtyard with her. She repeated her demand for a percentage of the company. Radin was adamant about her not getting any. She wept as he yelled at her.

Uncomfortable in their presence, Alagria, who had just met Laney for the first time, went up the winding staircase to the second floor. He stood in the hallway for fifteen minutes before Radin appeared, storming into the library to speak with Evans. The two men started shouting at each other.

"Why don't you give her a share?" Evans yelled at Radin. "She introduced us, don't you remember? She should get a piece of the deal. Look, I'll even split it with you, if you want. We can split the difference of what she wants. What's wrong with that?"

"No dice," Radin replied. He turned his back on Evans and walked out of the library.

"Meeting's over, Jose," Radin said to Alagria. "Let's go."

In the limousine, Alagria offered to help Radin out of his impasse. "You were so willing to give me ten percent of the company, Roy," Alagria said. "Why not go ahead and give the lady something?"

"I'm not giving her anything," Radin insisted.

A week later, on the afternoon of Friday, May 6, Grigg picked up Johnny Stoppelli and brought him to Radin's apartment for lunch. He conferred with Radin throughout the meal, and then Grigg drove the two of them to Evans' town house.

When they arrived, Evans was inside, along with Jose Luis Castro. They had just sat down when Laney and Frank Diaz walked in. Radin was alarmed to see her. He had hoped he and Evans could work out any problems between them and finalize a deal before Radin returned to Los Angeles that weekend.

As soon as he saw Laney and Diaz, Stoppelli whispered to Radin that he did not want to do business with them.

When Laney began to recite her litany of complaints against Radin, he lost his temper and told her she did not belong there in the first place.

She began to cry again, and Radin reiterated that he was willing to pay her a flat finder's fee but was against giving up a share of the company.

As the arguing escalated, Stoppelli picked up his coat and hat and left the house. Radin soon followed. In the limousine, the old man said, "I'm not doing business with drug dealers."

When Stoppelli stepped out of the car on his corner, Radin told him they would talk later. He looked hard at Radin and then proceeded into his building.

Radin returned to the Mayflower late in the afternoon. He slammed the door and began ranting about Laney Jacobs.

"I'll kill her," he yelled at Lawson.

Lawson asked him what had happened, and Radin recited his now familiar bill of particulars against Laney. His scorn was also aimed at Evans, whom Radin accused of sabotaging him by backing up her demands for part of the company.

"The deal is dead," Radin said. "It's dead."

On Saturday, Radin called Alagria and informed him that he intended to withdraw from the company. The only way he would stay in, he said, was if Laney dropped her demands. Alagria encouraged him to try to reach an accommodation, but Radin made no promises.

The following afternoon, Stoppelli came to the apartment to see Radin. He warned Radin not to have anything to do with Laney. He told him not to go back to Los Angeles. When Radin said he had to go, Stoppelli repeated his warning.

"Stay away from these people," he said. "Don't go back out there, Roy. You're buying yourself trouble."

FIFTEEN

EARLY ON THE MORNING OF MAY 9, RA-din prepared to fly to Los Angeles to attend the Bar Mitzvah of Red Buttons' son, Adam. Grigg drove Radin and Lawson to the airport. Radin was unusually subdued. He sipped coffee from a Styrofoam cup and tried to read the newspaper. When they reached their terminal, Grigg unloaded the luggage and shook Radin's hand, saying goodbye. Radin hugged him tight. "Take it easy, kid," he said, and walked off.

During the flight, Lawson made a point of reemphasizing what Uncle Johnny had asserted the day before. He strongly urged Radin not to disregard so direct a warning from someone with years of experience on the street, sizing people up. If Stoppelli's advice was to get away from Laney and Evans, then Radin certainly should do so.

"He knows what I know, no more, no less," Radin said. "He looks at them and sees trouble, that's all."

Lawson asked if that meant that Radin would not be walking away from the deal.

"No dice," Radin said, though two days before,

he had talked about giving it up. "I am not walking away from this. I'm going to make it happen."

Lawson asked what he planned to do about Laney.

"I can control her," Radin insisted.

"No way," Lawson said. "She can't be controlled."

"Uncle Johnny's wrong about this," Radin said. "It's just like the Joey Bishop thing. You have to push back."

"Roy," Lawson said, "I've never seen Uncle Johnny so insistent about anything before."

"If Evans wants her to have a share, let *him* give it to her," Radin said. "I won't."

Radin and Lawson arrived in Los Angeles on Monday afternoon. They went directly to the Regency, where they found they could not have their customary two rooms. They would have to stay together instead. This suited Lawson, because he wanted to keep a closer eye on Radin.

By evening, Radin's cockiness had disappeared. He began complaining again that he was being ganged up on, pushed out of the deal. Radin had always been a man who experienced wide-ranging mood swings, from exhilaration and self-confidence to seemingly bottomless depression. A profound nervousness seemed to sweep over him by the end of their first day back in Los Angeles. Lawson tried to keep him upbeat.

"When you think about it," Lawson said, "does it really matter if this particular deal falls through? There will be others, you know that. It's a temporary setback."

"That's not the point, Jonathan," Radin replied. He paced around the small living room. He still had his suit on, although the tie was nearly pulled off and several buttons on his shirt were undone. "That is *absolutely* not the point! I put the financial side of this together. I brought in Jose. I made the whole Puerto Rican thing happen—the money, the studios, everything.

"Evans couldn't do shit in this town. He couldn't rub two nickels together. I was going to make it happen for him! Then *she* comes along, and all of a sudden, just like that, he is telling me to give her *half* of my interest. He brought nothing to this deal. Hell, he couldn't even raise the money for a goddamn performance bond! They're pushing me out so she can get my share. She and her Cuban lover, two goddamn drug dealers, want to be movie producers. And I'm in the way."

Radin collapsed on the couch, his head back, his hands over his face. He told Lawson he was not budging.

The following morning, Evans called Radin at the hotel even though Radin had not told him or Laney about his trip to Los Angeles. Radin picked up the phone and listened for a minute to what Evans had to say. Then he said, "No, I don't want to do that." He said it again, then hung up.

Turning to Lawson, Radin said, "Can you believe that? He offered me a buy-out. He offered me two million for my share."

"Roy," Lawson said, "take it. For God's sake, take it. You've only been in this deal a few weeks. Take it!"

"No way," Radin said. He was smiling, almost laughing. "Hell, if he'll pay me two million, then he knows he has something good going. They can't make the movie without me."

Lawson doubted that was true. Moreover, he was immediately suspicious about the money itself. It was his understanding from everything Radin had told him that Evans was cash poor. It was Evans' responsibility to post the performance bond, which he had failed to do, yet now he was offering Radin a two-million-dollar buyout. It did not make sense.

Lawson asked Radin where the two million dollars was coming from. Radin disregarded the question.

That afternoon, Demond Wilson came over to the apartment to watch television with Radin. The cocaine was brought out, and the two men began inhaling it with the zeal of two street addicts. Wilson was an addict who used cocaine on almost a daily basis, and whenever he was around, Radin would get high. The actor was paranoid and often thought people were out to get him. As a result, he frequently had a gun with him, either stuffed into a holster in his belt or hidden in the pocket on the driver's-side door of his Mercedes.

Radin had a nickname for Wilson: Gree. He had started calling him Gree years before, when Wilson went on a vaudeville tour with Radin's troupe. The origins of the name went back to a Cajun song Radin liked. In the course of the afternoon, Radin told Wilson that he was working on a deal that could make him the next president of Paramount Pictures.

Later that night, Lawson was alone in the apartment when the phone rang. He picked it up, and an unfamiliar man's voice asked for Radin.

"Who is this?" Lawson asked.

The man said his name was Michael Scalese.

Lawson did not know the name. And he was puzzled because the man had dialed Radin's personal line, without going through the hotel switchboard. Only a handful of people—Laney, Evans, some close friends and family—knew the number.

Lawson told the caller that Radin was not there. "I'll be hearing from him; can I take a message?"

There was a pause, and then the man said, 'You know Radin is pushing his luck. He's stepping where he doesn't belong."

"Who *are* you?" Lawson asked.

"Radin's got a big mouth. This is your first warning. The second time, you're not going to get a warning. We won't call the next time. He's going to find himself in very big trouble." Then the line went dead.

Radin was having dinner that night with Anna Montenegro, but Lawson could not remember where they had gone. He called around and could not find him. Late that night, when Radin returned, Lawson told him about the call. Radin's response was that it was "bullshit."

But Lawson did not think so. It had sounded all too real. "My God, Roy, what do you mean, it's bullshit? What are you going to do about it?"

Radin asked what the caller's name was again.

Lawson told him, and added that he had a New York accent.

Early the following morning, Radin got out of bed and called Johnny Stoppelli in New York. It took several attempts to find him, and when he did he mentioned the name of the caller. He thought Stoppelli would know if there were any mobsters by that name in New York.

The old man thought about it for a minute and said no, he did not know anyone by that name. He asked for details on the conversation, and Radin tried to minimize it, saying it was no big deal, reminding Stoppelli that it had happened before, during his tribulations over the Melonie Haller mess.

Stoppelli renewed his request that Radin come back to New York immediately. Radin reassured him that he would be all right.

After speaking with Stoppelli, Radin called his apartment at the Mayflower. Sal Miglionico picked up the phone and, hearing Radin's voice, said, "Hey, how are you, buddy?"

"Not too good, Sallie," Radin said. "Some guy named Scalese called and said to keep my mouth shut and get out of L.A. You know that name?"

"Yeah, sure," Miglionico said. "But in Brooklyn, not California."

Radin wanted to know if he was sure.

"Sure I'm sure," Miglionico said. He asked Radin what was going on.

"He threatened me," Radin said.

"Buddy, you want me to come out, bring some fellas with me?" Miglionico offered.

Radin told him not to worry about it; he would be home on Friday anyway. "Hey, I can take it," he added.

"Sure you can, but that's not the point," Miglionico replied. "I come out with some fellas, we can give you real protection. No one would mess with you, leastwise some guy named Scalese."

"Really, I will be back on Friday," Radin said. "I'm getting out of here."

Miglionico handed the phone to Radin's mother, who had heard one side of the conversation and was alarmed. She asked her son what was going on, but he ducked the question.

"Do you love me?" he asked instead.

"What do you mean, do I love you?" his mother said. "What's wrong, Roy?"

He told her nothing was wrong and asked to speak with Miglionico again. "Sal, my mother's upset. Do me a favor, will you? Take her to see *My One and Only*."

Miglionico said he would be glad to take her to the musical. Radin thanked him and repeated that he would see him on Friday.

By midday, Radin was heavily into cocaine. He seemed so desperate that Lawson tried to keep out of his way, though they occupied the same apartment. He had seen Radin go through cocaine binges numerous times in the past, then come out of it and stay off the drug for weeks at a time. But this seemed worse than usual.

Wilson returned to the Regency in the middle of the afternoon and talked about "The New Odd Couple" being canceled. He was angry and needed guidance. Lawson suggested that he join the company of *Ain't Misbehavin'*, which was shortly to begin a tour in St. Louis. Wilson thought that sounded like a good idea and said he would look into it.

When Wilson left, Lawson helped Radin lay his clothes out for Adam Buttons' Bar Mitzvah. Radin had a date for the affair, an actress who had toured with his company years before. Lawson tried to urge him along, but Radin acted so unnerved that Lawson practically had to dress him himself. He seemed all right when he finally left to pick up his date, and Lawson hoped that he would come back in good spirits.

That evening, when Radin returned from the Bar Mitzvah, he found Anna waiting for him. Anna, who seemed genuinely to care for Radin, had been staying in Laney's Beverly Hills apartment while he was in New York.

He asked her where Laney was. Anna said that

she was out of town. He asked if she knew when she was coming back. Anna said she did not know, and she warned Radin to stay away from her.

When Evans had phoned Radin to offer a buy-out, Radin assumed he was in Beverly Hills. He made several surreptitious calls to determine Evans' whereabouts. While he had not gotten a clear answer, he thought about going over to his house, then decided to wait and see if he would call back to further discuss the buy-out offer. If the offer was three million dollars, he might take it.

While Radin was waiting to hear from Evans, Evans was trying to determine if a deal could be worked out without Radin's participation. Three or four days after the May 6 meeting at his town house, Evans called Alagria in San Juan and asked if the financing would still be available if Radin was no longer involved. Alagria made it clear to Evans that he did not favor doing anything without Radin's knowledge and approval. Personally, Alagria favored the two men working out their differences. If they could reach an agreement, Alagria said, the Puerto Rican government was willing to make the money available to them.

But there were other considerations, irrespective of whether Radin would allow a deal to proceed without him. Radin was to have contributed eight million dollars in collateral for the loan, so whoever replaced him would have to make that up. Alagria left Evans with the idea that if Radin's collateral could be provided by the other parties, it was possible that a deal could proceed without Radin.

After Evans' call, Alagria received a call from Jose Luis Castro, who along with Frank Diaz was representing both Laney and Evans. Castro asked if the deal could continue without Radin, and Alagria told him the same thing he had told Evans.

On Thursday morning, Lawson, who got up before Radin, had just finished making coffee in the kitchen and was sorting through some papers, when the phone rang.

"Good morning, Jonathan," the caller said. "Is Roy in?"

It was Laney. He recalled Anna's saying that Laney was out of town, yet she sounded as if she was in Los Angeles now.

"I want to see him," Laney said impatiently. "I want a meeting. Tonight."

Lawson told her he would talk to Radin about it. His voice was calm and unemotional.

"Look," Laney insisted. "I have to meet Roy. Tonight. Late, maybe ten or eleven."

"No possibility," he said.

"Where is he?" Laney asked.

"Listen," he said. "I will talk to Roy when I talk to him. All right? I'll tell him you called when he gets up."

She gave him her phone numbers, and he scribbled them on a "From the desk of Roy Radin" pad he kept by the phone.

"I really don't understand why he walked out of that meeting," she said.

"Laney, come on," Lawson said. "What are you talking about? He has nothing to discuss with you. Period. I have your numbers. I will pass on the message. Goodbye."

When Radin came into the kitchen, Lawson

told him about the call. There were black circles under Radin's eyes, and his face was pale. He had his bathrobe on, the belt wrapped loosely around his waist.

"She's here, then," Radin said. "She wants this deal as badly as Evans does. This could be good. Honest to God, this could be good. But I'm not meeting that bitch tonight. Demond's coming over, and I want to have dinner with him. Let's make it for tomorrow."

Early that afternoon, Wilson's secretary, Amelia Quintana, drove him to the Regency in his Mercedes. Before leaving his home, Wilson had called to tell Radin that a mutual friend had had heart surgery and was in the hospital, and Radin had suggested they go and see him.

As he prepared to go to the hospital, Radin felt ill, hung over from three long days of bingeing on cocaine. Earlier in the week, he had gone to the Beverly Hills doctor whom Laney had recommended for his nose problems. It was a waste of time, for the very next day he bought two ounces of crystal, or rock, cocaine at a price of two thousand dollars. He paid with a check.

Before leaving the apartment, Radin suggested that he and Wilson have dinner that night to talk about movie projects. But Wilson checked with his wife, and she asked him to come home instead.

"So how about tomorrow night, Gree?" Radin asked.

It was decided that Wilson would come by the apartment late in the afternoon on Friday.

"This might work out for me," Radin said. "I have some important people to see anyway, and I will introduce you. I'm trying to take over Paramount Pictures."

Ocean Castle—Roy Radin's home in Southampton, New York (1980) *(GEORGE ARGEROPLOS,* NEWSDAY)

Melonie Haller before her Grand Jury testimony (1980) *(UPI/BETTMANN NEWSPHOTOS)*

(upper left)
Toni Fillet and Roy Radin
in the Suffolk County
Courthouse (1980)
(NEWSDAY)

(upper right)
Toni Fillet and Roy Radin
(1981)
(OZIER MUHAMMAD, NEWSDAY)

(lower right)
Publicity photo of Melonie
Haller (1981)
(UPI/BETTMANN NEWSPHOTOS)

Publicity photo of
Demond Wilson
(1982)
*(UPI/BETTMANN
NEWSPHOTOS)*

Demond Wilson at
the pulpit, practicing
his new profession
(1984)
*(WAYNE SCARBERRY,
UPI/BETTMANN
NEWSPHOTOS)*

Roy Radin's mother, Renee (center), emerging from the church after her son's funeral (1983)
(DICK YARWOOD, NEWSDAY)

High school
yearbook photo of
Larry Greenberger
(1966) *(COURTESY OF
GREENBERGER FAMILY)*

Larry Greenberger and Karen "Laney" Jacobs after their Las Vegas wedding (1984) *(COURTESY OF GREENBERGER FAMILY)*

Laney and Larry Greenberger aboard a fishing boat (1985) *(COURTESY OF GREENBERGER FAMILY)*

Pictured above are: Laney Greenberger with Dr. and Mrs. Alejandro Quiroz

THE CENTER FOR PLASTIC SURGERY

Will host a champagne party at the Seminole Cove Clubhouse
on Friday, July l7th, 1987.

Guests of honor will be
Dr. and Mrs. Alejandro Quiroz.

Dr. Quiroz is an internationally famous plastic surgeon and is also associated
with The Center for Plastic Surgery, Inc., here in Okeechobee.

Dr. Quiroz is a member of the American Society of Plastic & Reconstructive
Surgeons as weil as being Board Certified.

Advertisement placed by Laney Greenberger in the
Okeechobee News

(OKEECHOBEE NEWS)

Alex Marti and Bill Mentzer at their arraignment in Los Angeles (1989) *(AP/WIDE WORLD PHOTOS)*

Robert Lowe, limousine driver on the night of Radin's disappearance at his arraignment in Los Angeles (1989) *(AP/WIDE WORLD PHOTOS)*

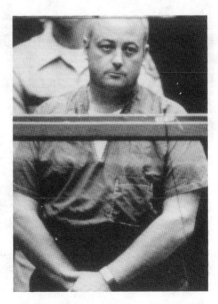

Bill Mentzer and Laney Greenberger at their arraignment in Los Angeles (1989) *(AP/WIDE WORLD PHOTOS)*

Robert Evans and his attorney Alan Schwartz leaving the Los Angeles Courthouse after the "Cotton Club" hearing (1989) *(LOS ANGELES TIMES PHOTO)*

"That's like trying to knock over a building," Wilson scoffed. "Give me a break."

They talked about which restaurant to go to, and Wilson suggested La Scala in Beverly Hills. "If you're taking me out to dinner, let's go to someplace classy," he said.

That same morning, Mike Pascal, acting for Laney, called Golden Rule Realty in Studio City and asked a sales agent named Laverne Henebry if she would be interested in listing a very nice home in Sherman Oaks.

Henebry said she would, and that afternoon she and a broker in her office, Frieda Law, went to the address provided by Pascal, 3862 Sherwood Place. When they stepped inside, they were greeted by Laney and her son, Dax, who was three days away from his first birthday.

Pleasant and affable, Laney showed Law and Henebry her house, and as they toured the rooms the agents commented on how beautiful it was. A considerable amount of expense had been invested in remodeling, including bars on the windows, which were surely not common in the quiet neighborhood. The house was well cared for, clean, and bright.

As they walked through the house, Law asked Laney why she was selling her home.

"I am moving to New York," Laney said, smiling. "I am going to be working for a movie producer, Robert Evans."

Laney indicated that she was in a rush that afternoon because she was giving a birthday party for her son. She quickly filled out the listing agreement provided by the sales agents, signing her name as Karen Jacobs.

* * *

Late that afternoon, after Radin had returned from the hospital, Anna came over. She was troubled and tense. She stood for a few minutes in the living room, talking with Lawson.

She had just come from Laney's Sherman Oaks house, where she had seen a number of men with Laney. They were "bad people," from out of town.

"You must be careful, you must be careful," Anna warned Lawson. "Something is going on."

"What are they, goons?" Lawson asked.

"You must be careful," she repeated. "Don't underestimate this woman. I know her. I know her background. Jonathan, don't underestimate this woman."

Lawson told Anna that Laney had called and wanted to meet Radin for dinner.

Anna began waving her arms. "No, no, no! You can't let him do this. You mustn't!"

She immediately went into Radin's bedroom and sat on his bed. "You must not go out with this woman," she said. "Listen to me. You can't."

Radin sat up. He still felt wired and fatigued. And frightened. The threatening phone call, Evans' buy-out offer, Laney's sudden appearance in Los Angeles, her call asking for a meeting—everything seemed out of control. And now Anna, whom Radin felt genuine affection for, was begging him to stay away from Laney. Anna started to cry.

"Oh, Roy," she implored. "Don't go out with her."

Radin explained that he had to face her.

Anna continued to plead with him, but he would not listen. She stood up, crying, and stalked out of the apartment.

A deep sense of foreboding swept over Lawson

after Anna left. He tried to talk sense into Radin, but he would have none of it. Radin had made up his mind; he was going to see Laney, if only to tell her off for the final time. Maybe just one more angry attack would convince her to take the finder's fee he had offered and get lost. Then, and only then, could he go back to Evans and try to finish the deal.

Radin was scared, too, but he tried to bury it under tiny spoonfuls of cocaine. He went on an ego-pumping binge and was soon mouthing off that he was going to turn Hollywood on its ear. He was totally full of himself, full of bluster about how he could control Laney Jacobs and Bob Evans and get his way.

At no time since Radin was a teenager putting tours on the road had he ever been backed into a corner he could not get out of. He had always been a man *in control.* After a decade and a half of putting deals together and coming out on top, he was now scrambling for survival. He could not even turn to Uncle Johnny, the way he had in Atlantic City. He was all alone this time.

After Anna left the apartment, Laney called. Lawson said Radin was not available.

"Roy will meet you tomorrow night," Lawson informed her. "He will go with you to La Scala." Radin, Wilson, and Lawson had agreed on the restaurant the night before.

"Why La—?"

"Because that's where he wants to go, Laney," Lawson said. "Understand? I've made the arrangements." He then hung up.

Radin returned around midnight after an evening with friends, and Lawson was waiting for him. "Look," Lawson began. "I'm begging you. Don't see her. There is no need to go."

"I'm going," Radin said. "I can control her."

"Look at the threatening call, look at the warning from Anna—what more do you want?" Lawson asked, but Radin was not listening.

"If you want, Roy, I'll cook here," Lawson continued. "You can stay in the apartment."

"No," Radin replied adamantly. "I'm going out with her tomorrow night; that's the plan."

"Then for God's sake call me from the restaurant. I'll come and pick you up."

On Friday morning, Marc Fogel was in his Budget office when the phone rang. It was Bill Mentzer.

"I have an important customer at the airport who has to be picked up," Mentzer said. "I need a limo, but I don't want a driver."

Fogel did not have any limousines on the lot, but he knew someone who probably did. He referred Mentzer to Dean Kahn, who owned a service called Le Express, based at the Hotel Bel-Air. Fogel called Kahn and asked if he had a car available, and Kahn said he did.

"Bill wants to rent it, and drive it himself," Fogel said. Kahn had never rented a limousine without a driver, but Fogel assured him it would be all right, and the two men agreed that Mentzer would leave a thousand-dollar deposit, half of which would be refunded if he returned the car in clean condition.

A few hours later, Carl Plzak, one of Bill Mentzer's weight-lifting pals, drove to Mentzer's apartment in the Valley. When he arrived, Mentzer was there, along with Alex Marti and a muscular, light-haired man named Bob Lowe. Marti and Lowe had recently returned from Tennessee, where they had spent a frustrating few days looking for Tally Rogers at Laney's bidding.

Plzak had been summoned to Mentzer's to participate in another effort on Laney's behalf. Mentzer said there was a certain producer whom Laney knew, and the belief was that this producer knew what had happened to the missing cocaine.

Mentzer's plan was for Lowe to dress as a chauffeur and go with Laney to pick up the producer for a dinner engagement. Once the producer was in the limousine, Marti and Mentzer were to get in the car and Laney was to get out. While this was under way, Plzak and another man, a pleasant and soft-spoken weight-lifting friend of Marti's named Roger Korban, were to wait at Laney's Beverly Hills apartment.

There, Mentzer explained, between 7:30 and 8:00 P.M., they were to look for a "tall, skinny, fag-looking guy," who was a friend of the producer's. Mentzer was referring to Lawson. Since Mentzer had never met him, this description of Lawson had evidently come from Laney.

As outlined by Mentzer, when Lawson approached Laney's white Porsche, they were to grab him. They were then to alert Mentzer immediately on a walkie-talkie and hold the man until Mentzer arrived.

An hour or so after Plzak arrived at Mentzer's, Korban drove up to the front of Mentzer's apartment building. In nearly all respects, Korban was a man out of his element. He was nineteen years of age on this spring evening, and nothing like the men he was now with. Within a minute of his arrival, he was certain he had made a mistake in agreeing to do this job.

Standing outside the apartment, Marti told Korban, "We are going to kill this guy."

"I don't want to kill anybody," Korban immediately said.

"Don't worry about it," Marti said, and they walked into the apartment.

Inside, Marti opened a gym bag and pulled out a pistol, which was equipped with a silencer. For a minute or two, Marti held it in his hands, turning it over and showing it around the room. On the floor in front of the couch was another bag, into which Mentzer was looking. It contained a set of handcuffs, a pair of cotton gloves, walkie-talkie equipment, and several small bombs, about three inches in length.

"We're going to take this guy out to the desert," Mentzer said. "We're going to put bombs in his mouth to blow up his face so he won't be recognized."

Marti was smiling. "This guy's a fat Jew pig," he said.

Upon hearing this, Korban announced he was leaving. Mentzer asked him not to go, and said, "You don't have to do anything, Roger. You just have to go and watch a car."

Mentzer began to pass around envelopes. Inside Korban's was five hundred dollars in cash. But there was no cash-filled envelope for Mentzer. He said he had received a four-thousand-dollar wardrobe as his payment for the job.

At four o'clock that afternoon, Mentzer drove to the Hotel Bel-Air. There, Kahn showed him a black Cadillac limousine with blacked-out windows and explained that he wanted the car returned clean.

In answer to a query by Kahn, Mentzer said, "I need it for—you know, I just need to drive some-one tonight." He quickly added, "You didn't see me. I didn't get a car from you. And if anybody asks, you don't know me."

SIXTEEN

THAT FRIDAY, MAY 13, AS MENTZER AND his buddies were gathering, Radin was confused and afraid. Every instinct he had honed over a decade and a half of business life, everything he had ever done that had brought him to this moment in time, now told him that he was in dangerous waters.

He had awakened late, past ten, having slept poorly after finally falling asleep just a few hours before dawn. Radin had been abusing himself all week, living on daily doses of cocaine, and he was now paying for it. After he got out of bed, he found that Lawson had slept poorly, too. Immediately, Lawson began to repeat everything he had said the day before, reiterating all the reasons why Radin was a fool to keep his appointment to meet Laney for dinner. But again Radin would have none of it.

Instead, he proposed a protection plan.

"I'll ask Demond to come to the hotel early," Radin said. "He'll bring his gun. Just before Jacobs is supposed to arrive, Demond will go outside and sit in his car. He'll wait until he sees me come out with her, then he'll follow us to La

Scala. At the restaurant, we'll happen to meet, and I'll leave with him."

"Oh, Christ!" Lawson said. "Do you really think Demond is a bodyguard?"

"He doesn't have to be," Radin explained. "He just has to watch my back. That's all I want him to do. Just watch my back. When we get to the restaurant and finish dinner, he can bring me home. It's simple."

Well into the afternoon, Radin talked over his plan with Lawson. The more he talked about it, the more certain he became that it was foolproof. Lawson, for his part, thought the whole thing was absurd. Wilson was no bodyguard. Like Radin, he was a cokehead.

By the middle of the day, Radin had gone through almost a gram of cocaine, and it looked as though he was going to lose his mind. Lawson told him he was out of control and begged him to stop.

Radin shrugged and said he knew what he was doing.

To keep himself focused on Radin's needs, Lawson forwarded all phone calls to the answering service. He knew Radin could not have handled phone calls anyway. After so little sleep and so much cocaine, he would have sounded like a blabbering idiot. But Radin insisted on making calls back east. Lawson practically had to dial the numbers for him.

At 4:00 P.M., Wilson returned to the hotel to keep his appointment with Radin. They went over the plan, walking back and forth between Radin's small bedroom and the living room. "Remember," Radin said. "Let's meet at the restaurant

and make it look as though we just ran into each
other there."

Wilson asked how Radin planned to get to the
restaurant.

"Laney's coming here. You follow. Just watch
and see if anything happens. Just watch my
back, 'cause if something happens, it will happen
going, during, or after dinner."

Wilson asked if this was because of the film
deal. Radin said it was, adding that *The Cotton
Club* was the root of all his problems.

Wilson stayed half an hour or so. Radin made
more calls back east to his family and friends. He
paced the room and watched television. Around
six, Lawson went to help Radin get dressed.

Shortly after seven o'clock, Wilson returned,
dressed for dinner. He called his secretary from
the apartment and told her to pick him up at
eight. While they waited for her, Wilson and Radin sat on his bed, talking. Wilson owned several
screenplays, including one he called *The Chicago
Story*, and he was hoping Radin could put together a production deal for him. Wilson wanted
to discuss his script after he joined Radin at his
table at La Scala.

While they talked, Wilson took out some cocaine he kept in a glass vial, and he and Radin
began inhaling spoonfuls of it.

At seven-thirty sharp, Gary Keys appeared at Laney's house in Sherman Oaks. Keys was a very
good chauffeur. His customers never missed
their airline flights because of his negligence.
Earlier in the day, he had been advised by the
dispatcher at Ascot Limousine that Laney needed
him to take her maid, Myriam Plaza, and Dax to
Los Angeles International Airport for a flight to

Miami. Keys calculated that the round trip from
Sherman Oaks to LAX was an hour, and he had
that estimate in mind as he stopped his limousine in front of her house.

Waiting outside her house, Keys saw a black
Lincoln park near the driveway. Two men got out
of the front seat. One was tall and thin and was
wearing a black leather jacket and Levi's. The
other was shorter, more husky.

The smaller man approached the driver's-side
window of Keys' limousine and said, "Hi. You
must be Gary Keys. I've heard a lot about you,
young man." Keys noticed that the taller man
had a set of handcuffs on his belt. Having had a
number of unpleasant encounters with the law
over the years, Keys was struck with the thought
that someone in Laney's house was in trouble.

As he sat in his car, Keys saw the two men go
into the house and then emerge with luggage,
which they placed in the trunk of the limousine.
Myriam came out, holding Dax in her arms. She
and the baby got in his car, and Keys headed for
the airport.

As he drove toward the freeway, Keys mentioned to Myriam that the men he had seen appeared to be policemen. "Is Miss Jacobs all
right?" he asked. "Is she in any trouble?"

"No," Myriam answered in halting English.
"She isn't in any trouble."

A few miles away from Laney's quiet cul-de-
sac, Roger Korban and Carl Plzak stepped into
Korban's Toyota pickup. They drove to West Hollywood and stopped at a bar called Osko's. Plzak
had once worked there as a bouncer and had remained friendly with the bartenders.

The two men went inside and had a few beers,
while Plzak talked to some friends. After forty-

five minutes or so, they got back in the pickup, continuing on to their appointed destination at Laney's apartment in Beverly Hills. When they got there, Plzak spotted Laney's white Porsche at the end of the parking lot.

They parked near the Porsche, turned off the engine, and doused the headlights. In the stillness of the night, they waited for Lawson to arrive, the truck illuminated by the lights from a nearby tennis court.

Wilson's secretary, Amelia, arrived at Radin's apartment at eight o'clock, just as "The New Odd Couple" was beginning. While the others watched the program, Radin made another series of phone calls. Afterward, he went into his bedroom to finish dressing. Wearing a dark three-piece suit and dark-colored Pierre Cardin tie, he sat on the edge of the bed, his head bowed, like a grieving man. Wilson came in and stood by him. He could see Radin's anxiety was eating him alive.

Concerned, Wilson asked if there was anything else he could do other than go to the restaurant.

"That's all I want you to do, Gree," Radin assured him.

"I can call someone if you want," Wilson said. "I can call the cops."

"Nah," Radin said. He stood up. "It's almost time." He pulled his wallet out of his pocket. "Here's some money for dinner for you and Amelia." He handed Wilson one hundred fifty dollars. "Take off and wait out front."

Outside, there was no light left in the sky. The air was warm and still. Wilson's Mercedes was parked on Hollywood Boulevard a half block west of the Regency. Amelia and Wilson got in the car and drove two blocks to a convenience store, where Wilson bought a pack of cigarettes. Then they returned and parked approximately where they had before, with a clear line of sight to where the driveway curved around and met the front of the hotel.

Sitting in the car, his gun in the door pocket, Wilson dipped a tiny spoon into a glass vial containing cocaine, held it tight to a nostril, and sucked in the white powder. His head floated back to rest on the seat, and he sniffed a few more times to make sure he had gotten it all. He repeated the procedure with the other nostril.

Perhaps forty minutes later, a black Cadillac turned into the hotel driveway and stopped at the front doors. A woman stepped out of the back seat. From where they sat, both Wilson and Amelia noticed her dress. It was long and tight-fitting, very shiny, the color of gold. They watched as the woman entered the hotel.

Inside Radin's apartment, the phone rang. It was the front desk, announcing Laney's arrival. Lawson nervously waited a minute before he opened the door.

"Hello, Jonathan," Laney said.

"Greetings and salutations," Lawson replied, an edge of sarcasm in his voice.

She was all smiles, her face toned from her recent face-lift. Lawson poured champagne into tall glasses, and presently Radin emerged from his bedroom. Despite the anxiety of the afternoon, he appeared fresh and ready to go out for the evening. Although Radin was seeing her for the first time since the debacle at Evans' New York town house, he did not let on that he harbored any bad feelings.

He told her they had a table at La Scala.

"Very nice," she said.

Radin and Laney went into the living room and sat on the sofa. Lawson turned on the stereo and went to the kitchen to get the hors d'oeuvres he had earlier prepared. Lawson had kept in mind that Radin's doctor in New York had ordered him to lose weight, just as his psychiatrist had thought it a good idea that he kick cocaine. Lawson had taken this weight-losing demand seriously, so tonight he put out cauliflower and carrots. Radin would have preferred Cheetos and sour-cream-and-onion dip, but Lawson considered that garbage.

Radin got up and went into his bedroom, where he put out a line of cocaine on his dresser and sucked it up his nose. In the living room, Lawson announced to Laney that he intended to drive both of them to the restaurant. But Laney protested, saying she had hired a limousine.

Laney was in good spirits, upbeat. Smiling, she said she hoped that the check Radin had recently mailed her to replace the one he had put a stop on was good. Lawson assured her that it was.

When Radin came back into the room, she rather politely alluded to their fight in New York. She was not looking for another argument. Instead of repeating her demand that she be brought into the company, she now mentioned that all she expected to get was a finder's fee.

This evidently pleased Radin, who assured her that if all went well she would get just that. As for her demand that she be given a piece of the company, Radin told her she would have to work that out with Evans.

Just before they were to leave for the restaurant, Laney asked Lawson if he would do her a favor: drive to her car, which was at that moment

parked in the lot near her apartment in Beverly
Hills. There were two grams of cocaine in the
glove box, and she wanted him to bring them
back to the Regency. That way, she and Radin
would have the cocaine when they returned from
dinner.

Lawson turned to Radin and shook his head.
"I'm not going," he told her. "I'm staying here
until you're done with the meeting."

"Roy, make him go," Laney insisted.

Before Radin could reply, Lawson pulled him
away from Laney. "Look," Lawson whispered,
"there is no way I am leaving the suite until I
hear from you after dinner. No way."

Radin walked back to Laney. "Jonathan is staying," he said.

"Come on," she said. "He works for you, doesn't
he?"

"No, Laney," Radin said. "He works *with* me."

She then turned and strode out the door, with
Radin behind her. Lawson waited a minute, then
followed them. He watched them pass through
the inside security door and go into the lobby and
out onto the street.

Seated in his Mercedes, Wilson told Amelia,
"There's the big guy."

As Radin and Laney emerged from the building, Bob Lowe, dressed as a chauffeur, jumped
out and opened the back door of the car. Laney
got in first, then Radin, and the door was shut
behind him. Presently, the limousine pulled
away from the curb and proceeded onto Hollywood Boulevard.

Wilson, who less than an hour earlier had held
a coke spoon to each nostril, now tried to get his
car away from the curb and behind the limousine. But he was partially blocked in, and it took

several attempts to position himself so that he could pull out into the line of traffic.

Standing just inside the lobby, Lawson looked for Wilson's car as the limousine turned onto Hollywood Boulevard. What he saw was a different car pull up directly behind the limousine. Amelia, waiting for Wilson to get going, saw this same car as it passed her and fell in line behind the limousine. Two men were sitting in it.

The limousine immediately picked up speed as it left the hotel. It made a quick right-hand turn and headed toward Sunset Boulevard. Wilson finally caught up to within six or eight cars of the limousine as he saw it move onto Sunset Boulevard. But the Friday-night traffic was heavy, and Wilson got bogged down. At the bend on Sunset, where the roadside is dominated by huge billboards, Wilson lost the limousine completely. Instead of looking further for it, he proceeded toward La Scala.

A few minutes later, Lowe pulled the limousine over to the side of the road. As he did, the car that had been following him stopped directly behind. Laney immediately jumped out, as did the two men in the following car. The men got into the back seat of the limousine—one on either side of Radin—and as the doors shut behind them, the limousine pulled away. Laney got in the other car, checked for traffic, and drove toward Beverly Hills.

Five miles away, Plzak and Korban sat in the dark outside Laney's Beverly Hills apartment.

They had been waiting in the pickup for approximately an hour, and both men were getting anxious. The man they had been told to look out for had not shown up.

Korban froze when a Beverly Hills police car approached. Plzak waved at the officer, who asked them what they were doing there.

"We're doing a job for Mike Pascal," Plzak informed the cop. "This is an investigation. We're just watching for somebody."

The cop asked for identification, and both men handed him their driver's licenses. He held a flashlight over them and handed them back. Satisfied they were not breaking any laws, the cop said good night and drove off.

"Chuck, I want to leave," Korban said as soon as the cop was gone.

"Let's just get this done, Roger," Plzak said.

After fifteen minutes had passed, Plzak picked up the walkie-talkie he had on the car seat and tried to reach Mentzer. There was no response, nothing but static, but he kept trying. Presently, a car drove up on the opposite side of the street from where the pickup was parked. It was twenty or thirty yards away, but Korban could make out the features of a blond woman wearing a bright, gold-colored dress.

"I'm going with her," Plzak said, and he stepped out of the truck. He had the walkie-talkie in his hand. "If you want, you could follow us, or you can just go home."

Korban said he would go home.

Plzak got in the car with Laney and shut the door. "Have you talked to Mentzer at all?" she asked.

"I haven't been able to reach him," he answered.

Quickly, she drove out of the parking space. It was approximately 10:00 P.M. Shortly, she stopped at a 7 Eleven. "I've got to reach Bill," she said anxiously. She stood at the outside pay phone and dropped quarters in the slot.

Unable to reach Mentzer through his answering service, Laney got back in the car, and she and Plzak drove around the area for an hour and a half. She stopped several more times at 7 Elevens, but all she was doing was talking to Mentzer's service. Nor did Plzak have any luck trying to reach him on the walkie-talkie. If Mentzer's walkie-talkie was turned on, he was out of range.

At some point as they drove around Plzak asked where Alex and Bill were.

"They grabbed the fat pig," Laney said. "They were taking him to the desert."

"What about the other guy we were waiting for?" Plzak asked.

"He wouldn't go get the cocaine," she said. "He was scared, for some reason."

Sometime around 11:00 P.M., Laney drove to the Westwood Marquis and pulled into the parking lot. "Look," she said. "My alibi is that I was with my lawyer all night. I'm going to make some calls from his house."

She got out of the car and Plzak slid over to the driver's side. "You haven't seen me all night," she added as she slammed the door shut.

At almost the same time that Plzak dropped off Laney, Lawson decided to call La Scala to make sure Radin was all right. He also wanted to tell him about a phone call he had received a few minutes before from a woman who had identified herself as Betty Rogers.

The caller had asked if Tally was there or whether Lawson knew where he was. Then she had asked to speak with Radin. "He isn't here,"

Lawson said. "But I will be hearing from him shortly. Can you give me your number?"

There was something about the call that was all wrong: "Betty Rogers" sounded like Laney. "This is Laney," Lawson said angrily. "What's going on?" The caller immediately hung up. He figured she was trying to trick him into giving her a number for Rogers, which of course he did not have.

Alarmed, Lawson dialed the number for La Scala. "Is the Radin party there?" Lawson asked.

"No," the maître d' said. "They never showed."

Lawson asked if Wilson was there. The maître d' said that he was.

"Can you please get him right away?" While he waited, Lawson nervously tapped the eraser end of his pencil on his notepad. When Wilson picked up the phone, Lawson practically yelled at him. "Where's Roy?"

"He never showed up," Wilson replied.

Lawson asked what he was talking about.

"He never showed," Wilson said. "I don't know where he is."

"You've been there for two and a half hours, Demond. Didn't you think to call? I mean, didn't you think it a bit strange that he never showed after three fucking hours?"

"We were going down Sunset, and they blew off and disappeared," Wilson said. "I followed them as far as I could."

"Oh, dear God . . . ," Lawson moaned.

"I don't know where he is," Wilson added.

"Why didn't you call me, Demond?"

Wilson claimed he did not know what the plans were.

"Demond, wake up!" Lawson was now yelling.

"Why were you following him with a gun, then? *Where the hell is Roy?*"

Lawson was shaking when he hung up the phone. He cupped his hands over his mouth and breathed deeply. Then he picked up the phone again and dialed Anna Montenegro. "Anna, this is Jonathan," he told her answering machine. "Get in touch with me as soon as you can."

Then he called a nightclub where Anna hung out and left a message there. *"I need you—Call."*

Lawson rummaged through all the phone slips on his desk until he found the numbers that Laney had left when she called to ask Radin to dinner. He called Laney's Sherman Oaks house, but there was no answer. He thought it odd that Myriam was not there.

After eight or ten rings, the service picked up. "I want to leave a message for Laney Jacobs," Lawson said. "This is Jonathan Lawson, and I need her to get in touch with me immediately."

Now Lawson was panicking. He thought about who else he could call who might possibly have spoken to Radin. It was almost two-thirty in the morning in New York, but he called the Mayflower, hoping to speak with Renee. There was no answer, so he called Uncle Johnny's apartment. Sylvia Stoppelli answered the phone.

"Hi, Sylvia, it's Jonathan. Is Renee there?"

"We're playing cards," Mrs. Stoppelli said. "Hold on."

When Renee got on the phone, Lawson said he was sorry to disturb her, but by any chance had she spoken to Roy in the last two or three hours?

She asked Lawson what was wrong.

"I just thought he might have called you," Lawson explained. "He went out for dinner, and I can't find him."

Again she asked him what was wrong.

"I don't know," Lawson said. His voice betrayed him, and Renee was frightened. "Look, if you hear from him, get ahold of me immediately. He had a meeting with Laney Jacobs, and I can't find him."

"Please," Renee said, "speak with Uncle Johnny."

Stoppelli picked up the phone and asked what was wrong.

"Uncle Johnny, I'm scared," Lawson said. "There is something very wrong. Roy had a dinner date with Laney Jacobs in Beverly Hills. He was concerned about it, and he asked Demond Wilson to follow him. I called the restaurant at eleven, but Roy never showed. Demond said he lost him somewhere on Sunset."

There was silence for a moment, and then Stoppelli raised his voice and angrily asked, "Why did you have that asshole following him? Why didn't he do something immediately when Roy didn't show?"

"I don't know. . . . Look. I'll be up for a while, Uncle Johnny. I will keep you informed."

Laney's alibi was Sol Besharat, who lived within walking distance of the Westwood Marquis. She had called him on Thursday and asked to see him Friday night around eleven o'clock. She added that she was leaving for Florida on Saturday for her son's birthday party.

At about ten-thirty, Besharat left his house for the hotel bar. He sat alone for a few minutes before Laney walked in. They had a few drinks, and he suggested they return to his house.

As soon as they reached Besharat's, Laney picked up his phone. She tried repeatedly to reach Mentzer, but without luck. Her last call was to Bob Evans, who was in New York. It was 3:21 in the morning there, certainly an unusual time for her to call.

(When asked years later why Laney had called at that hour and what she had said, Evans said he could not recall any details. All he remembered, he said, was that Laney informed him that she had had a fight with Radin.)

At about midnight, Anna Montenegro called the Regency. "I got your message," she told Lawson. "What's wrong? Where's Roy?"

"Anna, my God," Lawson moaned. "Where the hell is Jacobs?"

"Where's Roy?" Anna asked again, disregarding Lawson's question.

"He went with Laney to dinner and he hasn't come back and—"

"I told him not to go! Why did he do it?"

Lawson asked her to drive to the Regency. When he hung up, he sat on the sofa in the living room and covered his face with his hands, muttering to himself. He felt like a caged animal, having been in the apartment for nearly twenty-four hours. He reviewed the evening, step by step, in his mind.

When Anna arrived, Lawson hugged her and nearly wept. She mentioned that she had been to Laney's Sherman Oaks house earlier in the day and had seen four or five men there. "I thought maybe it was Milan sending these guys out to roust Laney about the rip-off," she said.

"Anna," Lawson pleaded, "I need help. Tell me everything, everything that might help Roy."

Anna paced the small living room and again went over the terrain she had mapped out before

—that Laney was a front for Milan Bellechasses, that he bought directly from the Colombians who controlled cocaine in Miami, and that both of them were capable of violent behavior to protect their interests.

Lawson asked her about the movie deal and why it had meant so much to Laney to have Radin turn over a percentage of his share.

The movie deal was a setup, Anna explained. She claimed it was a means for Bellechasses to launder his drug profits in Puerto Rico. Laney wanted the glamour and prestige and legitimacy of the movie business, and Bellechasses wanted a mechanism for investing and cleaning up his narcotics profits.

"We thought we knew it all, and we didn't," Lawson muttered.

He was now even more determined to find Laney. Perhaps she was holding Radin somewhere and was trying to force him to comply with her demands. Lawson wanted to believe this, and he began calling all the numbers he had ever been given for Laney. He reached her answering service again, and this time he left a sterner message.

"Get ahold of Jacobs *now* and tell her if she doesn't call me in thirty minutes I'm going to the cops," Lawson said.

For an hour, they waited in the apartment. Anna sat on the sofa and quietly cried. Then Laney called back.

"What is going on?" she said to Lawson. "What's this about the cops?"

"Where is Roy, lady? He is not here." He was breathing heavily, almost hyperventilating. "I want to know where he is."

"We got in the car—" Laney began.

"He left with you," he said, cutting her off. "Where is he?"

"We got in the car and he got out on Sunset because we had a fight," she explained. "He made the driver stop on Sunset."

"Where?" Lawson demanded.

"Near Tower Records," Laney replied.

"That's bullshit. Roy wouldn't do that. That's absolute bullshit."

"Look," she yelled. "He was going to call you."

"I haven't heard from him. *Where is he?*" He yelled frantically into the receiver.

"I don't know!"

"Produce him, lady, or I'm going to the cops and blow this whole thing."

"No . . . he didn't get out of the car . . ." She began to stutter. "He dropped me off at the Westwood Marquis and went on. That's what really happened."

"Then where's your car?" Lawson asked.

"I let him have it," she said.

"This is shit—where is he?" Lawson demanded.

"I don't have to put up with this!" Laney yelled hysterically.

Lawson shouted, "Where are you now?"

She hung up.

It was after 4:00 A.M. in New York, but Lawson called Stoppelli. "What should I do?" he asked. "I really think I should go to the cops."

"Do what you have to do," Stoppelli said. "I can't help you."

Lawson repeated that he thought he had to go to the cops.

"You gotta do what you have to," Stoppelli said. "Either just come back east or go to the cops."

Lawson got off the phone, and he told Anna

they were going to the police. They drove to a precinct house in West Hollywood and told a police officer what had happened. They were referred to a detective, and they sat in his office and filled out forms. The precinct was loud, with cops coming and going and the phones ringing.

"There really isn't much we can do for at least seventy-two hours," the officer informed them.

"But what if he's been kidnapped?" Lawson said.

The officer shrugged and said they would just have to wait.

Lawson and Anna returned to the apartment in the vain hope they would hear from Radin.

At 7:00 A.M. on Saturday morning, Dean Kahn went to work at the Hotel Bel-Air. One of the first things he noticed in the lot was that the black Cadillac limousine he had loaned to Bill Mentzer had been returned.

He walked over to examine it, opening the driver's-side door. The trip odometer told him the car had been driven seventy-eight miles since he had last seen it. Kahn was glad to see how clean the car was, particularly the inside, which appeared to have been carefully wiped out.

SEVENTEEN

SATURDAY MORNING. LAWSON PULLED himself out of bed. He did not remember falling asleep or even getting into bed.

He made coffee and, as it percolated, called New York to speak with Stoppelli again. No one knew Radin the way Stoppelli did.

Much calmer than he had been a few hours earlier, Stoppelli tried to assure Lawson that Radin had done this before.

"He just ran off—is that what you're saying?" Lawson asked. "How can that be? I've been with him almost twenty-four hours a day for more than a year. Wouldn't I know that?"

Stoppelli explained that when Radin had got into jams in the past, he would walk away for a while. He would turn up days later, or his office would eventually track him through his American Express card. Radin would show up this time, too.

Lawson got off the phone and sat at the kitchen table, cradling his coffee cup. Stoppelli's logic seemed faulty. Why would Radin just disappear on his way to dinner? Perhaps Stoppelli was just trying to be upbeat in order to cheer him up.

His mind reeled from unanswered questions. Did he get out of the limousine, as Laney had said, and walk away? Or, if she got out, where did the driver take Radin? Why didn't Wilson follow them as he was told to? Why hadn't Myriam answered the phone? Where had Laney called from? Was she still in Los Angeles?

Wilson's actions genuinely puzzled Lawson. He was told to follow Radin, and instead he had driven to the restaurant and had dinner with his secretary. He was either completely incompetent, wired on cocaine, or even somehow involved with Laney. Lawson went to the phone again and this time dialed every number he had for Wilson. After eight or ten calls, a friend of Wilson's said that he might be at a marina in Newport Beach. So Lawson called there. There was no answer.

By midmorning, the apartment phone at the Regency was ringing off the hook with calls from friends and family in New York. Radin's mother sounded so shaken that Lawson could barely hear her.

"Could he have gone somewhere?" she asked. "Is there someplace we could call?"

"I don't know where to call, Renee," Lawson said. "Honestly, I think I've tried everything. We'll have to wait it out."

"Is he alive?" she cried.

Lawson, who had come to the conclusion that his boss and friend was dead, did not want to reveal his feelings. "Maybe he went out to the airport. Maybe he'll call from Hawaii, or some such place. You know Roy. He likes to play tricks on people."

Early in the afternoon, it was suggested to Lawson by one of Radin's New York relatives that he call Radin's Beverly Hills attorney to see if he could recommend a private detective. Lawson was soon connected with a man named John O'Grady, a retired Los Angeles narcotics detective turned private investigator. Shrewd and cunning, O'Grady had once been Elvis Presley's chief investigator. He knew how to find missing persons, or corpses—whichever came first.

Very early that morning, Plzak was summoned to Mentzer's apartment in the Valley. He found Mentzer and Bob Lowe waiting for him. The two men were excited and talkative.

"What happened at the hotel?" Plzak asked as he poured himself a cup of coffee.

"We knew we were being followed," Mentzer said. "You know that guy who used to be in 'Sanford and Son'? He was sitting out in front of the Regency."

Lowe explained that he had lost him.

Mentzer said that when Laney jumped out of the limousine, he and Marti pinned Radin in the back seat. Radin was scared shitless, Mentzer said.

A few minutes later, a police car with the siren on roared up behind them, and the three men thought they had been caught. To keep Radin from shouting to the cop if they were pulled over, Mentzer shoved his pistol hard into Radin's mouth, splitting his lips, which bled profusely. The police car sped right past.

They drove north on Interstate 5, to a section of remote canyon land where Mentzer and Marti had gone target shooting in the past. The car stopped near a box canyon, Radin was pulled out, marched a short distance off a gravel road, and shot twenty-seven times in the head.

"Marti went crazy," Mentzer said.

Mentzer, who had consumed part of a bottle of wine to dull his senses, then administered a final shot to the head as sort of a coup de grace. Mentzer said that as it turned out, Radin knew nothing about the rip-off.

After hearing Mentzer talk about the murder, Lowe and Plzak left to take the limousine back to the Hotel Bel-Air. Lowe told Plzak he had personally cleaned out the car and wiped the blood from Radin's cut lips off the back seat.

"The fat pig was screaming," Lowe said. "They shot him . . . I couldn't watch it . . . and I walked back to the car."

When Plzak and Lowe returned from dropping off the limousine, it was announced that they were all going to Miami with Laney. The plan was to continue the hunt for Rogers, who, it was believed, was somewhere in southern Florida.

Later in the day, Mentzer, Marti, Lowe, Plzak, and Laney drove to an airport in Santa Monica. It was Mentzer's idea to use a Lear Jet that had been repossessed by Mike Pascal. That way, they could take their guns with them to Miami without a problem. A pilot named William Granwich would fly the jet east.

On board the plane, Mentzer and Lowe talked about when they were in Vietnam. And because they were the sort of men who liked to discuss their work, they again spoke about taking the fat producer out to the desert and shooting him.

Dressed casually in a designer jogging outfit, Laney sat with them and listened. If she was hearing for the first time the awful truth that Radin had been executed after she had got out of the limousine, she did not react to the news.

* * *

On Sunday morning, Jimmy McQuestion received a phone call from a relative in New York, asking him to help them find Radin. In his mid-thirties, almost the same age as his cousin Roy, McQuestion had long been of the view that Radin was living in overdrive and that eventually he was going to collapse or just flip out. He had seen Roy do enough cocaine for a half-dozen people, then go out and party all night. The man was a whirlwind of activity, and McQuestion wondered how long he could last.

What the relative told him was that Radin was missing and that Radin's mother had hired a psychic to help locate him.

"What the hell good is a psychic?" McQuestion asked. He was given several addresses to check out, one of which was Laney's house in Sherman Oaks.

"See if anyone is at her house," the relative said.

McQuestion went to the other addresses and found nothing. Then he drove to Laney's dead-end street, parked his car, and walked tentatively to the front door and rang the bell. A dog barked inside the house, but no one answered. He walked around the rim of the property, making a mental note of the iron bars on the windows. A few minutes later, he left and called New York to report that no one was at the house except a dog. Not an eager participant in this hunt for his cousin, McQuestion shrugged the whole thing off and went to work.

Midmorning on Sunday, Lawson met O'Grady for breakfast at the Brown Derby restaurant. He told him everything that had happened in the last month.

"It sounds like Laney wanted Radin out of that company and was willing to kill him for it," O'Grady said.

Lawson asked if O'Grady believed Radin was dead.

"Jesus H. Christ, man, you don't think they're holding him somewhere? Of course he's dead. That's why they grabbed him."

Lawson wanted to know why.

"She's a fucking drug dealer," O'Grady said. "They kill people for looking at them the wrong way."

"But Roy didn't steal her drugs," Lawson said. "She had to know that."

O'Grady said it did not matter. "The theft was when—March? Hell, if they'd thought he'd stolen the coke, they'd have whacked him the same fucking day. They wouldn't have waited until May thirteenth, for Christ's sake. It's perfectly obvious they didn't kill him for the drugs."

Lawson and O'Grady then went back to the Regency, where they met Anna Montenegro and Henry Fillet. Radin's former father-in-law had been enlisted in the search by anxious calls from New York.

Fillet told O'Grady he had been in Laney's Sherman Oaks house and it was obvious she was gone. The dresser drawers in her bedroom were pulled open as if she had left in a hurry.

"Any papers, any notes with phone numbers on them?" O'Grady asked.

Fillet showed him a photograph of Laney and Bellechasses, the one Lawson had seen when he first went to the house with Radin.

"That's her benefactor in Miami," Lawson said.

"Jesus, he's got drug dealer written all over

him," O'Grady said. "He ought to carry a neon sign around his neck."

"And that's Laney," Lawson pointed out.

"An attractive lady, huh?" O'Grady said.

"Laney was with bad people," Anna said. "I know something bad has happened to Roy. I'm sure of it."

O'Grady could see that Anna knew a lot about Laney, but he wanted to talk with her privately, away from Fillet and Lawson. He asked her to come to his office on Monday morning.

After spending several hours with Lawson, O'Grady returned to his office and called a prominent Los Angeles attorney, E. Gregory Hookstratten, who he knew was friendly with Bob Evans. He related to Hookstratten the details of the case and said he had to talk to Evans.

"Just give me a phone number I can call," O'Grady said. "I want to talk to him. And I want him to pick up the fucking phone and not hang up on me."

Laney and the others landed in Miami on Sunday morning and split up, with Mentzer staying at Laney's house. Plzak, Marti, and Lowe got a hotel room, and that afternoon Mentzer came to drive them to Laney's, where there was to be a party for Dax's first birthday. They did not take their guns, and if anyone at the party asked who they were, they were to say they were with a film crew.

Balloons were blown up, and everyone sang "Happy Birthday" when Laney brought out the cake. The hired guns stood outside by the swimming pool.

On Sunday night, Laney drove to Bellechasses' house on Ludlum Drive. There, she talked about

Tally Rogers and the theft and what she had
been doing in Los Angeles since her last visit to
Miami with Evans.

Then she told Bellechasses that Radin was
dead. At first, he did not believe her. Then he
blew up.

"Jesus Christ, why the hell did you do that?" he
yelled. "Do you know what kind of trouble this
could bring?" He looked as if he might kill her.
"God, I don't believe it! I don't believe it!"

Realizing that a murder investigation would
cause problems with his cocaine empire, Bellechasses grew angrier and angrier as Laney explained the details. She tried to assure him that
in spite of Radin's obvious disappearance, there
would be no murder investigation.

"They blew him up into a million pieces," she
said. "There will be no body to find. They stuck
dynamite down his throat. He'll never be found."

At ten-twenty on Monday morning, O'Grady
called Evans' Beverly Hills house. The butler answered the phone, and after a brief delay, Evans
picked up. His voice was guarded, and he seemed
on edge. Evans explained that he had no formal
contract with Radin to make a movie. He portrayed Radin as just another hopeful person who
had come to Hollywood to break into the movie
business.

Then Evans mentioned the phone call Laney
had made to him after midnight two days earlier.

"Why the hell would she call you so late?"
O'Grady asked.

"I don't know why; she just did," Evans responded. He told O'Grady he had someone with
him, and the call ended.

At eleven-thirty that morning, Anna arrived at

O'Grady's office, at 8721 Sunset Boulevard. She was alone, and by her anxious demeanor O'Grady could see that she felt she was in a bind between Laney and Radin. She explained, however, that her sympathies were with Radin. O'Grady offered her coffee and set up his tape recorder.

"I want to make a record of this, Anna," O'Grady said. When the machine was on, Anna spoke calmly for the next eighteen minutes. She described Laney as a major drug trafficker from Miami. She talked about Tally Rogers and the theft, and about the check Radin had canceled.

When Anna left, O'Grady returned to the Regency and asked Lawson to try to reach Laney through her answering service. Again he called her numbers and left messages. At one-ten in the afternoon, Laney finally contacted Lawson.

"Where is Roy?" Lawson asked, hoping Laney would not hang up this time.

Laney said she did not know.

"This is *Monday*," Lawson said. "You met him on *Friday*. Where is he?"

"He got out of the car," Laney replied. "I told you."

"Bullshit!" Lawson yelled. "You know where he is!"

"No, I don't," Laney protested. "Listen to me. Listen. He got out in the middle of the Strip."

"Bullshit!" Lawson exploded.

Laney slammed down the phone.

"What did she sound like?" O'Grady asked. "Where the hell is she calling from?"

"I don't know," Lawson said. "I don't know where she is."

* * *

On Tuesday, Mickey De Vinko and a Cleveland cop who had worked for Radin flew to Los Angeles and moved into Radin's apartment with Lawson. Lawson was an emotional wreck. He wanted to get away as fast as he could.

"I'll find out where Roy is," De Vinko told Lawson.

"You talk like he's alive," Lawson said. "Like he's staying at the Beverly Hills Hotel and isn't telling us."

"That's not impossible," De Vinko said.

De Vinko wanted to know where Radin's papers were—contracts, letters, any material relating to the movie deal with Evans. Lawson had placed the original paperwork between Evans and Radin, plus some PBA material and a quantity of cocaine, in a sealed package in the hotel safe.

Late that day, O'Grady came to the apartment. De Vinko handed him envelopes marked "Hold for John O'Grady," which had been in the safe. He opened one of them and saw the white powder.

"What the fuck is this?" he asked.

"It's coke," De Vinko said.

"Not the drink, I suppose," O'Grady responded. "Get rid of that shit now!"

O'Grady pressed De Vinko on what he wanted to do now, and De Vinko said, "We're not out here to start a war, O'Grady. We're here to give Roy a decent funeral."

After O'Grady had gone, Lawson and De Vinko argued about Radin's papers. De Vinko wanted to take them back to his office in Cleveland. With them, Roy Radin Enterprises could continue as a corporation. Lawson watched as De Vinko went through the apartment, collecting letters and contracts. The cocaine that Lawson had secreted in the safe was flushed down the toilet. Lawson blew up when De Vinko took a leather portfolio Radin had given him, which contained phone numbers, notes, and other material.

Lawson yelled that the portfolio was his, but De Vinko ignored him.

Lawson then called New York and spoke with Charlie Donchez, Radin's longtime confidant. "I'm losing my mind," he told him. "You have to get me out of here."

Donchez told him to buy an airline ticket and fly back to New York the next morning.

On Tuesday and Wednesday, O'Grady spoke to reporters and stated that Radin had been murdered. He pointed the finger at Laney Jacobs, who had picked Radin up for dinner. The papers called O'Grady "the number-one Hollywood private detective." The immediate result was that at five in the morning on Wednesday, O'Grady's answering service woke him and said he had received a telephone message. "Tell O'Grady it's just a matter of time."

That day when he left for work, O'Grady stuffed a .38 police special into his belt.

Thursday morning, May 19, O'Grady was visited at his office by Frank Rubino, Laney's Miami attorney. She had asked him to travel to Los Angeles to tell authorities that they could not interview her about the events of May 13.

Standing in O'Grady's cramped office, Rubino mentioned that he had seen O'Grady's quotes in the newspapers.

"Why don't you help us find Roy?" Rubino asked.

"I can't do that," O'Grady said. "That's a fucking conflict of interest, for Christ's sake. Have you been to the police yet?"

"Yes, and they are not interested in talking to her at this time," Rubino said.

"Well, good for her," O'Grady responded.

"You know," Rubino said, "she got out of the limousine that night."

"Oh, Jesus Christ, that is absolute horseshit!" O'Grady said. "She told Lawson that *he* got out of the car. She ought to get her fucking story straight."

Upon seeing how determined O'Grady was, Rubino turned and left the office.

O'Grady set off for the Regency, to talk with De Vinko. While he was there, a messenger arrived with a letter from Evans. O'Grady read it over first. It was short and to the point: Evans was now severing any relationship with Radin.

"He's canceling the deal when all he knows is that Roy is missing," O'Grady said. "I don't get it."

A few days after their arrival in Miami, Marti and Plzak were on their way to a restaurant for dinner. Marti mentioned that he had two .22 caliber pistols with silencers wrapped in white hotel towels in the trunk of the car.

Plzak suggested that they pull over to the side of the road and get rid of them. Marti agreed, and soon they stopped at a small lake. It was dark, but they could see an older man and a boy fishing in the distance. Marti handed Plzak the heavy towels, which were wrapped tightly with string. Plzak waded out into the water and threw them as far as he could.

A day or two later, Mentzer, Marti, Lowe, and Plzak went to Bellechasses' house. When they arrived, Bellechasses said that he had information that Rogers was in St. Thomas. He proposed a plan whereby the five of them would charter a fishing boat that would stop in St. Thomas. He argued that his plan would not arouse suspicion. Later, it was agreed that only Lowe would go, perhaps with a woman, to make it appear as if they were tourists. This plan was abandoned, however, when Lowe could not find a woman to go along with him.

Five or six days after their arrival in Miami, Mentzer, Laney, Plzak, Myriam, and Dax drove to Islamorada, a resort in the Florida Keys south of Miami. Laney had rented a two-bedroom apartment near a rocky beach, and she wanted Myriam and the baby to stay there with Plzak, while she and Mentzer returned to Miami.

On the way to the Keys, Laney directed Mentzer to drive to the Collection, the luxury-car dealership. She was short on money, and she wanted to retrieve the expensive watches that Joe Amer had given to Joe Rodriguez after his arrest. She asked Plzak to come inside with her; he was to say that he had been a cellmate of Amer's and was there at Amer's request to get his watches.

While Myriam stayed with Dax in the car, the others went inside. Joe Rodriguez was startled to see them. As Plzak spoke, Rodriguez reached into a desk drawer.

"Don't do that!" Plzak said. "We'll shoot you before you can get the gun out."

Laney tried to soothe him. She said she really needed the jewelry, but Rodriguez said he did not have it. He could get it, he said, but not before tomorrow. "Have it tomorrow, then," Plzak said. "Accidents can happen, you know. Cars can blow up very easily."

Laney and her group continued on to Islamorada. Later, Laney and Mentzer went back and picked up the watches. Soon after, Mentzer handed Plzak five hundred dollars in cash, as a down payment toward the work he had done to date.

EIGHTEEN

A WEEK AFTER HE HAD HELPED ARrange for the loan of the limousine, a frightened Marc Fogel called Fred McKnight.

"I think a man's been killed," Fogel said.

Over coffee at the Hyatt Hotel on Wilshire Boulevard, Fogel detailed what he knew about the limousine that Kahn had rented to Mentzer, concluding with the fact that it had been returned cleaner than it had gone out.

"Who would have been murdered?" McKnight asked.

Fogel had the name—Roy Radin. He had picked it up in conversations between Laney and Mentzer. "He's a producer who has been working with Laney Jacobs," Fogel informed McKnight. "He's a dead man, I'm sure of it."

McKnight returned to the police department and called the homicide squad. They had nothing on a murder victim by the name of Roy Alexander Radin. He called missing persons and was directed to a detective named Glen Sousa. Sousa had been working on the case since Lawson filed a missing persons report after Radin's disappearance.

"This man may not be missing," McKnight informed Sousa. "We have an informant who thinks he was murdered."

Sousa said he had no hard information that would lead him to that conclusion, but he thanked McKnight for the tip and hung up.

Approximately a week after she had left Los Angeles, Laney called Evans. She tried to initiate a conversation about *The Cotton Club*, but Evans cut her off. He was on his way to a meeting with Francis Ford Coppola to talk about the movie. She promised to call back later.

A few days before Memorial Day, Evans got in touch with Fred Doumani, who had a home in Los Angeles, and asked if he would give a friend of his a complimentary room at the Golden Nugget. The friend, Evans explained, was a Los Angeles police detective named Glen Sousa, who had been very good to him.

Evans was himself to spend Memorial Day weekend at the Golden Nugget, and shortly after his arrival in Las Vegas he met the Doumani brothers in their office. Later, speaking to Fred Doumani, Evans got right to the point. "You let me down regarding the *Cotton Club* movie, and now I've got myself in some kind of trouble."

Doumani asked him what was going on, and Evans told him about his recent troubles. He said he had met a New York producer named Roy Radin, who had promised to raise millions of dollars through the Puerto Rican government. But Radin was now missing, and the deal was as good as dead. Worse, Evans explained, the woman who had introduced him to Radin had probably killed him. Evans appeared to be frightened.

Evans went on to explain that the woman, Laney Jacobs, was a dope dealer with ties to suppliers in Miami, and that he had been sleeping and partying with her.

Inferring that Doumani had mob ties, Evans asked if he could help him. Doumani declined.

"Why do you believe Radin is dead?" Doumani asked. "He could just be missing."

"Believe me, he's dead," Evans said. "The bitch had him killed, and I'm next."

Midmorning on June 10, almost two weeks later, in the desert country north and east of Los Angeles, near the town of Gorman, Glen Fischer went looking for a place to store his beehives. Instead, he found a corpse.

Late in the afternoon, homicide detectives Carlos Avila and Willi Ahn arrived to inspect the fetid body. Standing over the remains, Avila noted that the head was facing west, the feet east. The right foot was crossed over the left, and only one foot had a shoe on it. The left arm was pointed skyward, resting against a bush. The right arm was extended in a southwesterly direction.

The corpse wore what appeared to be a dark-colored three-piece suit and a Pierre Cardin tie. The shirt was partially open, exposing a section of waxy-looking skin. Also, the pockets of the pants, front and back, were pulled out, as if the person or persons responsible had also picked the man's pockets. There was no watch on either wrist.

Later, after the remains had been carted off for an autopsy, Avila returned with a filtering screen and sifted the soil in the surrounding area. Approximately seven feet from where the body had come to its final rest, he found a portion of a jawbone containing several teeth. This was con-

sistent with someone's putting a bomb in the
dead man's mouth.

Several hours after the body had been discovered, Avila opened an investigation into the murder of Roy Alexander Radin. Since the body had
been found in the county, the missing persons
case that had been conducted by the Los Angeles
Police Department, and, in particular, by Detective Glen Sousa, was now in the sheriff's jurisdic-
tion.

Their two-week respite in the Florida Keys ended
shortly after noon on June 11, when Mentzer and
Laney came into the apartment and announced
that the newspapers in Los Angeles were carrying stories about a body that had been discovered. It was late in the day, and the sun had
nearly set. The ocean outside the apartment was
the color of wet slate.

"What body?" Plzak asked.

"The guy we wasted," Mentzer answered. Laney was standing next to him, looking angry. Myriam was playing with Dax in an adjacent room.

"I don't see how they will be able to identify
him, what with the number of times we shot
him," Mentzer added.

The news so alarmed Laney that the same day
she angrily conveyed the news to an acquaintance to whom she had earlier laid out the bill of
particulars against Roy Radin, as well as the
method of his execution. Her anger seemed almost uncontainable.

"This should never have happened!" she
yelled. "They weren't supposed to find the body!
They weren't supposed to find the body!"

* * *

In New York on this same afternoon, Jonathan Lawson and a friend from Spain were stepping off a railroad car at Grand Central Terminal. Lawson put his friend on an uptown bus, and he prepared to take a cab to the apartment in the Village where he had been staying after moving out of the Mayflower. His departure had been sparked by a particularly loud and angry fight with one of Radin's relatives, who had falsely accused him of taking Roy's clothes.

Before leaving the station, Lawson went to a pay phone to check his answering machine. There was one message: "Call the Mayflower. They found Roy's body."

Lawson ran out of Grand Central and hailed a cab. When he reached the Mayflower, he found a roomful of weeping people. Charlie Donchez, the big and burly former cop, was crying, too.

"Renee wants to talk to you," Donchez said.

Lawson put his arms around Radin's mother. "I'm so sorry," he said.

Renee was a heavy woman, and her whole body shook as she sobbed. Her hair was pulled straight back in a ponytail, but strands of it had come out and were hanging off her forehead. When she stopped crying, she said that Johnny Stoppelli wanted Lawson to call as soon as possible. Lawson picked up the phone and called the old man.

"We appreciate everything you did for Roy," Stoppelli said. "Would you help with what the cops need? Dental records, that sort of stuff. There will be questions you'll have to answer."

"Of course," Lawson said. Fearing public exposure, Stoppelli and his wife went only to the wake, avoiding the spectacle of the funeral.

Red Buttons was asked to read the eulogy at St.

Malachy's. An abundance of flowers filled the front of the church. Only a few show business friends of Radin's had shown up at the funeral. Radin had become an embarrassment, a scandal. Few people wanted to admit to knowing him. When he was through, Buttons handed Renee Radin a yellow sheet of paper containing his eulogy.

Henry Wadsworth Longfellow once said, "We judge ourselves by what we feel capable of doing, while others judge us by what we have already done."

As far as I'm concerned, Roy Radin did a lot. He packed a hundred years of living into thirty-three years of life, an envious accomplishment.

This was the Roy Radin I knew: He had an excitement about him. There was always something happening—something doing—something playing. I knew Roy in all his shades, all his colors, all his moods. *Yes*, he was temperamental, brash, cocky, outrageous. *Yes*, he was compassionate, charitable, sentimental, lovable. He had the devil on one shoulder and an angel on the other. And for Roy it was a perpetual tug-of-war. *Yes*, he was Peck's bad boy, and *yes*, he was not dull. He had wit. He had style. He had class. He was generous to a fault. There was no picking up a check when you were out with Roy Radin—a vanishing breed in today's world of short arms and long pockets. At the incredible age of seventeen, when most kids are still hustling their parents for spending money, Roy started producing shows. It's hard for me to believe that when I met Roy he was only twenty-two years old. He was an anachronism. When he was born, vaudeville was already long gone and forgotten, and yet he had this strong desire to relive that nostalgic era. That was the milieu he seemed to be most comfortable with. Roy had a deep and profound respect for performers who in the twilight of their careers found the going rough. His treatment of headliners long past their prime was a joy to behold. The affection and tenderness he displayed toward Georgie Jessel, as an example, was inspirational for all who were privy to witness it.

Roy was enthusiastic. There was a boyish charm about his enthusiasm: it had an infectious quality. Roy had plans—so many plans—always plans. He reminded me of a prizefighter in the gym, shadowboxing and chasing some elusive target. It saddens me to think of all the things he left undone. It came as no surprise to me when I learned he helped raise, with love, his three sisters—Katie, Lisa, and Diane. He loved his brother Joel. Roy loved his mother, and he loved his father, Al. He loved Loretta and he loved Toni. Roy adopted two children, who he dearly loved. That should tell you something about the man, and I sure hope God noticed that one. It came as no surprise to learn that Roy Radin played Santa Claus every Christmas Eve at an upstate orphanage. Roy loved kids. He was a big kid himself. He was flamboyant. He was fun.

He was my friend. I miss him already!

After the funeral, Radin was buried in Southampton. The next day, fearing for his own life, Lawson fled to Spain.

In the third week of June, Bill Mentzer called Fogel at the Budget office. He wanted to know if the cops had been around his office or the Le Express office at the Hotel Bel-Air. Fogel answered no, but by that time, had detectives come around, they would have discovered that the interior of the Cadillac limousine in question had been ripped out and new seats installed.

Not long afterward, and after repeated calls regarding the police, Mentzer and Laney drove up to the Budget lot and walked into Fogel's office. Laney appeared relaxed and talkative, and she suggested that they walk up the street to a restaurant. As they were leaving the lot, Fogel asked about the limousine that had been rented on the night of the murder.

"You don't want to know," Mentzer said.

Laney, Mentzer, Myriam, and Dax spent the summer in a large house at 2214 Yosemite Drive in Palm Springs. Laney tried several times to get hold of Evans, but was unable to reach him. Without him, she had no way of breaking into movies. Her Hollywood dream was now dead.

NINETEEN

T HE MAN'S NAME WAS BILL RIDER. HE had been a policeman in Ohio at one time, but had retired to become Larry Flynt's security director in Los Angeles. Rider was a gun lover, a man who invested what little money he had in firearms.

In the course of his duties working for Flynt, whose magazine, *Hustler*, had made Flynt wealthy, Rider had hired as bodyguards or met socially three men whom he considered tough and unpredictable. They were Bill Mentzer, Bob Lowe, and, the worst of them, Alex Marti.

Rider worked at Flynt's publishing office in Century City and also at his mansion at 364 St. Cloud, in Bel Air. It was at the mansion, on a morning in early June, that Rider first learned about the murder. Mentzer approached him and started talking about doing a "hit" and dumping the body up where he, Rider, and Marti had gone target shooting. The exact location was north of Los Angeles, just off Interstate 5 in a remote area called Caswell Canyon. The men had dressed up like commandos. Rider had brought along his MAC-10, which could fire a hail of bullets at the

touch of the trigger. The men had taken pictures
of each other—first Rider had photographed
Mentzer and Marti; then Marti photographed
Rider and Mentzer.

A few days later, while standing with Marti
near Flynt's swimming pool in Bel Air, Rider
asked about Mentzer and the shooting. "He was
chickenshit and had to drink a bottle of wine before he had the courage to shoot the guy," Marti
explained.

Rider had now heard from both these men that
they had committed a murder, but he was not
sure they were telling the truth. He thought they
were bullshitting him, until the pair brought
newspaper clippings about the discovery of
Radin's body. Rider glanced over them enough to
see that the body had indeed been found in Caswell Canyon. "The body of a New York theatrical
producer missing since May 13 was found yester-
day in a remote canyon north of Los Angeles. . . ."

"And you didn't believe us, did you?" Marti
said, pointing to the articles.

If Rider harbored any doubt at all, it was removed when Marti tried to sell Rider a Rolex
watch and a ring that he had stripped off Radin's
body. Marti laughed as he explained how he had
taken the jewelry off "Rodan."

"Who's Rodan?" Rider asked.

"That's the name Alex gave Radin," Mentzer
explained. "It's a monster in a Japanese sci-fi
movie."

"He was a big, fat Jew," added Marti, who left
Rider with the impression that killing Jews was
a labor of love for him.

Of the two men, Rider had always been closer
to Mentzer, who was easier to get along with.

Rider thought Marti, who had only recently turned twenty-two, was crazy as well as a born criminal. It made sense to Rider that it was Marti who had emptied his gun into Radin's head and that Mentzer had followed with a shot into the already dead man.

In addition to saving newspaper stories of Radin's death, Mentzer had taped televised news reports. Mentzer was his own best public relations man. When Rider visited Mentzer, he was shown the tape. Rider had watched it in rapt silence and had listened carefully when Mentzer said that Marti had "gone crazy" as he fired shot after shot into Radin. Maybe it was true, maybe it wasn't. Rider had no way of knowing.

Mentzer frequently brought up Radin's death. He evidently believed he had committed the perfect crime, which could never be unraveled, so talking about it so casually was not a danger. When Rider asked who had paid for the murder, Mentzer was quick to claim it was Laney Jacobs, a rich woman from Florida, and Bob Evans, the Hollywood movie producer. It all sounded incredible.*

Asked why it had been necessary to kill him, Mentzer told Rider two different stories. One story was that Radin had been killed because Laney believed he was somehow involved in the theft of cocaine from her house. The second story was that Radin had tried to cut her out of a promising movie deal with Evans.

* * *

* Evans has vigorously denied any involvement in Radin's murder or having any advance knowledge that it was to take place. He has not been charged in connection with the crime.

On the afternoon of September 19, 1983, a warm and sunny day that was noteworthy for the almost complete lack of smog in the air, Steve Slazes and several members of his undercover narcotics team sat in unmarked cars near the Pan American building at Los Angeles International Airport.

The airport was crowded, as it always seemed to be, with automobiles jamming the pickup and drop-off curbs. People jumped out of cars and limousines and shouted for luggage carriers; others rushed to crowded ticket counters. It was certainly not an easy location to pick out a man who had been described in the most general of terms.

Seated behind the wheel, Slazes eyed the crowd, looking for a man in his thirties, heavyset, balding, with short brown curly hair. The man's name was Robert Lowe, and if the informant who had spoken to Slazes that afternoon was right, he was about to step off a flight from Miami, his luggage stuffed with cocaine.

Slazes had heard of the man who the informant said was picking up Lowe—Bill Mentzer. The caller was a longtime friend of Mentzer's, who, in recent months, had decided to turn against him. The caller had further offered that the cocaine was for Mentzer and a woman by the name of Mrs. DeLayne.

After a long wait, Slazes, feeling that perhaps he had missed Lowe, decided to leave the airport and come back later. As he was driving away, he received a message over his car radio that his informant had called the office again, this time to say that Mentzer had only recently left for the airport to pick up Lowe and was driving a blue Mercedes convertible.

Suddenly, Slazes spotted the car, with Mentzer

behind the wheel, heading into the airport. Slazes turned around and followed the car back to the Pan Am building. He parked and watched as Mentzer stopped at the curb. A moment later, a man fitting the description of Lowe came out of the building and greeted Mentzer. Mentzer opened the Mercedes' trunk, and Lowe tossed in a brown carry-on suitcase.

The Mercedes pulled away from the curb, and Slazes tried to follow, but he was mired in traffic. He radioed ahead for other police units to stop the car before it left the airport. Officers approached the car with guns drawn and ordered the men out, to await Slazes.

"We're conducting a narcotics investigation," Slazes said. "We'd like to talk with you." Slazes asked them to accompany him to the airport's narcotics office.

At the office, the two men were separated. Slazes asked Lowe if he would consent to have his luggage searched. Realizing he had no choice, Lowe reluctantly agreed. When the bag was opened, the officers found two kilos of cocaine wrapped in cellophane and brown paper. Both men were informed that they were under arrest.

Over the next several hours, Slazes and the other officers spoke with Mentzer and Lowe. What Slazes wanted most of all was permission to search Mentzer's apartment, on Magnolia Street in Sherman Oaks. This was important because Slazes knew that Mentzer's name had been mentioned in a homicide case under investigation by the Los Angeles County Sheriff's Department. So when Mentzer agreed, Slazes called Carlos Avila.

Avila drove to Sherman Oaks. It was after dark

when he arrived, and it took a few extra minutes
to park and find the apartment. There, he found
Mentzer and several Los Angeles police officers
waiting for him. After speaking briefly with the
officers, Avila began slowly looking through the
small apartment.

Three months after the remains of Roy Radin
had been discovered, what Avila knew about the
crime was hardly enough to hold much promise
that the murder would be solved anytime soon.
Fogel's meeting with Fred McKnight had provided some insight into who was behind the murder, but nothing very solid. Fogel's relationship
with McKnight had led the cops to the limousine
used on the night of the murder. But there was no
physical evidence to be acquired—not only had
the limousine been cleaned; its interior had been
ripped out and replaced.

As Avila poked through Mentzer's messy apartment, he hoped for something substantial.

In Mentzer's dresser drawer, Avila found two
color Polaroid photographs, which he held under
the light of a table lamp. He could see that in the
first picture Mentzer was standing next to another man, who was shorter, with black hair and
a round face. Mentzer was wearing a green
T-shirt and beige pants, and the other man was
wearing a fatigue outfit of the sort sold in army-
surplus stores. This man was holding a shotgun.

Mentzer was also pictured in the second photograph, standing next to a different man, who was
holding what appeared to be a machine gun.
What caught Avila's eye was the background in
both photographs—arid and desertlike, it looked
remarkably like Caswell Canyon.

Among some papers, Avila found a pink slip
for the sale of a 1982 Cadillac. The car had been

purchased from Marc Fogel at his Budget Rent-a-
Car office by Karen DeLayne Jacobs; the owner-
ship was transferred to Robert Lowe on May 13,
1983, the day he had driven the limousine to the
Regency Hotel to pick up Radin. Avila also found
business records for Jamboni Enterprises, which
listed Mentzer as an official of the corporation.

Avila took the papers and the photographs and
left the apartment. On a hot and dry morning a
few days later, he drove north on Interstate 5 and
back down the rocky hardpan road into the canyon. He stood near the spot where the murder
had taken place and held the photographs in
front of him. The rugged skyline was the same,
as was the background.

With only the hum of the freight traffic on the
interstate to break the silence, Avila tried to
imagine what had happened on May 13. He could
envision Radin being pulled from a car and
walked down the dirt road; and he could envision
men holding guns to his head as he begged for
his life, followed by the explosion of gunfire,
which no one in the surrounding countryside had
apparently heard.

At the same time as Avila had almost by accident
placed the faces of possible suspects at the scene
of the murder, Laney Jacobs was in the process
of running away from the police. The discovery
of the body in June had ruined everything for
her. Her departure from Los Angeles abruptly
ended the estimated five-million-dollar-a-year
cocaine business that she shared with Milan
Bellechasses.

Bellechasses was understandably upset. His
anger at her had been evident the night she announced Radin's murder at his house. In and of

itself, the theft of his cocaine by Tally Rogers had been a temporary headache. Bellechasses was wealthy enough to cover the loss of the cocaine. The loss of his biggest market after Laney was forced to flee Los Angeles was another matter altogether. Finding a distributor to take her place would be a difficult task.

It would appear that someone other than the police was pursuing Laney, which may have hastened her departure from California. Perhaps someone from her drug-dealing days in Miami. When Jean Kappler, the co-owner of a Palm Springs house that Laney and Mentzer had rented that summer and wanted to buy for $350,000, went to the house after Laney had moved out, she found a telephone-answering machine that Laney had left behind.

Out of curiosity, Kappler turned it on. After some static, she heard a man's voice.

"I know you're there . . . you're hanging up on me," the man said, in a voice that sounded to Kappler as if the caller was from New York or New Jersey.

The man went on: "I know you're there because my people saw you arriving at the airport. They saw you picked up at the airport. Daddy will have to send for you, and you're not going to like it."

PART FOUR

OKEECHOBEE

TWENTY

MARCH 1984. TALLAHASSEE.
Joe Amer sat on the edge of the bed in his prison cell. He held the envelope but hesitated in opening it. At mail call, he had picked out the letter with Laney's handwriting on it immediately. She had not written him even once in the two years he had been in prison. Finally, he peeled the envelope open and pulled out the letter, which smelled of lavender.

He read her words out loud. ". . . I think it's time for Dax to come see his daddy." The letter went on to say that she would bring Dax to the prison the following weekend. For the next few days, Amer could not sleep. He wondered what he would say to her, and to Dax. He told other inmates that his son was almost two years old. "I was arrested, and then my wife gave birth," Amer said. "They couldn't have waited another few days to pick me up?"

When the weekend arrived, he had mentally counted out the months and days since Dax's birth and had a picture in his mind of a dark-haired baby boy with big brown eyes. Laney would be beautiful, as always, just the way he remembered her. He decided she was the best thing that had happened to him, and he wanted to look her in the eyes and tell her so. He wanted to say his relationship with Jackie Silva had not lasted. Amer had heard she was dating his lawyer, Frank Rubino, and they were planning to wed.

The visitors' area of the prison included a large brick patio, and Amer was nervously waiting there at the start of visiting hours. He walked back and forth between the patio and the enclosed area where the visitors were let in, until finally he saw Laney and the boy. Myriam was walking behind Laney.

"He's walking!" Amer yelled. "Oh, my God! He's walking!" He picked up Dax and held him tight. Then he put his arm around Laney and kissed her.

"You look great," he said. "I apologize for everything that has happened between us."

"It's all right," she said. "I just wanted Dax to see his father."

"Myriam, it's so good to see you," he said, kissing her on both cheeks. "Are you taking good care of Laney and Dax?"

She nodded yes and walked away from them so they could talk and be alone.

"It's so incredible that Dax is walking," he said. "God, he's so grown up." They sat down on a row of benches. He picked up the boy and put him on his lap. "You are so handsome, Dax. I am your daddy. I am your daddy!"

Amer asked if she had photographs of Dax he could send his parents in Honduras. She took a handful of color pictures from her purse and presented them to Amer. He looked them over, and his throat burned and his eyes were wet.

They talked while Dax played. She told him she had been in Los Angeles for about a year, but she offered no explanation as to why she had returned. Amer did know that she had taken his watches; Joe Rodriguez had written him and told him so. Rodriguez said Laney had come to his office with some men who had threatened him. He quoted Laney as saying, "I need the jewelry because I have to pay debts. If I don't, they will take Dax from me."

"Joe Rodriguez told me about the watches," Amer said. "What was wrong?"

"I owed people money," she said. "I'm sorry I had to do that."

He asked if everything was all right now.

"Yes, fine. Really, it is."

"You're amazing, you know that?" he said. "You're always in charge. You should run General Motors."

She asked when he thought he might get out of jail.

"I am hoping next March," he said. "One more year here."

"What will you do?"

"Go to Miami," he whispered. "I am owed five hundred thousand. If I can get it. Otherwise, find a job. Start over."

"Don't worry," she said. She put her arm across his shoulder and warmly looked into his eyes. "I will be there."

"I'd love to get back together, Laney. It was all my fault. I blew it. I really blew it."

She laughed and said, "Yes, you did!"

When Laney and Dax left, Amer returned to his cell. He wrote a long letter to his parents in Honduras and enclosed pictures of Dax. "This is my son," he wrote. "Can you believe it? I hope someday he will finally be able to meet his grandparents."

Laney had moved back into her house at 6660 Southwest 125th Avenue in Miami. She returned several times to Los Angeles to see Mentzer. Once, she traveled to Hawaii with Mentzer, where they ran into Marc Fogel, who had just gotten married. She now seemed to view Radin's murder as a forgotten chapter in her life. Her faith in her ability not to get caught appeared to be unshaken.

She also traveled to Las Vegas to see her friend Leslie Dekeyser, the owner of the Suzie Creamcheese boutique in the Fashion Square mall. But Laney found that Dekeyser was not as friendly as she had been in the past. Dekeyser had been arrested for selling cocaine to a Las Vegas undercover officer in late 1983 and had been placed on probation. She did not want to risk violating the terms of her probation, which would have resulted in a lengthy jail sentence.

In the late spring of 1984, an employee of Marc Fogel's car dealership, Robert Deremer, delivered a car to Laney in Las Vegas. She drove him to the airport, and he caught a flight back to Los Angeles. At a later date, Deremer delivered a Fogel car to her in Miami. As in Las Vegas, she took him to the airport for the flight back.

In between Laney's trips to Los Angeles, Mentzer and Marti were retained by Mike Pascal to guard a prosperous family named Cavalli. Deremer was also hired, as was a man named Tom Markel, who was a Los Angeles County sheriff's deputy and Mentzer's cousin. The group was to watch the house of the family's grandmother, which was near the Beverly Hills Hotel, as well as the son's house near Malibu, and an office building. All this was because a member of the family had been threatened by a transvestite named June Mincher.

On the night of May 3, 1984, Mentzer stood on Sepulveda Boulevard in Van Nuys, near an apartment building where a friend of Mincher's lived. Mincher and a man named James Christian Pierce came out of the building and began walking along Sepulveda. As the pair neared Mentzer, Mincher suddenly whirled around and began running back toward the apartment building.

Pierce turned to follow her, then heard Mentzer coming up behind him. "What do you want?" Pierce yelled. Mentzer answered by firing a shot into Pierce's chest, which sent him sprawling onto the sidewalk. Then Mentzer jumped over Pierce, grabbed Mincher by her hair, and began firing into her head. He emptied his pistol and, when he was out of bullets, kicked the body. Then he turned and kicked Pierce in the head.

Late that night, Lowe called Deremer and told him to come to Mentzer's apartment. When he arrived, Mentzer asked for a ride to pick up his car. Approaching Sepulveda, they encountered congested traffic and police cars on the side of the road.

"Don't stop," Mentzer ordered. "Just keep going."

"What's going on?" Deremer asked.

"The Cavallis won't have no more trouble," Mentzer said.

Deremer asked him what he meant.

"Well, I had to shoot two people here," he said. "Keep going."

They drove on another mile or so, and Mentzer directed Deremer into a parking lot. "Let me out

here," Mentzer said. "You go wherever you want
to go, but you just keep your mouth shut and get
out of here."

That spring and early summer, Laney saw
friends and occasionally dated. She wrote Amer
several times, leaving him with the impression
that they might get back together when he was
released from prison the following March.

Frequently, she was a guest on a yacht called
The Sleuth, which was co-owned by her lawyer,
Frank Rubino. His partner in the boat was a tall,
handsome Floridian named Larry Greenberger,
who loved deep-sea fishing and the serenity of
the open sea. At Rubino's Coconut Grove office
one afternoon, the lawyer introduced Laney to
Greenberger, and very soon they were insepara-
ble.

Greenberger was thirty-six years of age, with
thick light-brown hair and rugged outdoorsy features. He often dressed like a cowboy, with snap
shirts and jeans, and he spoke in a deep drawl.
He was a Southern version of the Marlboro man,
with the notable distinction that he drove expensive luxury cars.

Greenberger had been raised in Okeechobee, a
cow town in central Florida that sits at the north
end of the huge freshwater lake of the same
name. His parents, Jerry and Dahlis Greenberger, owned a clothing store on the town's
main street. They were quiet people, undemand-
ing in their approach to parenthood. Their son
grew up the way many small-town Southern boys
did—hunting and fishing and playing football.
He was the most popular student at Okeechobee
High School. Greenberger was named "Mr.

OHS," a tribute to his good looks, popularity, and honor society membership.

In 1966, Greenberger enrolled as a marketing major at Florida State University. He made a lot of friends, many of whom came from large Eastern cities, and they regarded Greenberger as a Southern rube. One friend who attended the university with Greenberger later described him as "the sweetest guy I ever met. He was like a real redneck, a cowboy type. But he would give you the shirt off his back. He loved people, and he trusted them. A friend was always a friend—that was Larry.

"He did have a sort of 'mysterious' side to him. I can't explain it much, except to say that he could be around you a lot, you'd do things together and have fun, and then he'd like pull away from you. He'd go away and you'd run into him months later and he acted like he'd never been gone. I would always wonder about him, but he was so outgoing and lovable that whatever questions I had just didn't get answered. You didn't press him for explanations about these gaps in his life. You'd see him once, and he'd be working at a fancy store at the mall; you'd see him again, and he'd have his own real estate company that owned office buildings. That was the 'mystery' to him.

"I met his parents many, many times, and I thought they were two of the nicest, best people I'd ever met. Two absolutely down-to-earth, unpretentious people. You loved Jerry, and Dahlis would fall over backwards to help out. Larry just adored them. Even though he'd just go off and disappear and you might not see him for months on end, he'd come back and talk nonstop about going up to Okeechobee. I thought it was backwater U.S.A., but Larry thought the sun rose and set over Okeechobee—the two-lane country roads, the cattle ranches. He'd go up there and go off and practically get lost in the sticks. The openness did something for him, which was sort of how he looked at the ocean. The openness cleaned him out."

In the early and mid-1970s, Greenberger was supposedly working and investing in real estate. Somehow, though, Tallahassee police came to the conclusion that Greenberger was actually a drug dealer with a large clientele. While they apparently believed this and kept reports about his activities, they did not have any solid evidence on which to arrest him. By 1976, according to police reports, Greenberger was able to put together large cocaine shipments that were off-loaded at Florida airports and stored at safe houses.

An Okeechobee friend, who was himself handling planeloads of cocaine at a remote ranch north of the town, saw Greenberger becoming increasingly wealthy over the years. "With some people you know it's drugs, it's just as clear as a billboard. Larry, though, was always so even-keeled, so basically the same, that I couldn't see him that deep into it, if at all. What I'm saying is, Larry didn't *act* like a drug dealer. He didn't have that edge.

"Now, he was gone from Okeechobee a long time. I don't think I saw him a half-dozen times for the first ten years after high school. You'd hear things about him, but you'd never actually see him. I once heard he was living in a mansion in Beverly Hills. God, I couldn't get over that. But was it true? And I guess I always thought about his parents, who I'd see at their western-wear store. I'd go in and pick up something for a hunting trip, and I'd talk to Jerry and come away thinking that the Greenbergers were just about the nicest people in this little old town. That made it even harder to accept the talk that Larry was a great big dealer, someone capable of handling real tonnage.

"Okeechobee is an odd place. Everyone knows everyone, and they make it their business to know everyone else's business. There was an odd kind of view here of the rest of the country. Smuggling, and I mean bringing planes in and landing them on dirt strips way back in the interior of the county, or just kicking out packages over some old boy's barn, was never seen as an evil thing. I'm saying people justified it, said it was all right. Therefore, why not take advantage of the sums of money to be made, why not make a little for yourself?

"Folks might have whispered when a rancher you knew was suddenly buying up property and buildings and driving a fancy car. But no one blew the whistle, no one said, 'Gee, what's that old boy doing? He oughta go to jail for that.' What you heard was, 'If America wants cocaine, that's not of my doing. But why not make a little money for myself?' That's the town Larry grew up in."

By 1977, Greenberger was married to a pretty and ambitious woman named Sharon Poole. He dearly loved her, calling her his "dream." They were considered the perfect couple by their friends. Nevertheless, perhaps because their views of the future were so different, they separated a year later, at just about the time that Greenberger met a young Colombian cocaine smuggler named Carlos Enrique Lehder Rivas.

In the late 1970s, Lehder had surrounded himself with a number of young Americans, some of whom he had met while serving a federal prison sentence for marijuana smuggling in Connecticut. The Americans were bright, enormously ambitious, and fearless. What appealed to them was being part of Lehder's grand plan to turn cocaine smuggling into a science of precision and planning. Cocaine was then a small part of the overall American drug picture, but Lehder, being the visionary that he was, saw an unlimited future for the drug.

Perhaps as early as 1977, Greenberger was said to be distributing cocaine to California, the place Lehder and his Colombian associates considered the major American marketplace for it. Greenberger and Lehder formed a partnership, and Greenberger loaned his new partner money to buy an airplane. In exchange, Greenberger became Lehder's number-one stateside distributor and the leader of a small army of couriers and dealers.

Once, Greenberger asked a friend of his if he wanted to fly to Norman's Cay, an island in the Bahamas owned and operated by Lehder as a drug transit point into the United States. The friend agreed, and the two men flew to the island late at night in a Sabreliner.

Security guards met them at the airstrip on the island. They were carrying Uzis and spoke German. There was a lagoon, a clubhouse, and a marina, which was closed down. There were some houses the help stayed in. The guards put Greenberger and his friend in Land Rovers and took them to Lehder's house. There, they sat in a room overlooking the ocean and had drinks.

The friend went with Greenberger a second time to see Lehder. When they arrived, they boarded Lehder's yacht and sailed to Nassau.

They moored in front of an estate, and when they went inside, Lehder introduced them to Robert Vesco, the fugitive financier who had long eluded the law in the United States. Lehder told Greenberger and his friend, "Mr. Vesco is helping us out." The friend could not believe he was meeting Vesco.

"In a way, it was like Larry was only along for the ride, for the adventure," the friend recalled. "He acted like this was a way of making a huge amount of money that could be with him for the rest of his life. It wasn't his disposition to be mean or pushy or deadly, for that matter. He was nothing like Lehder. He was among them, but he wasn't one of them."

Between March 1978 and June 1979, Greenberger shipped 2,200 kilos of cocaine into San Francisco. There were other shipments into Los Angeles. In May 1979, federal agents followed a Lear Jet into Palm Beach International Airport. After it landed, they saw Greenberger unloading suitcases, one of which turned out to contain more than $100,000 stuffed into brown bags. He was questioned, and released for lack of evidence.

Before releasing Greenberger, federal agents took a diary they had found on the plane. It belonged to Greenberger's girlfriend, Mayari Sergeant. They would later return the diary, but not before studying it and making extensive notes.

The following year, Greenberger was arrested while vacationing in Honolulu, in an indictment that also included Lehder. Frank Rubino flew over, and after a frenzied few days of legal maneuvering, including a rare Saturday morning bond hearing, Rubino managed to get Greenberger out of jail. Later, because the government was unwilling to expose the details of its investigation of Lehder, the charges against Greenberger were dismissed.

Greenberger returned to Florida. Almost immediately, he let it be known that he no longer wished to work for Lehder. Greenberger had grown tired of the drug business.

TWENTY-ONE

GREENBERGER AND MAYARI SERGEANT began living together in 1980. The dark-haired, attractive Mayari claimed to be the daughter of the king of Burma. They moved into a house in Pompano, where Greenberger ran a company, Guardian Properties, that owned commercial property, including an office building in Denver. The couple talked about moving to Hawaii and going into real estate there, but Greenberger decided he wanted to move back to Okeechobee.

He had been away for a long time, only returning for holidays and then leaving again. He had traveled extensively: to the Spanish coast, Greece, the South Pacific, all over the world. At heart a small-town man, Greenberger missed the presence of his parents and his sister, Janis, in his life. Mostly, he missed Okeechobee, that one-horse town.

Early in 1984, he began remodeling an old farmhouse that stood outside the Okeechobee business district. It was a pretty house, built around the turn of the century, set well back from the road and with a great deal of lush farmland around it. It was the sort of place a quiet man who wanted to be left alone would seek out. His plan was to move into the house with Mayari. Soon he was spending his weekends there, performing carpentry jobs or talking to painters and electricians.

In February, though, the couple broke up. His plans to live in the old farmhouse floundered, and instead he moved into a trailer in a remote area eight miles from town.

Then, in late May, he met Laney Jacobs.

Greenberger introduced Laney to many of his friends, including Richard Johnsen, an airlines pilot. Soon, Greenberger moved into her spacious Miami house. There, he began meeting some of her friends, including Ed Bolter, who was now running a company in Delray Beach called Eagle Outdoor Advertising.

Laney saw in Greenberger a stable man of great wealth who liked to travel. As her previous relationships seem to reveal, she tended to become involved with men who were progressively bigger members of the drug underworld than their predecessors. Apparently, she had now reached the zenith. If all the whispered allegations about Greenberger were true, she had finally met the man of her materialistic dreams.

On the morning of September 3, 1984, Laney and Greenberger flew to Las Vegas, where they planned to get married in one of the city's many chapels. Dax was left behind with Myriam in Miami. Greenberger brought along Richard Johnsen to act as his best man.

Upon their arrival, they went to the county clerk's office to buy a marriage license. On it, Laney listed her address as Sherman Oaks, although she had not lived there since May 1983.

And she did what she had done on every one of
her previous marriage certificates. On the line
that asked for the number of this marriage, Laney wrote that it was her second, although in
truth Greenberger was her sixth husband.

The following afternoon, they were married at
the Little Church of the West, which sat in front
of the Hacienda Hotel, surrounded by a parking
lot. A neon sign in front of the church flashed the
word CAMPERLAND day and night. The chapel was
a wedding mill, averaging one hundred twenty-
five marriages a week. Its stained-glass windows
were actually made of painted plastic. Inside, ten
wooden benches faced a raised altar flanked with
electric candles and a mock organ. Music was
piped in through a sound system.

When they returned to Florida, Greenberger
brought Laney to Okeechobee to see his remod-
eled farmhouse. They kept to themselves. One afternoon, Greenberger's sister saw them sitting in
a silver 450SL Mercedes near the Pizza Hut. The
car's top was down, and Janis noticed her brother
was in the passenger seat.

"Hey, Larry," she yelled as she slowed to a stop
by the Mercedes. "How you doing? I heard you
got married."

He introduced his wife, referring to her as
Karen Amer. Janis could not help but notice the
way his new wife clung to him. Driving away, it
occurred to Janis that she had never seen any
woman hold on to her brother that way.

A few days later, Janis went over to the farmhouse to see her brother. Greenberger was busy
finishing up some of the remodeling work. A
porch facing the driveway had been enclosed,
leading into a large kitchen with a bar in one
corner. The ceiling in the kitchen was covered

with stamped tin. In his office, he had placed artwork on the wall near a large desk and couch. He
had his real estate business cards in a neat pile
on one corner of the desk, alongside a pen-and-
pencil set.

Janis said she thought the work looked lovely.
Then she asked how her brother had met Karen
Amer.

"In Frank Rubino's office," Greenberger said.
"You can call her Laney. Karen's her first name,
but everyone calls her Laney."

Janis asked if they were going to live in Okeechobee.

"Not right now," Greenberger said. "We'll start
bringing stuff up, though, and maybe move up
next spring."

Laney was walking through the house, deciding where to put the collection of Chinese furnishings that she had acquired over the years.
She had many expensive pieces and wanted to
showcase them throughout the house. She also
owned a collection of masks, which she wanted
to hang on a wall in the living room.

Janis sat down on one of the barstools. She
asked Laney what she did for a living.

"I own stock in Suzie Creamcheese," she replied. "It's a clothes boutique. We have stores in
Las Vegas and Houston. Very expensive, real
classy. I have done very well with it."

March 1985. On the day Joe Amer was released
from prison, he arranged for a ride to Miami. He
had five hundred dollars cash to his name and
some clothes in a suitcase. The man who had
once been able to buy anything he wanted, any
watch, any new suit, any gold ring, anything at
all, was now a vagabond in search of a home.

He also had with him Laney's letters, wrapped tight with a rubber band. After Laney's visit the year before, Amer had felt there was a chance they could get back together. But after receiving her last letter, he knew it was out of the question. She had spelled out her new relationship with Larry Greenberger. Her closing line was, "I'm very sorry it didn't work out."

He was sorry, too. But he had his son to consider. And Dax was his son. She had said so herself. Now he wanted to be part of his son's life.

When he arrived in Miami, he called Frank Rubino, who filled him in on Laney's marriage to Larry Greenberger. He advised Amer to stay away from them.

"But what about Dax?" Amer asked.

Rubino explained that Greenberger was the boy's new father and that he even intended to adopt the boy. Amer was sad and angered. Rubino said that Laney had wanted him to pass on the message that she did not want Amer to make waves. That meant not to come around and not to inquire about the boy.

A few days after speaking with Rubino, Amer called Michael Rodriguez, Joe's brother. Rodriguez offered Amer a place to stay and said he was sure that his brother would have a job for him at the Collection.

A few nights later, Amer saw Joe Rodriguez. Rodriguez was then the subject of a huge federal drug investigation, and he was nervously anticipating his arrest. Amer mentioned his watches, saying he could not believe Rodriguez had turned them over to Laney. Amer protested that he could have started over had he had the watches to sell.

"She had trouble in California, Joe," Rodriguez said. "Frank told me. Some kind of murder case."

"Murder?" Amer asked in disbelief. "Laney?"

"That's what he said, Joe. But I think she beat it somehow. That's all I know."

Rodriguez offered Amer a job as a salesman at the car dealership. There, one morning several months later, he was standing in the lot with a couple who were looking at an Audi, when he saw Laney. She was picking up a black Mercedes. He was stunned to see her, and for a minute or two he could not move. Slowly, he walked toward her, until she turned around and saw him.

"Hello, Laney," he said softly.

She was quiet for a moment, looking him over as if she could not believe he was standing there.

"Joe," she said. "Frank said you were out. How are you?"

He stepped closer to her, and as he did, she walked a few steps away from him, toward her car. Greenberger was behind the wheel, and Dax was standing up, his head out the driver's-side window.

"Hey, Dax!" Amer yelled.

Laney quickly got in the car, and Greenberger backed up as Amer ran to get closer. Laney said something to Greenberger, and he pulled out of the lot and into traffic. Amer stood there for several minutes, until he could no longer see the car.

In May, Laney invited Greenberger's sister and her boyfriend to Miami to stay at her house. In many ways, Dick Markham resembled Larry. He was strong and muscular, with rugged features honed by outdoor work. Markham was very fond of Janis, and he particularly liked Larry. He thought he was a good-natured, down-home kind of family man, a man of his word.

Laney also invited Ed Bolter and his wife, Diane, for the weekend. When they arrived, Laney, Diane, and Janis went to Laney's favorite hairdresser at a local mall. Laney knew everyone in the shop and claimed to have put the owner in business. While they waited to have their hair and nails done, the three women sipped champagne. Laney paid for everything, peeling cash off a roll she kept in her purse. That night, Larry took everyone out to dinner at a swank Miami restaurant.

The following morning, Laney gave Janis a tour of the house and property. It was built for privacy, with an electric gate across the driveway. The area around the pool had been landscaped with a rock garden and tiny trails. An outdoor bar dominated one corner of the pool. Inside the house, in the sunken living room, she pointed out her favorite black pillows, with the letter *L* painted on them.

Laney explained that she loved her house but wanted to move to Okeechobee. "I'd like Dax to grow up in the country," she said. "Miami's just a crazy place to raise a kid, it really is."

In the bedroom, Laney showed Janis a Rolex watch and said she'd wanted to buy one for her. She took a diamond necklace from her jewel box and presented it to her as a gift. She opened her closet, which was filled with dresses and furs. She took several out and showed them to Janis.

While Janis was touring the house, Markham was out by the pool, watching Dax as he played near the water. His attention was drawn to an adjacent property, where he heard a man yelling at a German shepherd in Spanish. There was a tall chain-link fence around the neighbor's property and a radio tower in the backyard. Markham

was no fool. He could guess that the owners of
the house might be in the drug business.

May 15 was Dax's third birthday. Soon after,
Laney, Greenberger, and Dax moved to Okeechobee.

For Laney and Greenberger, Okeechobee was to
be the start of an entirely new life. Greenberger
now hoped to manage his investments, work
around the house, travel, and spend the winter
skiing in Colorado. He wanted to be a country
gentleman, far from the way of life he had once
lived working for Carlos Lehder.

Greenberger considered himself an extraordi-
narily lucky person. Though he had been in the
top echelon of cocaine smuggling and distribution, he was not in prison. He did not believe any
state or federal agency was after him, particularly now that the federal indictment that had
resulted in his brief arrest in Hawaii had been
thrown out, owing to the excellent legal work of
his flamboyant attorney, Frank Rubino.

The one bad aspect of Greenberger's plans was
that he was again using cocaine. He had once
used it heavily, back in the days when he would
oversee airplane off-loads of hundreds of kilos.
He had used it enough that it scared him into
quitting. But after meeting Laney, he went back
to using it.

As Greenberger's new wife, Laney hoped to put
her past behind her, as well. At some point after
their marriage, she told Greenberger about the
murder of Roy Radin in California. But in explaining it, she had made it sound as though she
had very little to do with it, adding that "someone" had had Radin killed because he partici-
pated in a drug rip-off.

Settling into her new life and making new friends, Laney repeated her oft-told tale that she was a clothes designer and an investor in the Suzie Creamcheese boutiques. To one friend, she explained that she had worked in commodities and by the time she was thirty-five had acquired three and a half million dollars. She had done well enough to want to settle down and get married again.

Just after the move, Laney told Myriam that Dax was big enough so that it was no longer necessary for her to live with them. But Myriam loved Laney and the boy, and nearly every weekend she would drive north on Interstate 95 from Miami to West Palm Beach, then north and west on State Route 710, past the huge cattle ranches, through the little hamlets, and into Okeechobee. She had lived with the boy since his birth and considered him her child, too. Sometimes she would stay for longer than a weekend and help around the house, ironing or watching Dax.

Myriam considered Laney a woman who lived in a dreamworld. She was restless and always looking for someone to make life better for her. She viewed money as the source of all happiness. In the months before she met Greenberger, Laney had cried to Myriam that she did not have any money. Laney claimed she was broke, although she had enough money to drive a Mercedes and live well. On meeting Greenberger, all her money problems, if in fact she really had any, vanished.

After they moved into the new house permanently, Laney and Greenberger saw a few friends and family. Ed Bolter would come around to see them. Greenberger's sister would often sit and talk with Laney. In their conversations, Laney would speak about herself and about people she knew and places where she had been.

Once, she told Janis that her goal was to do something so great that she would get into the history books.

Laney was happy to be in Okeechobee, although it was certainly unlike any place she had ever lived in before. There was nothing glamorous about the community, and the shopping area was only a few blocks long and oriented toward the town's blue-collar residents. The restaurants were plain, certainly nothing like the ones she had gone to in Beverly Hills and Coconut Grove. She could be seen driving around town in her Mercedes, eating at Caso's, an Italian restaurant, or getting her hair done at a beauty salon near her house.

She talked a lot about spending Greenberger's money. One idea was to build a resort on the Pacific coast of Mexico, where people could go to get plastic surgery. She said she had lined up a Mexico City doctor, with whom she was also talking about opening plastic surgery centers in the United States, perhaps in Colorado and Florida.

Laney was a big believer in plastic surgery, and talked about having face-lifts, liposuctions, tummy tucks, breast implants, cheek implants, and a variety of other procedures designed to improve her appearance. She tried to talk her husband into having certain of these procedures performed. He considered her plans rather silly and was unresponsive to her dreamy talk about raising millions of dollars to build a Mexican resort. Just because he had a lot of money did not mean he wanted to throw it away.

For her part, Laney had no trouble spending money. She would drive to Fort Pierce or Palm

Beach to shop, buying clothes, artworks, and furnishings for the new house. Around Okeechobee, she wore designer clothes and leopardskin or snakeskin boots, and her hair was always done up perfectly. She would sit on the porch of the house with Janis and Dick Markham and hand them free airline tickets. Markham, a workingman who loathed handouts, would not accept them. Before she went skiing in Colorado, she bought the most expensive ski clothes.

She told Janis she wanted to help set her up in a lucrative business. But in offering her assistance, Laney counseled her that she should look for a rich husband. Get someone with promise, she told Janis, and not some blue-collar worker with a limited future. A commonsense woman, Janis ignored her sister-in-law's advice. When he learned from Janis that Laney had bad-mouthed him, Markham laughed it off. He considered Laney a bimbo, sponging off her new husband; a world-class phony with a closetful of shoes she almost never wore.

Janis would listen when Laney whined about how she wanted to live in a five-million-dollar house. She was puzzled when Laney said she wanted more. What more was there, for heaven's sake?

Laney explained that she had been born in a house with a dirt floor. She painted a picture of a family that was poor and hungry. At the first opportunity, Laney told her, she had left her family and settled in Miami, where she worked as a paralegal in a law firm.

"But I decided," she said, while sitting on the porch one hot summer night, "that I was not going to be a working-class hero. I didn't want to go to work every day. I didn't like that, not at all."

Janis asked her what she did.

"I pulled a scam," she said. "I didn't want to work any longer, so I pulled a scam."

For the most part, Greenberger's parents got along well with Laney. They loved their son, so they loved his wife. She was just a Southern girl to them, one who had quite obviously done well for herself, traveled, and picked up some class and sophistication along the way.

In late 1985, Greenberger legally adopted three-year-old Dax. The boy was now Dax Greenberger, and his father wanted him to grow up the way he had, working at odd jobs when he got older. Laney, however, wanted to ship the boy off to private school when he was twelve.

Once, when Myriam mentioned to a friend of Laney's that Greenberger was not Dax's real father, Laney pulled her into another room and warned her not to say that ever again; Greenberger was very sensitive about it. And Greenberger did not want Joe Amer to come around the house, not ever.

In December 1985, Laney and Greenberger packed their ski gear and moved into a condominium in Dillon, Colorado, for the winter. A friend drove one of their Mercedeses out. Dax remained in Okeechobee with a new housekeeper.

TWENTY-TWO

WHEN SHE RETURNED FROM COLO-
rado, Laney began planning for what she
foresaw as the next phase in her business life. A
Mexico City plastic surgeon, Alejandro Quiroz,
wanted to expand his business into the United
States. She offered him financing to start a chain
of plastic surgery boutiques in Colorado and Florida, the two states in which she intended to spend
most of her time.

In addition, Laney envisioned a world-class resort in Mexico, perhaps near Acapulco, where
wealthy Americans could travel for cosmetic surgery. It was to be something like a Club Med for
the liposuction crowd, a place where women and
men with a lot of money to spend could go and
have themselves reshaped. Laney believed cosmetic surgery would be the craze of the 1980s
and 1990s, the next phase for the consumption-
oriented, self-centered crowd with whom she had
closely identified since her early twenties.

Reshaping one's body went along with having
the best jewelry, the best watches, the most expensive clothes, the finest cars, the biggest
houses, the best vacations, the most cocaine. Why

live with fat thighs if all you had to do was pay someone a few thousand dollars to suck out the fat with a tube? Her idea was to take the process one step further by building a resort totally devoted to beauty and cosmetic surgery. It was a natural extension of her hedonistic lifestyle.

Laney was married to a wealthy man, and she hoped she could persuade him to go along with her investment plans. Soon she was talking about spending $500,000 of Greenberger's money toward the construction of clinics in the United States and the resort in Mexico. She had no idea what the final cost of completing such a resort would be, but she was convinced that she would now have the money to get it off the ground. Once it was properly launched, she was certain the necessary capital to finish the project could be pulled together.

Greenberger, however, remained uninterested in the plastic surgery concept. He did not see the glamour in it that she evidently did, nor was he convinced it was such a good investment. His view of money differed sharply from Laney's. He had his money wisely invested, a large amount of it through a Prudential Bache office in Palm Beach; he had other investment accounts, as well. In addition, he had sizable funds in the Bahamas, in an oil company set up by a Denver attorney, and in real estate holdings.

After moving back to Okeechobee with Laney, Greenberger had also invested $250,000 in Ed Bolter's Eagle Outdoor Advertising company, which made him a partner in the firm.

Greenberger was very tight-lipped about his finances. Talking about money, or crying about it, as Laney had so often done, was not part of his personality. He had it, and he intended to have it when he was an old man. What he wanted to do with it was spend it on those things that gave him pleasure, such as deep-sea fishing, skiing, and travel. He was particularly fond of expensive fishing gear, including large brass saltwater reels.

The boat he owned with Frank Rubino, *The Sleuth*, was worth in excess of $250,000, and Greenberger and Rubino had shared in many of the equipment and maintenance costs. The boat was moored at Islamorada and captained by a man named Larry McCandless. Greenberger would go out on the boat, fish off the Bahamas, and enter fishing tournaments. Laney often went with him, and throughout the house she had placed pictures of the two of them, a smiling couple standing at the stern of their boat.

Although Greenberger was reluctant to invest his money in his wife's plastic surgery scheme, he did agree to help set up an office in Okeechobee that would serve as a referral center for Dr. Quiroz. She called it the Center for Plastic Surgery, and its offices were on the second floor of a red-brick building near the center of town. An awning was erected over the door, carpeting was installed on the stairs leading to the second floor, and desks and offices were set up. It was a strange location for a cosmetic surgery business, but Laney hoped to get business throughout Florida.

After the center opened, acquaintances around the town, and men and women Laney ran into at the beauty parlor, in restaurants, or at the market, were encouraged to come by and pick up brochures. She would hold formal parties at a hotel in Palm Beach, inviting Quiroz to come up and give seminars on the benefits of face-lifts and cheek implants.

Laney overwhelmed people with her zeal for cosmetic surgery. She was very frank about what work she had had done, and she would point out that there were no scars around her eyes and cheeks. In tiny Okeechobee, Laney stood out. Her style didn't dovetail with the blue-jeans crowd. The Center for Plastic Surgery did not help: It was seen as an odd business in an odd location. People wondered why she had not set up her business in Palm Beach.

Laney continued to use cocaine. When Greenberger's parents came to the house for a visit, she would often go up to her bedroom and "bump her nose," as she put it.

Many of Greenberger's old friends knew he had moved back to Okeechobee. They saw him driving around town in his Mercedes. But Greenberger kept mostly to himself. It was as if he was living in seclusion.

One friend heard he kept guns in his house, even one in his car. The boy who had been voted the most popular student at the local high school had developed into a man of mystery.

There was much that was mysterious about Greenberger's hometown, too. Beginning in the early 1980s, cocaine traffickers discovered that the area around Okeechobee was a perfect drop site for cocaine. There were few cops in the area, few homes, and more than a few dirt landing strips deep inside cattle ranches, where light planes could land and unload. Minutes later, a plane could land at Palm Beach International Airport, where, if for some reason it was searched, nothing would be found.

Soon a number of drug organizations were using Okeechobee exclusively. Huge amounts of co-

caine were being dropped over pickup sites and
unloaded at remote airstrips or even on deserted
roads at night. Because the area was so far removed from the Miami metropolitan area, far to
the south, law enforcement officials were slow to
catch on. The result was that Okeechobee
quickly became a mecca for smugglers. Some
even stored their loads in barns and warehouses.

To protect themselves, the smugglers reached
out to local landowners. Ranchers were paid off
to allow planes to land on their property at night.
Seeing no way they could ever get caught, other
property owners sought out the smugglers, setting up systems whereby they could take a percentage of the profits derived from the sale of the
cocaine. By the mid-1980s, there were residents
of Okeechobee who were buying up large
amounts of commercial real estate, opening restaurants, and buying more ranchland.

The sight of vans and even eighteen-wheel rigs
rumbling down country roads after midnight
was not uncommon. Nor was it uncommon to
hear the engine noise of airplanes circling overhead at night.

One Okeechobee resident who got rich transporting cocaine onto his property bought large
amounts of commercial real estate in the area.
He was a popular man who suddenly had a great
deal of money to spend, and he did not conceal it
from townspeople. Harry Collins, as he will be
called here, worked with a group in Miami that,
in a few years, unloaded tons of cocaine on his
property. Collins was convicted and sent to federal prison. He said he bought every building he
could that was for sale.

"I bought houses, cars, ranches, boats, and did
whatever I felt like doin'. I graduated from Okee-

chobee High. We were all right financially, but I couldn't quite find my own way. You know, it was the late sixties and all that hippie stuff, and drugs kind of presented themselves as no big deal.

"Basically, I met a guy who knew a guy who was a young Colombian. We made contact in Miami. Had dinner, talked it over. He was likable as hell, really. He certainly didn't look evil or anything. You expect after reading all about those guys that they'd have horns or something, but then you meet them and they're like anybody. I never saw a gun or heard a shot fired.

"He did all the arranging. I gave him the locations, the times, et cetera. That's all I did. I never put my hands on a single kilo of cocaine. The mules who'd bring it up would cut out a little for themselves. It reminded me of a cowboy herding cattle who'd cut out an old steer, butcher it, and eat it. Before you knew it, they were dropping in load after load, storing it for a few days sometimes, then trucking it down to Miami. You'd see the mules driving around town, pulling into the grocery store to use the public phone.

"From where I am now, I could certainly argue that those ol' boys tricked me into doing something I shouldn't have done. But at the time, it was a way to get rich and not get my hands dirty. I certainly didn't help create a drug problem. It existed long before I came along, and I am very sure it will exist long after I am gone."

Collins knew Greenberger well but had not made contact with him after Greenberger remarried. When Collins was arrested, he half expected his old friend to call him and wish him well, but he did not.

"Larry was the most laid-back guy you ever

saw," recalled Collins. "I would drive to Tallahassee on the weekend and drop in on him, and it
would be like high school all over again. We
never, ever discussed what he was doing, and
later we never, ever discussed what I was doing.
Frankly, to this day I don't know what Larry did
or how he made his money. Don't much care, either, considering I liked him and his family.

"But the point is that Larry, tooling around
town in his Mercedes, kind of blended into the
general mysteriousness of Okeechobee, this town
that was like a giant landing strip for drug pilots.
People had a way of accepting what was going
on, even after their neighbors were arrested.
You'd see some guy you knew in high school,
someone from a relatively middle-class family,
and now he was living in a big farmhouse on a
dozen acres or so and driving a Mercedes or a
Jaguar. You didn't think he'd hit the Lotto."

Frank Rubino, handsome and suave, cut an impressive figure. Shrewd about the limits of the
law, Rubino had a high-priced clientele of accused drug traffickers who expected to either get
off on technicalities or win at trial.

Born and raised in Philadelphia, Rubino became a Secret Service agent after college. He was
on the presidential staff when Lyndon Johnson
was in the White House. Later, he moved to
Miami and went to law school, working as a private detective to pay the bills. After passing the
bar, he quickly established himself as a brilliant
federal practitioner.

By the winter of 1986, a year and a half after
Laney and Greenberger had married, Rubino
found himself in an awkward position with
Greenberger. Laney had cut off her husband

from some of his closest friends, including
Rubino. Worse, she began to challenge Rubino's
half-ownership of *The Sleuth*.

By spring, Laney started accusing Rubino of
mismanaging the boat, which was often rented
as a commercial charter, with the profits going to
both men. Rubino would take clients out on the
boat, the way some lawyers would take clients to
their country clubs. Until Laney came along,
Greenberger had never complained that what
Rubino did on the boat was somehow unfair to
him.

The relationship deteriorated so quickly that
Rubino decided that the best thing to do was to
stay away from the Greenbergers. As with many
of Larry's old friends, Rubino now saw that
Greenberger had developed a severe drug habit
after his marriage. He would sit alone in a room
for hours, shaking and sweating. It seemed to
some that Laney was consciously avoiding helping her husband.

In July, Greenberger called Rubino and asked
if he could drive down to Miami and see him. He
said he wanted to talk about the boat. When he
arrived at Rubino's office, he brought out some
MasterCard bills and asked Rubino about various
charges he had incurred.

Rubino looked them over and said they were
legitimate expenses, such as rags and mops. Satisfied, Greenberger apologized for accusing
Rubino of misusing the boat and left the office.

He was back a few days later, this time with
fuel bills. Again Rubino went through them and
showed Greenberger they were indeed legitimate
expenses.

"All right," Greenberger said. "I can see that."

"What's going on, Larry?" Rubino asked. "You and I have known each other for years."

"Laney made me do it," Greenberger admitted. He stood up to leave the office. "She's a white-haired bitch."

"Look," Rubino said. "This has reached a point where either you have to buy me out or I'll buy you out."

"I'll buy you out," Greenberger said.

"Fine," Rubino said. "Let's do it. That'll solve this problem once and for all."

Rubino looked over his calendar and made an appointment for the following Friday afternoon; the two men would go over the numbers and agree on a buy-out price. Then Greenberger left the office.

On Friday, Rubino was surprised when Laney, Greenberger, and two men walked into his office. Rubino recognized one of the men as Bill Mentzer. He had gotten Mentzer off on cocaine charges after his arrest at the Los Angeles airport in 1983. Greenberger, his hands shaking, picked up a piece of paper and scrawled a note on it, handing it to Rubino.

Sign the boat over to me or they'll kill your wife and you, the note read.

Rubino laughed. "Oh, come on, Larry," he said. "You and I have been friends for years. What is this bullshit?"

As Rubino put down the note, Laney began screaming at him. She seemed out of control. "Sign it or they'll kill you!"

She yelled so loudly that Greenberger led her out of Rubino's office, leaving the two men behind. As they headed outside, Greenberger turned to Mentzer and said, "Make him sign it."

The three men stood there for a moment. "I

like you, Frank," Mentzer said. "You've been good to me. But Laney says you have to sign this or I'll have to kill you."

"This is stupid, Bill," Rubino said. "I can't believe this. It's obvious there isn't any more talking about this, huh?"

"Just sign it," Mentzer said.

The second man was Mentzer's cousin Tom Markel, the Los Angeles County sheriff's deputy who had worked part time for Mike Pascal, the private detective Laney had hired to help her find Tally Rogers. He stood silently in front of Rubino's desk.

To Markel, Rubino said, "And you don't look like you have the intelligence to understand what I'm talking about."

Both men pulled guns out from under their coats and leaned them against Rubino's head. The boat papers were on the desk.

"You won't do this right here," Rubino said.

"We'll take you out the back door, and they'll never find you," Mentzer said. "Sign the papers."

Rubino picked up a pen and in a few seconds signed over his share of the $250,000 boat to Greenberger. When he was finished, Mentzer stripped the Rolex watch off Rubino's wrist. Then he picked up the keys to Rubino's black Ferrari and left.

Sometime over the weekend, a cinder block was thrown through a window at Rubino's house. That evening, Laney and Greenberger drove to Greenberger's parents' home in Okeechobee. Janis was there when they arrived, and she could see that Laney was enraged about something.

Inside the house, Laney said to Greenberger, "Frank is ripping us off, Larry. We have to take care of this."

Janis moved closer to them, and Laney said, "We had a rock thrown through Rubino's window."

Laney began ranting about Rubino. "We have to take care of this," she repeated. It seemed to Janis that she was talking about killing him.

On Monday afternoon, Mentzer called Rubino and demanded the title to the Ferrari. "And we want all your wife's jewelry," Mentzer added. Rubino hung up.

Later, Mentzer called again and said, "Give me the title, and we'll forget everything."

Afterward, a man came to Rubino's office and picked up the title. Realizing that going to the police could result in his murder, Rubino did not report the incident. But to protect himself and his wife, Jackie Silva, he asked several clients to watch over them for the next few weeks.

TWENTY-THREE

JANUARY 1987. LOS ANGELES.
Within a few months of his finding the photographs in Mentzer's dresser drawer, Sergeant Carlos Avila acknowledged that his investigation had ground to a halt. He did not know who the other two men in the photographs were, and any thought that Mentzer might be persuaded to help him vanished after he beat the drug charges pending against him following his arrest at the airport.

In early 1987, Avila left for a year's training sabbatical at the FBI Academy in Quantico, Virginia. In his absence, two Los Angeles County sheriff's deputies, Sergeant Bill Stoner and Detective Charlie Guenther, picked up the Radin investigation. They were quiet, efficient workers. They spent several days reading Avila's reports and looking over the autopsy report as well as other available information.

The files were voluminous, complete with the usual tips and rumors that homicide investigators pick up in their work. Also included were numerous newspaper clippings about the murder, and a lengthy *Newsday* article called "Snowblind: The Hollywood Murder of Roy Radin."

The story detailed the last month of Radin's life, the fight with Laney Jacobs over the theft of her cocaine, and her demand that Radin turn over part of his share of *The Cotton Club* to her. Although Stoner and Guenther considered the fight over the movie company to be a possible motive for Radin's execution, Laney's huge cocaine racket and the theft from her garage seemed the most promising line of inquiry. After reading everything that was available, they began looking for people to interview.

Toward the end of the month, the detectives started to pull together information from the Los Angeles Police Department's files. There was also material that Steve Slazes and Fred McKnight had written pertaining to drug trafficking, as well as reports by Sergeant Glen Sousa, who had been in charge of the missing persons investigation before Radin's body was found.

Stoner and Guenther learned that Sousa had retired and gone on Evans' payroll as some sort of police consultant. McKnight had become suspicious of Sousa's relationship with Evans when he went to Sousa's retirement party and encountered the producer. Evans stood at the podium and spoke about Sousa as if they were the best of buddies. Later, McKnight ran into Sousa at the Paramount Studios commissary, and Sousa explained that he was working for Evans. It made McKnight sick to his stomach.

It was February 1987 when Stoner and Guenther learned where Laney was living. They had interviewed a relative of Leslie Dekeyser, Laney's friend in Las Vegas, who was now in prison on cocaine charges, and had learned that Laney had called, looking for her. She had left a number with a Colorado area code.

A Colorado police officer traced the number to a condominium used by Laney and Larry Greenberger. The officer, Sergeant Devault, then went to the complex to examine paperwork on the apartment, which showed the Greenbergers' addresses—6660 Southwest 125th Avenue in Miami and Post Office Box 1198 in Okeechobee.

"They are not here now," Devault told Stoner and Guenther. "But they're due back next week, on the fifteenth to be exact."

Stoner thanked him for his help and hung up.

The detectives hoped to find someone who could identify the men in the photographs found in Mentzer's house. After weeks of searching, they located Mentzer's ex-wife, Deborah, and on March 23 they met her in suburban Los Angeles.

One of the detectives asked her what she could tell them about Mentzer.

"Well, he used to own a limo service, Rodeo Limo, in the San Fernando Valley," she said. "I know he was a bodyguard for the guy who publishes *Hustler* magazine, Larry Flynt. Bill was a very private person, honestly, and never really spoke about what he did. He had some close friends. Bob Lowe, who was a real leech as far as I'm concerned. Bill Rider's another. Plus Mike Pascal, who's some kind of private detective. Does mostly divorce cases, as I understand it."

The detectives asked if Mentzer owned guns.

"Yes," she replied. "He did. I believe he had a gun permit. He used to go shooting at the Beverly Hills Gun Club. His guns were always loaded in the apartment."

"Did he ever go out to the desert to shoot?"

"Not anytime when I went along, no. I know he got arrested out at the airport, but that was after the divorce. Once, Bill came to me and asked me to sign a paper so he could refinance his Mercedes to pay for his lawyer. He said the case cost him every penny he had. He told me at that time someone might come and want to talk to me."

"What did he tell you to say?" one of the detectives asked.

"Told me never to talk to anyone, not to say a thing," she said.

Stoner showed Deborah one of the photographs taken from Mentzer's apartment. He asked if she knew who was in it.

"Well," she said, looking the pictures over closely. "That's Bill, of course. And that's him and Bill Rider."

Stoner asked whose Jeep was in the background, and Deborah said it was Rider's.

"Do you know where Rider lives?" Guenther asked.

"Used to live in Woodland Hills. But that was in eighty-three. He worked for Flynt, too. A lot of Bill's friends worked for Flynt as security guards."

"What happened after you split up?" one of the detectives asked. "Did Bill see anyone?"

"He was running around with a girl named Linda. Linda Jacobs. She had a small child. I heard they were out of the country. But I don't know where they were. I called Bill, it might have been February or so, the year we split up, because I found some of her clothes in our apartment. I said her name, and he went nuts. He really got crazy on the phone. He said, 'You shouldn't have mentioned her name!'"

They asked if she knew who else Mentzer hung out with.

"He used to go running with a guy named Alex. He worked at a car place on Wilshire. A real mean guy. He acted like he liked to go around hurting people. I could probably get his last name if I asked around. But after Bill met this Linda Jacobs, he seemed to have real nice cars and jewelry. She must have been buying him expensive stuff and giving him money. I heard she gave him a blue Mercedes, in fact."

Guenther showed Deborah the second photograph the detectives had brought with them.

"That's Alex," she said, pointing to a short, squat man holding a shotgun. "Alex threatened a guy once."

"Who was that?" Stoner asked.

"Marc Fogel," Deborah said. "He lived with Bill and me at one point. He was definitely afraid of Alex."

Tally Rogers had moved from South Carolina, where he had fled after the theft from Laney's house, to Louisiana in the fall of 1983. He believed no one would find him, if in fact anyone was still looking for him.

Rogers' relationship with Betty was over. It had been on rocky ground for years. Soon after moving back to Louisiana, he began to date. One of his new girlfriends had two sons, and one night Rogers got drunk and sexually molested them. He was arrested, convicted, and sentenced to a lengthy term in Angola State Prison.

Stoner and Guenther learned of his whereabouts and flew to Louisiana on May 5. The following day, they drove to the prison to interview him. They encountered a bitter and hostile man who argued that he had been framed and should not be in prison.

Stoner, who had a soft voice and a gentle manner, tried to duck any discussion of the circumstances that had led to Rogers' imprisonment. "We just want to know if you can help us tie up some loose ends in the Radin murder," Stoner said.

"I'll tell you what I know," Rogers said. They were in a lounge in the prison, and the noise of doors slamming and men yelling could be heard all around them. The air smelled of sweat and greasy food. It looked like a hellish prison, one of the worst Stoner had seen. "Let me say at the outset that I liked Roy. Liked him a lot. I feel bad for what happened to him. I honest to God do. He didn't deserve it. No way.

"I'll start pretty much at the beginning," he went on. "I met Laney, Laney Jacobs, in eighty-one. She was involved in cocaine with a Cuban named Bellechasses. In Miami. I got involved with them through a guy named Tim Whitehead, from Crystal Springs, Mississippi. To him goes the dubious honor of getting me started in cocaine trafficking.

"So I went to Miami, and from what I saw, Bellechasses was buying from young Colombians in the area and then was shipping the narcotics out to the West Coast for distribution. I met his attorney, another Cuban, Frank Diaz. Diaz was not involved in the cocaine business.

"In about eighty-one, the year I met her, Laney moved to the West Coast. I would guess it was shortly after her son, Dax, was born. So check that date, and it was after that that she actually moved. Okay. Now, she went to California to start the dope business for Bellechasses. My job was to ferry it out to her from Miami. I didn't touch it, I didn't use, I just drove it. That's the God's honest truth.

"My personal involvement was to transport ten kilos of cocaine that I would pick up from Belle-chasses and take it in my personal car to Laney. She would sell it to other dope dealers, I'd say in kilo form. As I say, that was my job. I was a mule.

"Shortly after we got there, Laney told me she had met this Mr. Evans, a Hollywood movie producer. What she told me was that he was interested in obtaining narcotics dollars to produce movies. She said she and Anna, Anna Montenegro, went over to Evans' house to talk about this very subject. Laney told me that there were eight or ten other Hollywood people interested in producing movies with drug money."

Rogers fidgeted in his chair, nervously tapping his foot on the concrete floor. Occasionally, he would cross his legs and continue moving his foot up and down.

"I met Roy I'd say in early eighty-three. Laney introduced me. Roy thought I was a movie producer when he first met me. Within a couple of weeks or so, we were running around together and doing coke and partying. I moved into his hotel so I could be closer to him. Roy bought from Laney, I know that. I believe Laney only charged him the amount the coke had cost her."

The investigators asked how much cocaine Laney was selling.

"About ten kilos every six weeks," Rogers said. "She was getting about sixty grand for a kilo and paying about forty-five. She and Milan bought on the come, so when they got paid the Colombians got paid. When she'd piled up a lot of money, I'd run it up to San Francisco for her."

"Where did it go in San Francisco?" one of the detectives asked.

"A Colombian, a guy, and two females," Rogers said. "One of the females was a Latin, the other was white."

"How much were you being paid, Tally?" one of the detectives asked.

"Twenty grand a trip, or whatever Bellechasses agreed to. Twice, she shortchanged me. Milan agreed to pay me thirty grand for two trips, and Laney gave me only twenty. She took advantage of me. I didn't appreciate it."

Rogers was asked what he did about it.

"Stole ten kilos and a ton of cash, that's what," Rogers said. "She put a price tag on my head. Fifty grand. Sent people out looking for me."

"Let me ask you this," Guenther said. "Did Roy have anything at all to do with that theft?"

"No, sir. He sure didn't. He knew it after the fact, but that was it. Laney went to him and raised all kinds of hell trying to get him to intervene to find me and the money. Roy wouldn't help her, and I'm sure it pissed her off to no end."

"What did you do?" Stoner asked.

"Drove to South Carolina. My wife knew where I was. In fact, she called me when she read about Roy's murder. That's the first I heard of it. But I just hid out. I didn't want no part of those people. Tim Whitehead took some men from Miami to Memphis to try and find me. Probably still looking for me, as far as I know. As I understand it, since they bought the coke on the come, Laney and Bellechasses would be held responsible. They'd have to make it up to the Colombians."

"How many runs did you do for Laney before the rip-off?" one of the detectives asked.

"Six or seven," Rogers replied. "Ten kilos each."

The investigators mentally calculated the dollar amounts. Seventy kilos transported equaled $4.2 million in gross sales.

Two months after Mentzer's ex-wife identified Bill Rider in the photograph, Guenther tracked him down in the Midwest, where he had moved to be closer to his family. The detective phoned and said he had some photographs he would like Rider to look at. To Guenther's surprise, Rider agreed to fly to Los Angeles.

On June 4, Rider was met at Los Angeles airport and taken to a hotel. Afterward, Stoner and Guenther sat with him in the hotel restaurant, and they chatted for a couple of hours. The investigators mentioned the Radin homicide, and Rider nervously admitted that he knew who was involved. He was frightened to even mention the killers' names but seemed determined to help Stoner and Guenther catch them. At heart, Rider was still a cop, and he knew now that he had to do the right thing, no matter what the risk.

"You know," Rider told them, "Mentzer's got a cousin named Tom. He's a deputy sheriff. So I'm not so damn sure I can trust you guys with notes and information. If I help you, I don't want any notes, any pictures taken, or any tape recorders used. If you can agree to that, then maybe we can talk."

The investigators said that that would be all right.

They showed Rider the two photographs, and he agreed to guide them to the canyon where the pictures had been taken. The next day, they drove north to the Hungry Valley exit, where

Rider told them to turn off. He directed them to within a few yards of the spot where the body had been found.

At one point, Rider declared that Mentzer and Marti were killers. "I'm afraid of these guys," he said. "If they knew I was talking to you, they'd kill me and my family. They used to work for me when I worked for Larry Flynt. They were security guards."

Asked how he got the job with Flynt, Rider said, "He's my brother-in-law. The wives are related. I was a cop, and he hired me to handle security for him."

Rider revealed that on a number of occasions Mentzer and Marti had talked about killing Radin. Marti spoke about it as if it were the high point of his otherwise dull life. "Marti just went crazy," Rider explained. "He just went crazy and started shooting him in the back of the head. When it was Bill's turn, he shot him once, kind of a coup de grace."

Rider stayed in Los Angeles for several days, and Stoner and Guenther would meet him for coffee and talk. Once, they asked him who it was who wanted Radin dead.

"Bill told me Bob Evans was involved in the hit, along with Bill's girlfriend, Laney," Rider explained.

They asked him about Bob Lowe.

"He's just as bad," Rider said. "After leaving Flynt, I did private investigative work. I had a job in Texas, and Lowe was down there. So I asked him to help me out. Lowe started talking about Mentzer blowing away some transvestite."

"Where was this?" he was asked.

"On Sepulveda in the Valley. Mentzer supposedly shot her several times. He shot some guy

who was with her, too. Right in the chest. Mentzer got carried away, and Lowe had to yell at him
to get him to stop. He kept kicking and shooting."

The worst thing about it, from Rider's point of
view, was that Mentzer had used Rider's gun for
the job. It was a .22 equipped with a silencer.

One of the detectives asked Rider what the gun
was for.

"I used to shoot rats at Flynt's mansion," Rider
said with a straight face. "They're all over the
place. Bill returned the gun a couple of months
later."

"What did he say he wanted the gun for in the
first place?"

"He said Mike Pascal wanted it for a job,"
Rider said. "God knows why they killed the transvestite, but it was something about how she was
bothering a wealthy family."

Stoner and Guenther knew they needed Rider
if they were going to make a case against Radin's
murderers. When they asked him to assist them,
he backed off.

"I have to consider my family," he said. "Let
me think about it. I'll help if I can, but I have to
think it over."

They gave Rider their phone numbers and said
goodbye.

TWENTY-FOUR

IN THE FALL, STONER AND GUENTHER went to Miami. Four and a half years had passed since Roy Radin's murder, an exceptionally long time in terms of homicide investigations. The investigators were working on theories only, without a rich body of physical evidence or a confession.

Their first major break, the introduction to Bill Rider, had been important because it helped direct and focus the investigation. Based on what Rider had said, it now appeared that the murder was centered on the deal-making to produce *The Cotton Club* rather than on the stolen cocaine.

Cocaine surely had played a role, though. Perhaps the movie had become more important to Laney Jacobs *because* of the theft of the cocaine. Cocaine complicated relationships and distorted realities. It made a failure feel like a success. It inflated egos. In drug-smuggling organizations, even the smallest ones, blood was inevitably spilled. It seemed probable to the investigators that Laney had brought her cocaine ethics to Hollywood, and when she could not get what she wanted, she committed murder.

After arriving in Miami, Stoner and Guenther spoke with detectives from the Metro Dade Police Department, who helped them locate business records for the Jamboni corporation. The firm was identified as an interior decorating business, with Karen DeLayne Jacobs as its president. Only a fool could possibly believe that Laney went all the way to the Netherlands Antilles to incorporate an interior decorating business.

The investigators had copies of letters mailed to Radin before his murder that pertained to *Cotton Club* matters. On the stationery were phone numbers that belonged to Jose Luis Castro, one of the two attorneys who had tried to help Laney and Evans set up a movie company. When Stoner and Guenther looked for Castro, they found that in July 1986 he had been convicted in Miami federal court on a multimillion-dollar coffee scam.

Frank Diaz, the other attorney, was also gone, literally. He had been kidnapped near his law office by two men with automatic weapons. Police investigators came to the conclusion that Diaz had staged the event to avoid federal criminal charges pending against him. He was later reported to be living in Brazil, where he was subsequently arrested and jailed. Somehow, though, he managed to walk out of the prison one afternoon, and he was again a fugitive. Diaz's association with Laney suggested to the investigators that money laundering might also have been involved as part of the effort to produce movies.

One of the reasons for going to Miami was to follow up on information provided by Tally Rogers about Milan Bellechasses. When Rogers fled to South Carolina, he had written a long letter to himself detailing everything he knew about Bellechasses. The letter was sort of a last will and testament: if something happened to him, if he was murdered for stealing Laney's cocaine, the authorities would at least know whom he'd been dealing with and what sort of people they were. In the letter, which Guenther and Stoner procured, Rogers said that Bellechasses had two addresses in the Miami area—8925 Southwest 102nd Court and 1611 Southwest 102nd Avenue. At the latter address, Rogers claimed, he had picked up cocaine.

When Stoner and Guenther went to the second address, they showed a neighbor a photograph of Bellechasses. "That's Milan," he said. "But he's gone now. He moved away in eighty-three."

Rogers had also gone to another house Bellechasses owned at the dead end of Ludlum Drive. Following the directions in Rogers' letter, the detectives drove up to the house and parked. Not knowing if anyone was inside, they spoke to neighbors first. One neighbor said the house had recently been raided by U.S. Customs agents and Bellechasses had moved out.

In fact, a Customs agent had learned of Bellechasses' house when he obtained the address book of a drug dealer. Going to the Ludlum Drive house, which was actually at 6740 Royal Palm Drive, the agent, Frank Figueroa, found a hidden, windowless room. In it were papers used in wrapping cocaine; there was cocaine residue on the rug.

Before they left Miami, Guenther and Stoner met a Drug Enforcement Administration agent named Karl Kotowski, who was busy investigating a conspiracy case that involved Bellechasses. Kotowski's information was that Bellechasses was trying to import five hundred kilos of cocaine from an island in the Bahamas. On the day

the detectives visited Kotowski, he was looking
for Bellechasses so that he could arrest him.

The DEA file on Bellechasses contained bio-
graphical material as well as informants' reports. It said he was born December 6, 1947, in
Santiago, Cuba; he was five feet eleven inches
tall, weighed 175 pounds, had brown hair, brown
eyes. A driver's license photograph of Bellechasses clearly showed a harelip on the left side of his
mouth. Bellechasses had served in the U.S. Army
and had become a United States citizen on February 3, 1971.

Other information in the DEA files showed
that Bellechasses had moved into an apartment
at Del Vista Towers in North Miami after the
raid on his Royal Palm Drive house. The rest of
the information was murky. Bellechasses had
told people that he was in the construction business and owned a restaurant in Costa Rica called
Monte Carlo. A man there had told Kotowski that
Bellechasses was, in fact, a part owner of the restaurant and was receiving a salary of eighteen
hundred dollars a month.

In the fall of 1987, Kotowski received information that Bellechasses was trying to smuggle a
load of cocaine from Colombia to a tiny island
called Rum Cay in the Bahamas. From there, it
was to be flown to the Florida mainland. The
Cuban's problem was that he could not find a reliable pilot to make the trip from Colombia, so
his operation was stalled.

There was very little activity on Rum Cay,
which was what made it such a good off-load site.
There was a fishing club, a diving club, and a
tiny airstrip suitable for a light plane. Bellechasses was so taken by the little airstrip that one of

his associates had made a video of it, which had been forwarded to high-ranking drug distributors in Colombia. Perhaps Bellechasses wanted the Colombians to see how useful the airstrip could be. The island had only a handful of inhabitants, none of whom would have paid much attention to a plane landing and unloading boxes. From the island, Bellechasses had arranged for a thirty-one-foot Hatteras, a fishing boat, to transport the cocaine to Florida. The boat was owned by a Panamanian company.

Prior to Kotowski's interest in Bellechasses, Florida officials had learned that he was a financier in a ring that smuggled marijuana to Florida from Kingston, Jamaica. The informants in this case had told state investigators that Bellechasses was a rich and powerful man, a "man in the shadows" with impressive contacts in the drug underworld. Investigators had surveillance photos of Bellechasses at meetings with other dealers; he was dressed all in white—white pants, white shirt, even a white hat.

On their way back to Los Angeles, Stoner and Guenther stopped at Angola State Prison to see Tally Rogers again. They discussed what he had told them earlier about the theft of the cocaine. This time, though, he implicated his wife. This account was, of course, the opposite of what Betty Rogers had related. The investigators listened with interest, but they had no way of knowing which Rogers was telling the truth.

"She was in Las Vegas to keep her eye on Laney while I did the theft in L.A.," Rogers said. "That was the whole reason for her being there. Once I took the stuff, I called her and told her I had done it. I wanted her to get out of Vegas."

Rogers was asked what had happened to the cocaine.

"Hell, I sold it," he said. "Immediately. I couldn't drive around with ten kilos in my car. And I want to state again, 'cause I'm sure it's going to come up, Roy had absolutely nothing to do with it. Nothing. He wasn't involved with the stealing or the sale of the coke."

One of the investigators asked if Rogers would testify in court in the event of arrests.

"Yes, I will," Rogers said. "Roy was an okay guy. I'm sorry it happened, I really am."

A few weeks after their return to L.A., Stoner and Guenther received a phone call from Kotowski.

"Bellechasses is in jail," he said. "He's in the can in Fort Lauderdale."

The investigators flew immediately to Lauderdale. There, they learned that Bellechasses had been arrested in a cocaine conspiracy case. For Stoner and Guenther, the arrest afforded a rare opportunity to speak with someone close to Laney who might also have knowledge about Radin's murder. They wanted to propose some sort of trade that could be beneficial to Bellechasses if and when he was convicted of the drug charges and came up for sentencing.

The initial response from Bellechasses' attorneys was that he wanted to talk with them about the murder. Evidently, Bellechasses did not want the detectives to think he had had anything to do with it. But his attorneys wanted to evaluate the federal charges first; they would get back to the detectives.

While Stoner and Guenther were trying to speak with Bellechasses, he was sitting in the federal Metropolitan Correctional Center. In an ironic turn of events, Joe Amer was there, too, having been picked up on additional drug charges after working for several months at the Collection.

For Amer, the short period of freedom in Miami had ended abruptly. He found he could not stay away from friends who dealt cocaine; the money was just too appealing.

One afternoon, Amer and Bellechasses met near the center of the prison, where inmates gathered to talk and sun themselves. The two men shook hands and sat down on a bench and discussed life in prison. After years of doing cocaine, this was a first for Bellechasses. Mentioning a girlfriend, whom he had spoken with on the phone that morning, he said he hoped he would see her again. He was not acting like the tough guy Amer had met by Laney's swimming pool.

"You gotta be tough in here," Amer said. "It's really not a bad place. Honest to God. There's a lot to do."

Then Amer asked if Bellechasses had seen or heard from Laney.

"No. She moved away," Bellechasses replied. "She's living with a guy up in Okeechobee."

"Larry Greenberger," Amer said. "I saw them together at the Collection. She looked great. I also hear she had some trouble on the West Coast. Like real trouble."

Bellechasses was silent for a minute. Then he said, "She made me lose some money."

"What are you talking about?" Amer said.

Bellechasses shook his head. He did not want to answer.

* * *

Shortly after two on the afternoon of December 14, Stoner and Guenther met Anna Montenegro. Her attorney, Allen Soven, had earlier agreed to set up an interview, so after their failed attempt to see Bellechasses, the detectives called him and asked if they could see her.

Like Jonathan Lawson, Anna had left Los Angeles in a hurry after Radin's kidnapping. To her credit, she had tried to keep Radin away from Laney, but he had stubbornly ignored her advice.

At her lawyer's office, Anna sat across from Soven's desk, her hands folded on her lap. She was pretty and well dressed, her black hair flowing over her shoulders. She spoke in a soft, Spanish-accented voice and talked about dating Bellechasses and Frank Diaz, adding that it was Diaz who had introduced her to Laney.

She was asked if she had ever met Bill Mentzer.

"I went with Laney to the Budget car office and met him," Anna said.

"Did you know the owner of the agency?" she was asked.

"Marc Fogel. I know he lost some cocaine once for Laney, and he offered her cars free of charge. I went out to dinner in Hollywood with Mentzer and Laney and met a guy named Mike Pascal. He said he was an ex–CIA agent. I got a kick out of that."

They asked if she had ever met Bob Evans.

"I went to his house once with Laney," Anna said. "They were going to discuss the financing on *The Cotton Club*."

"What about the theft from Laney's house?" one of the detectives asked. "What did you know about that?"

"I heard Tally and Laney fighting about

money," she said. "Tally was saying she was screwing him on a payment."

She went over the last two days of Radin's life, May 12 and 13, and talked about going to Laney's house and seeing Mentzer and being told she could not come inside.

"I told Roy all of this," Anna said. "He knew. He was afraid of Laney, but he must have thought she wouldn't do something real bad. He felt he had to keep the meeting on Friday to straighten out the whole *Cotton Club* mess. That was his problem. He felt he *had* to make that meeting, no matter what I told him."

One of the detectives asked if Bellechasses could possibly have been involved in the murder.

"Definitely not," she said immediately. "No way. He's too financially successful. The loss of ten kilos and some cash would not cause him to commit a murder. It just wouldn't have hurt a guy that rich."

They asked if Anna was aware that Bellechasses had been arrested.

She expressed shock and said she did not know. "I still date him," she said. "He never talks about Laney anymore. Sometimes he talks about the baby, but never Laney."

TWENTY-FIVE

AS THEY HAD EACH WINTER SINCE their marriage, Laney and Greenberger went to Colorado at the end of December 1987. When they returned three months later, Laney seemed distant from her husband's family. She stayed in her second-floor bedroom when Greenberger's parents called on them. It was as if she suddenly found it painful to live in Okeechobee.

In the morning, she would sit at the table on the side porch of their farmhouse, drinking coffee. She loved coffee and drank a potful of it as she planned her day—shopping in Palm Beach, a drive to the beach. Sometimes she would drive all the way to Miami to see a friend, returning to Okeechobee late at night. Laney was restless.

Her plan as the new year unfolded was to dig deep into her husband's pockets. She had investment plans, big ones, and to accomplish them she had to persuade Greenberger to tap his considerable fortune. Her principal goal was to build the resort in Mexico for plastic surgery buffs, for which she needed a half-million-dollar down payment.

One afternoon, she met with some friends to

talk about her plan. She had drawings and charts, which she laid out on a table. Greenberger walked in on the meeting, looked over the plans, and said, "Well, all you need is money, right? Well, you're not getting it from me."

A few days later, a woman who had attended the meeting reported to Janis Greenberger that Laney had erupted in anger at her husband's announcement. "If looks could kill, Larry would have been a dead man," the woman told her.

Laney had a money button, so to speak, and to get her angry, all you had to do was push it. Radin had pushed it, so had Frank Rubino. Now her husband was doing the same, and she reacted with disdain and flashes of anger. First, though, she cried. Her anger was always preceded by fits of crying.

Now, in the early spring of 1988, she was crying a lot. She claimed Greenberger was not sharing his money with her, and specifically that he kept his money in accounts that were in his name only. For example, he had a large sum of money in the Prudential Bache account, and he had accounts in the Bahamas, out of the reach of United States tax officials. Laney wanted the funds in joint accounts, but Greenberger had refused.

Bill Rider sat around his house in the Midwest for ten months before deciding to get in touch with Stoner and Guenther. Mostly, it was fear that kept him from calling to offer further assistance. Sometime after the Radin and Mincher murders, Alex Marti, whom Rider considered a goon who would kill his own wife if the price were right, phoned to say that Larry Flynt had placed a $75,000 bounty on Rider's head.

Rider was confused. He and Flynt were related by marriage, but hardly anyone in the extended family was talking to one another. Consequently, Rider had no one whom he could trust to pass on reliable information. Besides, how did he know Marti was telling the truth? Maybe he was trying to scare him. Anything seemed possible with a halfwit like Marti. It was as if he was taunting him, goading him to come out into the open. Rider tried to fade away.

On April 8, 1988, Rider contacted the Los Angeles County Sheriff's Department and said he would help. Charlie Guenther had retired from the department at the end of March, and Carlos Avila was back after his year at the FBI Academy. The detectives were delighted, and they offered Rider bodyguards as well as financial compensation to induce him to relocate to California as well as help them full time. By relocating him, the detectives hoped to keep him out of sight.

When Avila and Stoner saw him, Rider turned over a .22 caliber Ruger semiautomatic pistol fitted with a silencer. This was the weapon he had loaned Mentzer, who had used it to gun down June Mincher as she ran across the sidewalk in her high heels toward the front door of her apartment building. Laboratory tests confirmed that the slugs removed from Mincher's head had been fired from the Ruger.

The investigators' plan was to have Rider get in touch with Mentzer and Bob Lowe. He had not spoken to either of them in quite a while, and he was nervous about making contact again. They had learned that Lowe was in Maryland, managing a restaurant called the Scoreboard Café in Frederick. On May 5, Stoner and Avila flew east and rented two rooms at the Crystal City Marriott Hotel in Arlington, Virginia, not far from where Lowe worked. Two Virginia state troopers fitted the room with listening devices.

The following afternoon, Rider arrived at the hotel room and phoned Lowe at the restaurant. After a few minutes of chitchat, Rider explained that he was in the area doing a job, a divorce case, and needed help. He asked Lowe to help him with surveillance.

"I can't help you," Lowe said. "I manage this place, and I can't get away. Go see Bob Deremer."

Deremer, who had driven Mentzer past the scene on Sepulveda Boulevard where June Mincher had been gunned down in 1984, had moved back east and was living near Lowe. He had had sporadic contact with Lowe over the years, and was surprised to hear from Rider. Deremer had not seen Mentzer, who was now in Los Angeles, since shortly after the murder.

Of course, Deremer had had nothing to do with the Radin murder. But he feared that he could be charged with involvement in the Mincher murder. The investigators would have preferred that Rider speak with Lowe, but now that Lowe had suggested Deremer, they were compelled to send Rider to see him.

On the evening of May 10, Deremer arrived at the Marriott and rode the elevator to Rider's room. They chatted for a while, and Rider explained he was following a certain party around as part of a divorce investigation. The two men left the room and drove around the area in Rider's rented car.

Rider hoped that Deremer had picked up information about the killings in conversations with the participants. In the car, he brought up

Mentzer's having to get drunk before he could kill people.

"We went to a bar, Ana's, before the transvestite killing," Deremer explained. "Mentzer drank to build up his courage. I stayed at the bar during the killing so I'd have an alibi. I drove him to the murder scene to pick up his car."

Under prodding from Rider, Deremer said he had got the equivalent of three months' rent for assisting Mentzer.

"What did Lowe get for the Radin murder?" Rider asked Deremer.

"A black Caddy Seville and some cash," Deremer said.

"Isn't that something," Rider commented.

The next night, Rider drove to the Scoreboard Café. For the better part of the evening, Lowe and Rider watched a basketball game on the large-screen television in the lounge. While watching the game and drinking beer, Lowe talked about driving Mentzer to where he had gunned down the transvestite. He told Rider he knew Mentzer had borrowed Rider's gun for the job.

Rider asked about the Radin murder.

"I was the driver on that one," Lowe responded. "Mentzer and Marti shot Radin thirteen times, seeing as how it was Friday the thirteenth."

"Who wanted it done? Who paid for it?"

"Laney Jacobs and Bob Evans was what I was told."

Throughout June and July, Greenberger was estranged from his family. He had become a recluse, hidden away in his farmhouse. His drug habit had worsened considerably. Laney, who in spite of years of using cocaine did not display the behavior of a true addict, did not intervene.

Greenberger's parents tried to get along with their daughter-in-law as best they could. But they were perplexed when they went to the house and she avoided them, or their son stayed in the big upstairs bedroom with the door shut.

"How's Larry?" they asked Laney.

"Oh, he's fine," Laney responded. The Greenbergers had heard their son was in a bad way, and they wanted to see him and offer their help. But Laney positioned herself in such a way as to keep them away.

Janis felt estranged from her brother, too. She was surprised one morning in mid-July when he called to talk with her. Dick Markham answered the phone. "Hey, Larry, where are you?" he asked.

"I'm in town," Greenberger said. "How are you guys?"

Markham was surprised to hear from him, noting that his voice sounded upbeat. "Your sister is here. You want to talk to her?"

Greenberger said he did.

"Hey, Larry," she said. "You're in town?"

"Yeah," he said. "At least for now. Where are Mom and Dad?"

"In North Carolina," she replied. "What do you need?"

"I need some papers that they have in their safety-deposit box at the bank," he explained. "Some stuff on a T-bill. Can you meet me there?"

"Heck, Larry, I can't get into their box," she said. "Is it real important?"

"Well, yeah, it is," he answered. "When are they coming back?"

"Actually, they are on their way back this morning," she said. "They ought to be home by tomorrow sometime. Can it wait?"

He said it could, and he hung up.

Janis turned to Markham. "That's weird," she said. "It sounded like the old Larry. Warm and talkative. I wonder what's going on and why he needed those papers so bad."

"He did sound good, for a change," Markham agreed.

"You know, Laney don't hardly fit into this town," Janis said.

Markham scoffed. "Like a turd in a punch bowl, babe."

On July 7, Avila and Stoner rented two rooms at the Holiday Inn on Church Lane in Los Angeles. Listening devices were installed, and when they were certain they were working properly, Rider called Mentzer and invited him to the room.

Mentzer—who had been doing odd jobs in Los Angeles, most of them illegal, since his trip to Miami to harass Rubino—was characteristically talkative. Rider hardly needed small talk to induce Mentzer to talk about the two murders. He spoke about harassing Mincher before killing her, and of placing a bomb under the gas tank of her car, which failed to detonate.

Rider then asked about Radin.

"Alex called him 'Rodan—the big fat Jew.' It was a wild night. When we drove up to the hotel, we got right behind that black actor." He thought for a moment and then said, "Demond Wilson. He had a woman in the car with him. Then the limo with Lowe and Laney came, and we waited. When the limo left, we blew past Wilson and got right behind them. We lost Wilson pretty quick."

"Then what did you do?" Rider asked.

"The limo stopped, and me and Alex got in."

"Who's exactly where now?" Rider prodded.

"Lowe's driving, me and Alex are in the back with Radin. All of a sudden, Jesus Christ, a cop car whizzes by with its siren on. Marti dives to the floor and sticks his gun into Radin's crotch. I tell Radin, who's got my gun in his mouth, 'If you don't wanna lose everything, shut the fuck up.' The cop car went right by. I think maybe Radin wanted to kill Laney. We took a gun off him that night."

"What the hell was this whole thing over, anyway?" Rider asked.

The Cotton Club.

"Really, that was it?" Rider asked. "A movie?"

"Yeah. That was it. The movie."

"What the hell is Marti up to these days?" Rider asked.

"He's got a big dope business," Mentzer said. "He's rich. He hired me to kill some Iranian dealer, but I didn't do it."

Three weeks later, Rider met Mentzer again, this time at the Holiday Inn at Long Beach Airport. Shortly after Mentzer arrived, Rider offered him a job watching a drug dealer. Mentzer readily agreed, saying he needed the extra money.

The following day, Rider picked up Mentzer in a rented car that had been equipped with a recording device. They drove to a prearranged spot, where they met an undercover police officer posing as a drug dealer. The plan was to get Mentzer to talk about himself some more.

"There's a lot of things I can do," Mentzer told the man. "I got police contacts in L.A. who can get stuff for me—you know, run information on plate numbers, that sort of stuff."

"I got a party in San Francisco who owes me a

couple grand," the officer said. "I'm not real happy about that."

"If the price is right," Mentzer said, "I'll do anything you want me to do."

In early August, Laney announced that she wanted to get her real estate license. Her Center for Plastic Surgery had been only a modest success, and Greenberger's decision not to loan her money to build a resort in Mexico had ruined her plans.

She arranged to attend classes at the Bert Rodgers real estate school in Orlando. At one of her first classes, she met a twenty-two-year-old man from western Pennsylvania named Terry Squillante. He was short and thin, with dark hair and a boyish grin. Laney liked him so much that she invited him to Okeechobee.

Squillante was soon staying in the guest room that Greenberger had had built onto the back of the house. Greenberger liked Squillante, too, and within a few weeks of meeting him was jokingly referring to him as Dax's older brother. He was around the house so much that Greenberger had him doing errands and helping with household chores.

On August 20, Janis had a party for Markham's daughter. At some point that week and for mysterious reasons, Greenberger had flown to Los Angeles. After years of maintaining that plastic surgery was nonsense, he mentioned that he was going to see a doctor in Los Angeles about doing work on his cheek and around his left eye. When he left, Myriam drove up from Miami to spend a few days with Laney and Dax.

The afternoon of the party, when Janis went to her brother's house to pick up Dax, Myriam explained that Laney was off somewhere with Squillante.

"They're good friends now, I hear," Janis said sarcastically. She changed the subject. "Is Dax ready to go?"

Myriam said he was, and she got his things together and walked him to the porch door.

"You know," Janis said, "I really can't stand Laney anymore. She's a bitch. Why doesn't Larry just divorce her?"

"I think she loves him," Myriam said. "I really do."

"No, she doesn't," Janis said. "I can't understand it. I mean, why the hell doesn't Larry just divorce her?"

"They can't divorce. Larry doesn't want Laney to get her hands on everything he has set up for the boy," Myriam said furtively, for she was now betraying Laney. "He doesn't want her to have anything to do with it."

Janis walked out to her car, and Myriam called after her, "Dax can't stay with you tonight. Laney insisted you bring him home after the party."

A few days later, at eleven in the morning, Janis was home when her brother called from Los Angeles.

"Oh, hi, Larry. I'm on my way to the beach," she said. "What's up?"

"I've been trying to reach Laney," he explained. "The phone is off the hook. Could you please go over to the house and hang it up?"

Janis said that she would.

"I want you to see what cars are there," he added. "I want to know just what is going on."

"That's no problem," she replied. "Where are you? Do you have a number?"

"I'm in a doctor's office," he said, and he gave her the phone number.

Janis went to the house and saw that the gate across the driveway was pushed open. She drove up, parked, and knocked on the porch door. There was no answer. The door was locked. She could see a black Jeep in the garage.

"I wonder whose that is," she muttered to herself.

Laney's big black Mercedes was gone. Greenberger's Mercedes was parked, as was his Jeep and a truck that belonged to Eagle Outdoor Advertising. Janis left to call her brother.

"No one's home, but there's a black Jeep in the garage," she explained.

Greenberger was silent for a moment. The Jeep belonged to Squillante.

"Hey, Larry, what's going on with Laney anyhow?" Janis asked. "She wouldn't let Dax stay with me after the party."

"Who knows?" Greenberger said. "I gotta go."

In Los Angeles, on the afternoon of September 7, Avila and Stoner rented another room at the Holiday Inn on Church Lane, hoping to tape Mentzer saying more about the Radin murder. While the earlier encounters with Mentzer had been productive, the investigators needed more specific information about his role in the murder.

This time, when Rider called Mentzer to try to set something up, Mentzer instead invited Rider to join him and a friend named Vinnie, who was from Miami, for dinner at an Italian restaurant.

Rider drove to the restaurant, followed by an undercover team from the Sheriff's Department. When he walked in, he found Mentzer, who introduced him to Vincent De Angelo, a tall, hand-

some man with thick light-brown hair and
muscular, outdoorsy features. The three men had
dinner, and then Mentzer said goodbye to De Angelo. Afterward, Mentzer sat with Rider in his
car in the parking lot.

"You know, I'm really pissed at you for borrow-
ing my gun to kill that transvestite," Rider told
Mentzer. "I was so freaked out about it that I
threw it away when you gave it back. I didn't
want anyone to trace it to me."

"Why did you do that?" Mentzer was surprised.
"Hell, I would have bought it from you. I used
hollow-point bullets. They can't be traced. They
flatten out like shotgun pellets. Man, the only
reason I borrowed the gun was because mine got
thrown in a lake in Florida."

"I hope I don't have anything to worry about,"
Rider said.

"The only thing I'm worried about is Lowe,"
Mentzer replied. "My worry is he talks a lot, and
someone might try to tape him or get him to
snitch."

"Hey, that drug guy I introduced you to," Rider
said. "He might want to use you on a hit."

"If the money's right, I'll do it. That's what De
Angelo wanted to talk about, too. He wants me to
kill a couple in Miami in a few months. One hundred thousand for both hits. I'll split it with you if
you help me."

"Who is this De Angelo guy?" Rider asked.

"He's a drug partner of Carlos Lehder," Mentzer said. "He also wants me to go to Miami in a
couple of weeks and burn a house down. Vinnie
and his wife own it, and Vinnie wants the insurance money."

After Mentzer left, Rider met with Stoner and
Avila. They showed him a number of photo-

graphs they had collected over the years as part of their investigation. He identified one as Vincent De Angelo. Two undercover officers who had been in the restaurant and seated near Rider also picked out the man whom Mentzer called De Angelo.

He was Larry Greenberger.

TWENTY-SIX

AROUND OKEECHOBEE, AMONG THE townspeople who knew the Greenbergers as a nice family, the talk was that Larry had made twenty million dollars in the cocaine trade. A friend of Greenberger's once told a story that Okeechobee's sheriff had claimed that Greenberger was worth one hundred million dollars.

Apparently unknown to Greenberger, his name had been mentioned at the trial in Jacksonville of Carlos Lehder. Lehder's arrest in Colombia had made headlines, and his trial was followed closely. A number of witnesses testified that Greenberger had loaned Lehder a large sum of money to buy a plane and that in return Lehder had granted Greenberger a huge slice of his American business.

When Lehder was sentenced, on July 20, 1988, he received life in prison without parole, plus one hundred thirty-five years. If Greenberger read the news accounts the following day or watched television at all, he would have learned of his former associate's fate. Perhaps he did, and perhaps he was not bothered, believing still that he was beyond the reach of the law.

* * *

On a hot evening, Thursday, September 8, Greenberger deplaned at the Palm Beach airport and was picked up by Laney and Terry Squillante.

On the way back up Route 710 to Okeechobee, Greenberger and Laney argued. When Greenberger pulled the Mercedes into the garage beside the house, Laney stalked off.

The next morning, Greenberger called his broker at the Prudential Bache office in West Palm Beach to inquire about his treasury bill. Prior to his leaving the house to meet with the broker, Laney made it clear that she wanted him to cash in the note. He refused. Laney phoned him when he reached the office, and they argued again.

On Saturday, Myriam packed her suitcase and said goodbye. In the driveway, she picked up Dax, kissing him on both cheeks. She regarded Dax, now six years old, as a spoiled little boy, but she loved him as if he were her son.

There was much about Laney that Myriam did not understand, particularly now. Laney had always been a woman who seemed to love being married, but when Myriam had visited in recent weeks, Laney would be off with Squillante. It seemed to Myriam that Laney was flirting with him. Myriam found herself being Dax's nanny again.

Myriam considered Laney's and Greenberger's relationship altogether strange. Greenberger was a man who seemed to withdraw from everyone around him. Laney would go to bed early, while he would sit on the side porch and listen to the crickets. Most times he would bring a pistol with him and sit in the darkness in a wicker chair, rubbing the gun with an oily rag. He could do it for hours. Myriam would look in on him from the kitchen, where she was ironing, and think what a lonely man he was. His gun seemed to be his best friend.

He fired his pistols a lot in the field behind the house or alongside the garage. The neighbors would hear the shots at dusk and know it was Greenberger. He knew how to handle a pistol—how to load it quickly, fire off six shots, and then reload. His favorite was a Smith and Wesson .44 magnum, a massive gun, four pounds or better in weight, with a six-inch barrel. It felt good in the palm of his hand as he sat on the side porch on a dark and humid summer night in air redolent with lake smells, wiping the pistol over and over with an oily rag.

Monday morning, September 12, Greenberger awoke late and discovered that Laney and Squillante had gone off to the beach. He stepped outside and was met by Carl, the housepainter, who was doing the trim on the farmhouse.

"You don't get too much work done at the beach," Greenberger said in disgust. He went back inside the porch. "You don't shit where you eat."

At nine-thirty the following morning, Tuesday, September 13, Greenberger stopped at his parents' home on his way to meet Ed Bolter, his partner in Eagle Outdoor Advertising, near West Palm Beach. He seemed particularly upset. He sat down with his mother in the kitchen.

"Mom, I don't know what I'm doing with Laney," he said. "Honest to God, she's off her rocker. She's spending my money like water."

A pretty woman with short brown hair and an upbeat personality, Dahlis Greenberger tried to comfort her son. "You have to do the right thing," she said. "We'll always support you—you know that, Larry."

He drove to West Palm Beach and spent most of the day with Bolter. At dusk, Greenberger headed back up Route 710, through the little communities that always looked so backwater and so poor, and pulled into the driveway of his farmhouse. There was still light in the sky.

Laney and Squillante were in the house. Greenberger poured himself a glass of port and sat on the porch. A pizza was ordered for dinner. A little after dark, Greenberger took his Smith and Wesson from a small storage area under the staircase, and he, Laney, and Squillante stepped outside. It was a warm night, and the air was still. With so few lights in town, the sky was ablaze with stars. Greenberger carefully loaded the pistol and squeezed off a round at a target set up near the garage. Then he handed the pistol to Laney, who did the same. When she was finished, Squillante took his turn.

Sometime later, Laney went off to bed in the big bedroom at the top of the stairs that she shared with Greenberger. Shortly after, Squillante retired to the guest quarters, which were separated from the main part of the house by an enclosed garagelike structure and a sitting room.

As was his habit, Greenberger took his pistol and oily rag to the side porch and sat with his back to one wall. From where he sat, he could see out through the screens to the front yard, the driveway, and the tall gate and fence that enclosed the front of the driveway. He could see anyone who drove in along the road that led to the house.

Seated on the porch in a bathrobe, Greenberger

smoked a marijuana cigarette and snorted a small amount of cocaine. And he wiped his pistol with the oily rag, over and over, until it gleamed in the moonlight.

A few minutes after midnight, Laney picked up the phone in the kitchen and called Greenberger's parents.

"Jerry," she said excitedly. "Can you come quick? Larry just shot himself."

Jerry Greenberger hung up and phoned Janis. He asked her and Dick Markham to go to the house, too.

They sped over the darkened country roads and arrived just before twelve-thirty. The driveway was filled with police cars, and an ambulance was parked near the side porch. Janis and Markham walked to the side of the house away from the porch, into the alcove that separated the kitchen from the guest wing.

Laney was standing with some police officers. "Where's Terry?" she cried. "Where's Terry?"

A few feet from where Laney stood was Greenberger's body, slumped back in his favorite chair on the side porch. He was sitting upright, his head against one wall, his eyes open. There was a single bullet hole near his left eye. The bullet had passed through his head and entered the wall near the window. His bathrobe was saturated with blood. The big .44 magnum revolver was clutched in the fingers of Greenberger's right hand.

Dick and Janis stayed in the alcove. Laney fidgeted nervously, while Janis cried. Outside, Squillante was seated in the back of a sheriff's car.

"I can't believe he did this," Laney moaned. "I

just can't believe he would kill himself. Oh, dear God."

Markham went upstairs and carried Dax down to his van, gently laying him across the rear seat. Inside the house, a sheriff's detective told Laney not to take a shower; the detective wanted to test her hands for gunpowder residue. When he was through speaking with her, she went outside, and as Janis and Markham backed out of the driveway, they saw her hugging Squillante. They had not seen her shed a tear.

Halfway to the Greenbergers' home, Dax bolted up in his seat. "I didn't hear anything," he said. "My door was shut."

When they arrived at the house, Markham carried Dax into one of the bedrooms. Markham and Janis sat up talking, and sometime near four in the morning, Laney came and picked up Dax. She said she was on her way to Miami but did not tell them where she would stay. She had to get away, that was all.

Seven hours after the shooting, and perhaps at about the time Laney and Dax arrived in Miami, Greenberger's body was brought to the office of Frederick P. Hobin, the district medical examiner. The bloody robe was removed, and the cool body was laid out on a large stainless-steel table equipped with drains to catch any fluids.

Hobin examined the bullet wound beneath the left eye. What he noticed about it was that there was a pattern of gunpowder tattooing around the wound, with an outside diameter of nearly twenty centimeters. This was wide for a point-blank gunshot wound. Also curious was the fact that there was very little tattooing (the imprints made by gunpowder as it strikes the skin) in the eye itself. In fact, there were no gunpowder grains on the surface of the eye.

This discovery indicated to Hobin that the eyelids were elevated and the eye itself was open at the time of the gun blast. This meant Greenberger was staring at the gun when it went off. The absence of grains of gunpowder on the damp surface of the eye suggested one further finding —that the pistol was held a distance from the head that was significantly greater than the length of Greenberger's arm.

The bullet entered just beneath the left eye and exited at the back of the head, roughly at the level of Greenberger's mouth. To Hobin, this signified that the pistol was pointed down at Greenberger.

On the cover sheet of his report, under "Manner of Death," Hobin typed "Homicide." Beneath it, he wrote: "Based upon the objective findings, it is my opinion that the subject was shot by another person. I would conclude that this is a homicidal gunshot injury which another person had contrived to disguise as a suicidal injury."

The funeral was held at the end of the week at the Bass Okeechobee Funeral Home. Visitors came and spoke with Jerry and Dahlis Greenberger, while Laney sat off by herself. The farmhouse was now off limits, although Okeechobee police were deliberately close-mouthed about the medical examiner's findings.

When Janis approached Laney, Laney hugged her and said how dreadfully sorry she was.

"Why, Laney," Janis said. "It's me who should be saying I'm sorry to you. After all, you lost your husband. Dax don't have a father anymore."

Laney turned to a woman named Jeanne

Baker, who was seated next to her. "She thinks I did it," Laney said. "But they don't know what I had to put up with."

The eulogy was delivered by a Denver attorney named Paul Vranesic, who had driven Laney to Okeechobee from Miami that morning. He had been Greenberger's lawyer for several years and had become one of his closest friends. He had set up a company called Asher Oil, in which Greenberger and Ed Bolter invested.

After the service, Jeanne Baker found Janis and told her something that sent shivers up Janis's spine. Greenberger had once told Jeanne's husband, John, that Laney had had someone bumped off years before.

"Larry told that to John?" Janis asked. "Now isn't that something. So what do you suppose happened to my brother? I know him as well as I know myself, and I can tell you for certain that he didn't take his own life. Damn it, I just know that."

The discovery that Greenberger had been murdered strongly suggested that Laney was a liar. In order to believe her account, it would have had to be accepted that someone entered the house, murdered Greenberger, and staged it to look like a suicide so that when Laney ran downstairs and found his body, she assumed he had killed himself.

Greenberger had been found with the gun in his right hand. But it was a heavy revolver, and the force of the blast as he fired the gun would have sent it sailing across the porch. Also, he could not possibly have shot himself on the left side of his face at a downward angle with his right hand.

But the most telling discovery was that the gun

had been fired from six to eight feet away. His murderer, whom he was looking at directly as he or she approached him, must have stepped through the door that separated the kitchen from the porch, reached across a glass-topped table, and fired. Then the assailant or assailants put the pistol in Greenberger's right hand, closing his fingers around the grip. But had Laney run downstairs immediately on hearing the shot, the killer would not have had time to rig the scene.

It was also noteworthy that Laney and Squillante had been target shooting that evening. Thus, when Okeechobee authorities performed tests on their hands after Greenberger's shooting and found gunpowder residue on them, it was deemed meaningless.

Immediately after the funeral, Vranesic drove Laney and Squillante to a hotel in Miami. Meanwhile, word that Greenberger had in fact been murdered spread through the town.

In Los Angeles, Stoner and Avila learned of Greenberger's murder through police contacts. They had wanted to continue their investigation into Radin's murder, but this changed everything. They feared that Laney might be tempted to flee Florida rather than face questions by police about the exact circumstances of her husband's death. So they hurriedly set up another interview with Bill Rider, to go over the details of their case. They also conferred with Los Angeles Deputy District Attorney David Conn about writing an arrest complaint, so that Laney could be picked up.

The complaint was signed on September 27, and Stoner and Avila made plans to arrest her. The investigators had heard of rumors in Okeechobee that Laney planned to leave the country.

The Greenbergers had heard that she intended to fly to Spain. At about the same time, a high school friend of Greenberger's flew to the Bahamas and withdrew funds later estimated at $200,000 from an account of Greenberger's. It appeared Laney was in the process of gathering his funds together.

During the last two weeks of September, Lieutenant Don Fisher in Okeechobee tried to track Laney down to ask her to come in for an interview. She was moving from hotel to hotel in the Miami area, apparently with Vranesic.

On Friday, September 30, she was in Denver. From there, she phoned the Country Kids school in Okeechobee and left a message for Dax's teacher. A few minutes later, she called back and asked a secretary to destroy the Denver phone number she had given.

Finally, though, Fisher coaxed Laney and Vranesic into meeting him. Laney had expressed a desire to go back into the house to get some belongings, but in order to receive permission, she had to agree to be questioned. As a precondition for the meeting, Vranesic made Fisher promise that he had no arrest warrant for Laney and Squillante in the Greenberger murder.

On Sunday, October 2, Laney, Squillante, and Vranesic flew into Orlando and, at the Holiday Inn, met Fisher and an investigator with the Florida Department of Law Enforcement. Laney was questioned first. She claimed her husband had been depressed over a droopy eye and had killed himself. When she was through, Squillante was brought into the room.

As Squillante walked in, Fisher and the investigator stepped out into the hallway. Laney was standing there by the door, nervously waiting for

Squillante. Had she looked up, she would have noticed that Fisher was holding an arrest complaint. He approached her and began reading.

"You are wanted in Los Angeles to answer charges in the 1983 murder of Roy Alexander Radin," Fisher said. Laney stared at him in disbelief. "I have a warrant for your arrest, Mrs. Greenberger."

He handed her the complaint, and her eyes seemed to fix on Radin's name. So much time had passed since his murder. Surely she had convinced herself she would never be arrested. She shook her head back and forth, as if this was all some grotesque misunderstanding.

"Oh, my God," she said in a quivering voice.

She yelled for her attorney, who was with Squillante. As he came out into the hallway, handcuffs were quickly clipped to Laney's wrists, and she was led away to the elevator.

EPILOGUE

*There are mistakes too monstrous for
remorse . . .*

EDWIN ARLINGTON ROBINSON

LANEY WAS TAKEN TO THE ORANGE
County Jail in Orlando. On the day of her arrest, Bill Mentzer, Alex Marti, and Bob Lowe
were also picked up. Lowe was arrested in Maryland and, like Laney, filed court papers to fight
any attempt to remove him to Los Angeles.

In New York, word of the arrests delighted
members of Roy Radin's family. In the years
since the murder, the family had come to believe
that no one would ever be charged. Some in the
family even suggested that Radin might still be
alive, physical evidence of his death notwith-
standing. Radin's good friend Tiny Tim even
claimed to have seen Radin at a concert in Aus-
tralia.

Renee Radin, who had waged a letter-writing
campaign with Los Angeles authorities to prod
them into apprehending her son's murderer, did
not live to see the arrests. A courageous woman

of principle and conviction, she died of cancer in July 1987.

Some in the family claimed that Radin made an appearance at his mother's home after her wake.

For the most part, Laney found the jail comfortable. She was an instant celebrity, enjoying extensive press coverage that included almost daily revelations about the "secret" life of her murdered husband. Many of her friends could not believe she had committed a murder; nor could they believe Larry Greenberger's death had been anything but a suicide.

"I talked to Laney a couple of times while she was in jail," said one old Miami friend. "What she said was, 'It didn't happen that way in Los Angeles. Radin ripped people off, and someone killed him for it.' She sounded very convincing that at best she was some sort of minor player on the sidelines in a game that got out of hand.

"Larry was a mystery to me. The papers said he was a big dealer. So how come no one arrested him? To believe it was a murder, you'd have to accept that she was involved, and I can't see how a woman could kill her husband.

"Look, Laney was as determined a woman as ever walked the streets of Miami. What she wanted, she took. Men were a tool to be used, nothing more. She set her eyes on a goal, and the goal was money. She didn't want to be a little Alabama girl with an overdrawn checkbook and a boring job. Maybe Laney's fabled luck just ran out."

In the aftermath of her arrest, Laney hired a new attorney, Edward Shohat, who was bright and

well regarded. Years before, Laney had worked in
Shohat's law office as a secretary. As Carlos
Lehder's lawyer during his celebrated trial,
Shohat had learned something of Larry Green-
berger.

Shohat moved to bar any attempt by the Los
Angeles County District Attorney's office to extra-
dite his client to California to stand trial on murder charges. He proclaimed her innocence,
saying the case in California was weak.

Shohat dismissed as ridiculous any speculation
that his client would be charged with murdering
her husband in Okeechobee. Indeed, the police
investigation of Greenberger's murder all but
ended with Laney's arrest on the Radin murder
charge.

While Shohat worked on Laney's behalf, she
was a model prisoner. She talked about getting
out of jail and living with Terry Squillante and
Dax. The two of them visited her every weekend,
and Squillante became the boy's guardian.

Squillante's relationship with Laney was so
close that some people in the prison thought they
were married. When her son visited, she would
walk with him around the visitors' area of the
prison and hold his hand. She would sit with
Squillante and Dax, and cry when they left.

Mostly, she waited for word from Shohat regarding the necessity to travel to Los Angeles to
stand trial.

When he first met her, John Richter, the jail's
counselor, told her she had "crazy eyes" like
Charles Manson. Richter came to like her, and
Laney sent him little cards to thank him for his
help.

One of them read:

. . . Any day now your worst fears will be realized. Someday (even if space travel to Mars is
common and you've passed male menopause
and your wit and wisdom is shadowed only by
your latent charm) we will *all* be free! The beat
will go on and Campbell's will still be making
soup!

Regards,
Laney

She told Richter she had lived in the fast lane
until 1983 but had maintained a quiet and orderly life since then. She insisted that she was no
murderer.

One day, she told him that she was afraid of
being "hit" in the jail, but would not elaborate.

"I want them to know I can keep my mouth
shut," she told Richter. He did not know what she
meant.

In late December, Laney professed a willingness
to go back to California and fight the murder
charges. She was confident she would succeed.
On December 30, 1988, she wrote for the last time
to Richter.

Dear "JR,"
Just a note of sincere thanks for all of your help
during this untimely crisis. I truly appreciate
your wit and humor as a refreshing departure
from cell C-4. I'll keep in touch and let you
know how OCJ compares to the great L.A. Hope
your New Year is a good one!

Laney

In January 1989, nearly four months after her arrest, Laney Greenberger prepared to fly to Los
Angeles for criminal court hearings on the Radin

murder charge. She said goodbye to Squillante
and Dax, vowing she would return soon.

Avila and Stoner, the two gifted detectives
whose meticulous way of going about their business had paid off, flew to Orlando to pick her up.
They escorted her to a waiting plane. After the
plane took off, Laney took a Bible from her bag,
opened it, and began silently reading passages
from the New Testament.

Shohat prepared for the first of several hearings
in Los Angeles County Municipal Court. His
strategy was to secure Laney's release on bail
pending a hearing to determine if there was
enough evidence to hold her on the murder
charge.

On Friday, January 20, Shohat and his cocoun-
sel, Marcia Morrissey, appeared before Judge
David A. Horowitz. Deputy District Attorney
David Conn, who had been assigned to the Radin
case in early 1987, came to court with investigators' reports bound in notebooks stacked on a
cart.

Court officers brought Laney in from a holding
area behind the courtroom. She sat quietly at the
defense table.

Conn was an articulate and soft-spoken man of
moderate build, with thick brown hair that he
brushed straight back off his face. He explained
to Judge Horowitz that the charges pending
against Laney Greenberger and the other defen-
dants carried with them the death penalty. For
that reason, Conn argued that she should be denied bail.

Shohat strenuously disagreed. "We are talking
about the freedom of a woman in this particular
case who has a six-year-old son, who has no prior

criminal record, and who is only being held because of an arrest warrant."

To the argument that Laney had no criminal record, Conn pointed out her 1982 arrest for possession of marijuana and cocaine. Then he said: "In the past, she was married to a man by the name of Milan Bellechasses. He was a major drug lord who is now being prosecuted by the federal government. It was a common-law marriage. Through him she was dealing narcotics in California. . . .

"In addition to that, Your Honor, after she left California following the murder of Roy Radin, she went to Florida and married Larry Greenberger. He was the right-hand man to Carlos Lehder, who is the biggest drug kingpin on the East Coast: a man that counsel knows very well, because he represented him in his federal trial in Florida.

"Larry Greenberger himself was extremely wealthy from his drug dealings, and just before Laney was arrested on this charge, Larry Greenberger was shot in the face and killed in his home while the defendant was home. That killing has been ruled a homicide, and she remains a suspect in that homicide.

"Because of her connections to these very powerful individuals and because the defendant has a tremendous amount of financial ability here—she has millions—she could very easily put up bail of several million dollars and flee, and we would never see her again. . . . She would be a fool not to leave when she has the financial resources to flee the state and pick up her child and be gone forever. . . .

"In this case there is great public danger. Our key witness is a man by the name of Bill Rider. I can tell this court unequivocally that as a prosecutor assigned to organized crime, I am familiar with witness protection at the state and federal level. I can tell this court that the protection that was provided to this witness in this case is unprecedented because of the danger which the Los Angeles Sheriff's Department perceives to this witness from the defendant and her codefendants. In my experience I have never seen a greater amount of human resources committed to the protection of a single witness either on the state or federal level."

When Shohat spoke, he called the investigation that led to his client's arrest the most intensive he had ever seen. One of Florida's most experienced criminal attorneys, Shohat spoke forcefully and passionately about the charges pending against Laney Greenberger. He conceded that there was evidence that his client had been "involved in cocaine distribution." Then he added that Rider had nothing to fear from Laney Greenberger.

As for Conn's comments that Laney was a suspect in her husband's murder, Shohat said she had had nothing whatsoever to do with Greenberger's death. "Mrs. Greenberger lived and worked and played and loved Larry Greenberger to the minute he died. . . . They lived a good life, they had a nice home."

Shohat agreed that Larry Greenberger had been Carlos Lehder's right-hand man, but he added, "Larry was the smart one who got out of the business, who retired from the evil of the cocaine business . . . he was living a legitimate life when he died in Florida."

After hearing legal arguments, Judge Horowitz denied bail.

Later in January, Conn and Shohat were back
before Horowitz, to again discuss the question of
bail. Sergeant Stoner was called as a witness.
Stoner testified that Larry Greenberger had continued in drug trafficking after leaving Lehder in
1980, and that Laney had continued to sell cocaine after the Radin murder in 1983. Then
Stoner was asked about the manner of Greenberger's "suicide."

"Mr. Greenberger was found sitting in a chair
with a .44 magnum revolver in his right hand
. . . he was shot in the left side of the face, which
is not normal in a suicide to cross over and shoot
yourself in that direction, in a downward motion. . . .

"Normally, in that type of shooting with that
powerful a gun, the gun would leave the hand,
and it was found still with his finger in the trigger, and when they did tests it showed that the
gun was anywhere from six to eight feet from his
head when it went off. . . .

"Mrs. Greenberger indicated she was upstairs
when the shooting occurred. She immediately
ran downstairs to see what it was and found
Larry sitting there, that Mr. Squillante . . . ran
in . . . and if that's true, then if somebody else
reported it to be a suicide and it actually was a
homicide, that that person would not have had
time to put the gun in the man's hand and safely
exit the location without one of them seeing.

"Therefore, they [the Okeechobee authorities]
assume that one of them may possibly be a suspect."

Stoner went on to say that Laney had sent "contract killers" to find Tally Rogers after the theft
from her Sherman Oaks house.

To this, Shohat responded that Rogers was

never found. "Nobody was hurt," he said.
". . . Several people were contacted. . . . No one
was as much as touched, period. They were looking for cocaine that had been stolen, nothing
else."

Judge Horowitz denied bail again, and Laney
was handcuffed and sent back to her cell.

In May 1989, Conn prepared to bring Laney
Greenberger, Bill Mentzer, and Alex Marti into
the courtroom for a hearing to determine if there
was enough evidence to hold them for a trial.
And in particular, whether there was enough evidence to keep the "special circumstances" contained in the murder charge, which carried with
them the death penalty, as part of the prosecution's case.

As the hearing began before Municipal Court
Judge Patti Jo McKay, the fourth defendant in
the Radin murder, Bob Lowe, was being held in
Maryland, pending court proceedings on the
question of his extradition to Los Angeles.

The prosecution's first witness was Robert Evans. His scheduled appearance brought out a
horde of reporters and television camera crews,
who photographed him entering the courtroom
with a sullen look on his tanned face. He wore a
dark-blue suit, and his black hair was cut perfectly and brushed back in a high wave off his
forehead. He wore his trademark tinted sunglasses.

The information the prosecution had been
given about Evans was, essentially, that he had
had a relationship with Laney; that he had spoken to the Doumani brothers in Las Vegas prior
to Radin's body being discovered in a way that
suggested that he knew Radin had in fact been

murdered; that he had once traveled to Miami to meet Bellechasses. Conn called him a suspect in the murder but added that he did not have enough evidence to arrest him.

He wanted Evans to talk about his relationship with Laney, and it was to that purpose that he called him to the stand to testify.

Evans took the stand, was sworn in, and answered just one question put by Conn. "Mr. Evans, did you know a man by the name of Roy Radin?"

Evans immediately responded, "Based on the advice of counsel, I refuse to answer the question."

His attorney, Robert L. Shapiro, explained to Judge McKay that Evans would not answer any questions pertaining to the case. His argument was based on the fact that Conn had made statements to the press that Evans was a suspect in the Radin murder, although there was not sufficient evidence to warrant an arrest.

In arguing that Evans should be required to testify, Conn told Judge McKay, ". . . very often in the course of a criminal investigation we are certain about the involvement of some persons and we are not certain as to exactly what role, if any, other persons may have played in regard to a particular criminal act. It is my position that the mere fact that we cannot say with certainty that a particular person was or was not involved in a crime does not automatically grant to that witness the fifth amendment privilege."

Shapiro, however, argued that Conn was unfairly trying to force Evans to testify. "Mr. Evans is totally uninvolved in this case, and he wants to testify and he wants to clarify it," Shapiro said. "But I will not allow him to testify when I don't know what his official legal status is by the people." He added that dragging Evans into court was a publicity stunt on the part of the district attorney's office.

"The unfortunate reality is that innocent people are sometimes charged with crimes," he said. "And the testimony that is given in good faith and honestly may be interpreted by prosecutors in a different vein, especially prosecutors who are most eager to couch a case in terms that have wide appeal in both the public media, in the press and in television. And that's exactly what has happened in this case."

Shapiro went on to label as "an outright lie" the comments made by Bill Mentzer, as quoted by Bill Rider, that Laney Jacobs and Bob Evans ordered the murder of Roy Radin.

In response, Conn suggested that Evans himself was playing a game. On the one hand, Conn argued, Evans said he knew nothing about the murder of Roy Radin; on the other hand, however, he would not testify because it might incriminate him.

After several hours of hearings, in two courtrooms, Evans was permitted to exercise his privilege not to testify at the hearing. He walked out of the courtroom and through a phalanx of reporters and camera crews, and was soon out of the building.

In a number of newspaper articles in the *Los Angeles Herald-Examiner* and the *L.A. Times*, Evans was portrayed as a man who had achieved stardom as a producer. Now, the stories suggested, he was down-and-out, with only a small number of friends willing to give him work in movies.

The articles said Evans was working as a producer on *The Two Jakes*, a sequel to *Chinatown*, which Jack Nicholson was in the process of directing. The movie was to have been one of the films Evans would produce with Radin.

For two and a half months, the prosecutors, David Conn and Sally Thomas, brought a number of witnesses before the court to explain the facts surrounding Radin's murder. One witness was Jonathan Lawson, back from Spain, where he had fled after Radin's body was discovered. At the time of his court appearance, Lawson was living secretly in an American city.

No one knew more about Radin's final days than Lawson. He was privy to all the negotiations with Evans and Laney; he had attended most of the meetings to discuss *The Cotton Club*. As he prepared to testify, Lawson was frightened. He said his life had been ruined by the murder.

Lawson testified about Radin's cocaine habit, saying his boss "used coke the way some people used chocolate." He also spoke about the collapse of Roy Radin Enterprises and about Radin's mercurial temper and his relationship with entertainers such as the comedian Joey Bishop, which had produced an ugly fight in Atlantic City.

Upon hearing the testimony, Shohat suggested that both De Vinko and Bishop had reasons to kill Radin. Later, he added to the list of possible killers Melonie Haller, the actress who had accused Radin of rape and assault.

One day, Lawson appeared drunk in court and was excused. When his testimony was complete, he left Los Angeles and returned to his hiding place.

* * *

After Radin's murder, Demond Wilson found God. When he testified, he explained that he was a fundamentalist preacher.

Shohat labeled him a liar and a cocaine addict. He said Wilson had so badly bungled his bodyguard duties on the night of May 13 that his actions suggested he may have been involved in the murder.

Speaking of Radin, Wilson said, "One of the reasons we came together is because we both had heart. . . . I used to say he had more heart than any white man I had ever seen in my life."

As for Radin's dream of becoming a movie producer, Wilson said, "His desire was to be a producer, and it was his dream always. It was what we talked about all the time."

Carl Plzak testified under a grant of immunity. He said his actions on the night of the murder, when he and Roger Korban were to kidnap Lawson and hold him for Mentzer, were the result of fear more than of criminal intent.

Shohat portrayed him as a steroid junkie whose testimony could not be trusted.

Robert Deremer also testified under a grant of immunity. Mostly, he was called to speak about his relationships with Lowe, Marti, and Mentzer. He knew nothing about the Radin murder.

Perhaps the oddest testimony at the hearing came from Mike Pascal, the Hollywood private detective whom Laney had hired in the aftermath of the cocaine theft from her house. He testified to helping her track people down but said he had no idea she was a drug dealer. Nor had he known about the Radin murder, he said.

At one point during his testimony, he claimed that he was being pursued by the KGB.

Tally Rogers did not testify. The drug courier whose theft of the cocaine had set off a chain reaction that had ended with Radin's execution was serving out his prison term in Louisiana on the sexual molestation charges.

In a brief personal interview, he said he regretted what had happened to Radin. Life in prison was hell, he said.

"They are frying my brain with microwaves," he complained. "It's some kind of government plot, and I don't understand it."

Bill Rider, the prosecution's most important witness, testified for several days. He was living under a new identity in an undisclosed location. Prior to his taking the stand, the courtroom was cleared for a bomb search.

In his remarks in and out of the courtroom, Shohat portrayed Laney Greenberger as a woman who had made serious mistakes but was not a murderer. Then Shohat revealed the man he called Radin's real murderer: Milan Bellechasses.

Awaiting trial in Florida on drug conspiracy charges, Bellechasses was said to deeply resent his former girlfriend's attempts to blame him. But he said he would not testify.

As for Laney's involvement with Radin on the night he was murdered, Shohat said events became "out of hand" after she got out of the limousine on Sunset Boulevard and Mentzer and Marti got in.

He also suggested that Radin had made so

many enemies during his brief life that any one of them could have had a motive to kill him.

In his remarks, Conn argued that there was substantial evidence to hold Laney and her codefendants for trial. And he maintained that the "special circumstances" of the murder required the death penalty.

Conn asserted that all of Laney's actions indicated her belief that upon Radin's murder, she could continue her relationship with Bob Evans.

Referring to the testimony of Jose Alagria, the Puerto Rican banker whom Radin had brought in to raise $35 million to make three movies, Conn said, "He acknowledges that Mr. Evans was willing to give [Laney] some share of the deal, something that Mr. Radin was not willing to do. This goes right to the heart of the dispute that Mr. Radin had with her.

"Because if Mr. Evans was willing to give her a greater share of the deal . . . then it would become apparent that if Mr. Radin was no longer a member of that deal, then perhaps she could continue in business with Mr. Evans and get exactly what she wanted. . . . I would submit that there was reason to believe that if Mr. Radin were to be killed, the deal could go through."

Describing the motive for Radin's death, Conn said there appeared to be two reasons that the murder took place.

"One reason is as a result of *The Cotton Club* dispute. It is the theory of the prosecution that Mr. Radin was an obstacle to the further negotiations concerning *The Cotton Club*. . . .

"The other apparent motive for the killing . . . was in connection with the drug dispute. It is clear that she, Miss [*sic*] Greenberger, accused

Mr. Radin of being involved in the drug rip-off
which was actually committed by Tally Rogers.
She suspected that because of Mr. Radin's relationship to Tally Rogers that he was in some
sense involved in that, or could assist her in obtaining the drugs or recovering the drugs and
was unwilling to do so, and that she held him
responsible."

During the hearing, Marti was charged with another murder for hire in Los Angeles. Also during
the hearing, Mentzer and his cousin Thomas
Markel, the Los Angeles County sheriff's deputy,
were arrested for the armed robbery of Frank
Rubino. Markel was held pending extradition to
Florida.

On July 12, Judge McKay ruled that the evidence
presented at the hearing was sufficient, and she
ordered Greenberger, Mentzer, and Marti held
without bail for trial. In a victory for the prosecution, she also kept the death penalty provision as
part of the case.

Throughout the fall of 1989, there were additional hearings, pertaining to Shohat's requests
that his client be tried alone, and not with Mentzer, Marti, and Lowe, who had finally been
brought back to Los Angeles from Maryland. His
requests were denied, as was his application that
Laney be released on bail so that she could spend
Christmas with Dax.

When it became clear that she would not be
allowed to post bail, Laney wept in the courtroom.

*   *   *

In Okeechobee, the police investigation into the murder of Larry Greenberger had reached an impasse.

The anguish of Jerry and Dahlis Greenberger was only increased by their having no access whatsoever to their son's adopted child. "We would love to see him, or at least speak with him," Dahlis Greenberger said. "We have been shut out of his life completely."

Who killed Larry Greenberger?

In a letter to Jeanne Baker, Laney suggested that the killer was a dealer who had also worked with Carlos Lehder and who was arrested in Florida a few days after Greenberger's death. She did not explain how he could have gotten into the house, or how he could have rigged the murder to look like a suicide without Laney seeing him, or even why she no longer believed the death had been a suicide.

She wrote that she prayed for Greenberger's soul every day and yearned to visit his grave.

Ernst Muller, the assistant United States Attorney who prosecuted Lehder, was so interested in Greenberger's life that he visited the Okeechobee farmhouse after his death. Muller's investigation into Americans who dealt with Lehder, a case called "Son of Lehder," was completed several months after the murder, with dozens of indictments. Greenberger would have been among those indicted.

Muller said he was convinced that Greenberger had been murdered. "From what I learned, it would have been impossible to have been a suicide," he said.

Muller called Laney's statement that another dealer killed Greenberger "bullshit."

"He had no quarrel with Larry," Muller said of the dealer.

And Muller postulated a new theory—that Greenberger might have wanted to have Laney killed. Perhaps, he said, the couple that "Vincent De Angelo" told Bill Mentzer he wanted killed were Laney and Squillante.

Throughout the summer and fall of 1989, there were legal fights over Greenberger's estate. His will said he was worth approximately $3.5 million, but nearly everyone who knew Greenberger believed there were substantial funds hidden. It was doubtful any of these funds could be recovered, however.

In the fall of 1989, Janis Greenberger filed a civil lawsuit against Laney, accusing her of involvement in her brother's murder. The suit, written by Okeechobee attorney Lester Jennings, followed a number of court moves designed to keep Laney from collecting any of Greenberger's assets.

Jennings, a mild-mannered and shrewd attorney with a deep Southern drawl, said the Greenbergers would fight for as long as it took to keep Laney from profiting from Larry Greenberger's death.

Meanwhile, Ed Bolter, in whose business, Eagle Outdoor Advertising, in Delray Beach, Larry Greenberger had invested $250,000, could not collect on an insurance policy on Greenberger's life because of the circumstances of his death.

Bolter refused to speak about his years with Laney. In a letter, Bolter conceded that he had made mistakes in the past, but he would not elaborate. No charges have been brought against him.

As for Greenberger's death, Bolter said he was

horrified and did not believe all the talk that his business partner had once been a drug smuggler.

A few years after returning from California with Laney and Dax, Myriam Plaza married. In the fall of 1989, she was divorced and living alone in an apartment in Miami.

Myriam, who was with the Greenbergers the weekend before Larry Greenberger's murder, said she grieves for him. Mostly, she said, she grieves for Dax.

"Dax was like my son. I was with him from his birth. I hope he will be all right, I really do."

As for Laney, Myriam said she wanted to believe only good things about her.

"Since Laney was little, she wanted a better life," Myriam said. "She wanted no bills and a nice life. She always put her heart into everything. She's a lady with taste and was born with it. Really, she lived in a dream."

Early on a warm Christmas morning in 1989, Dahlis and Jerry Greenberger drove to their son's gravesite north of Okeechobee. As the sun rose, they stood over his grave, wondering out loud how his life could have ended the way it did.

All the talk and all the newspaper stories about their son's secret life in cocaine had shocked them. They did not believe it, did not want to believe it. They had loved him and they missed him, which was all that mattered on Christmas morning.

When they turned to walk back to their car, they saw Myriam approaching the grave. She had driven nearly three hours from Miami to come here and say a silent prayer.

When they returned to the grave to speak with

her, she looked up and smiled. "I hope you don't mind me coming here," she said.

They said they did not mind.

"Oh, God," Myriam said, choking back tears. "I hope Laney doesn't have to die in California."

"Have you spoken to her recently?" Mrs. Greenberger asked.

Myriam said she had not.

"Do you speak with Dax?" she asked.

Very rarely, Myriam said.

"Laney told Dax that Larry died during an operation," Myriam said in her heavy Spanish accent.

"That's her explanation?" Jerry Greenberger asked. "My Lord, she could actually tell that boy something like that?"

"Laney signed over legal guardianship of Dax to Terry," Myriam added. "Terry's his daddy now."

The Greenbergers were incredulous. They started to walk back to their car. Myriam remained behind.

"I just want to stay a few minutes," Myriam said. "I want to remember things the way they used to be."

POSTSCRIPT
TO THE
PAPERBACK
EDITION

Q: Mrs. Greenberger, you heard [a witness] tell us about a time when you delivered some cocaine to him with Dax in the car.

A: Yes.

Q: Did you do that?

A: Yes, I did.

Q: Why?

A: I don't know—I guess we both needed money . . .

Q: When did you first become involved in selling cocaine?

A: In 1979.

Q: How old were you then?

A: About thirty-two.

Q: How did you first become involved in selling cocaine?

A: Some people just asked me to do something and I did it and made a lot of money and it went from there . . .

Q: Why did you stay in that business from 1979?

A: It's kind of like being on a roller coaster that's going and you can't get off.

The journey is over now. This is as far as I
can go.
　　　　—Athol Fugard, *The Road to Mecca*

September, 1990.

After nearly two years of intense publicity, the
search for the truth—who killed Roy Radin, and
why—began on a warm fall morning in Los Angeles County Superior Court. Laney Greenberger,
Alex Marti, Bill Mentzer and Robert Lowe were
brought to a holding cell in handcuffs, then escorted into a packed courtroom. Laney smiled at
several people in the front row, then sat down
next to her attorneys.

Two months later, a jury was empaneled, and
in November, witnesses under the direction of
the brilliant prosecutor, David Conn, began taking the stand.

Meanwhile, Laney's friends in Miami were
watching to see what would happen to her. The
woman they had known—cocky, confident, and
self-assured—sat in the courtroom, listening
carefully, sometimes taking notes, whispering to
her attorneys. Those who observed her thought
she exuded an unnatural confidence, as if the
case unfolding before her was not really about

her at all, but about someone from a regretful past, someone now dead and buried.

Her friends watched news programs about the trial, catching glimpses of a woman who now looked older—her hair, which had once been so blond, earning her the nickname "La Rubia"— had gone gray. To them, she looked more like a grandmother.

Was this the cocaine broker who dealt so expertly with the Cubans? Was this the woman who married so many men, who knew so many Miami drug dealers, who lived the life of a cocaine princess, whose last husband, Larry Greenberger, was murdered in their Okeechobee farmhouse?

In Okeechobee, Larry Greenberger's family tried to stay in touch with events unfolding in Los Angeles. They were in a court fight of their own with their son's former wife, over the dividing up of his large estate. Moreover, they wanted visitation rights with Dax, whom their son had legally adopted. Laney and her attorneys blocked any attempt by the Greenberger family even to speak to Dax, who was living in western Pennsylvania with Terry Squillante.

And worse to the Greenbergers was the impasse in the murder investigation by Okeechobee authorities. The case seemed dead, never to be resolved.

Watching the trial proceedings from afar was Jonathan Lawson, still haunted by his friend's murder.

"Maybe someday I'll forget about everything that happened to Roy and me," he said. "Maybe, maybe not. I keep replaying the night of May 13. I told Roy not to go out that night. Had Roy listened, he would be alive today. But he wouldn't let go of the dream, the dream of being a movie producer. That was his downfall—he wouldn't let go of the dream."

April 24, 1991.

On a clear, dry Los Angeles morning, Laney Greenberger was called to the stand by one of her attorneys, Marcia Morrissey, to testify in her own defense. Her life had been a secret she could not reveal, and now, as she walked to the stand, she knew she had to let go.

After several nervous moments, she slowly began answering questions, reluctantly letting go of the pieces of her life story.

"Where were you living in May of 1982?"

"I was living on 125th Avenue in Miami . . ."

"Now, in May of 1982, Mrs. Greenberger, was there anything important that happened in your life?"

"Yes, my son Dax was born."

"Who is Dax' father?"

"Joe Amer."

She described her short marriage to Amer, their breakup, and her living with Myriam Arias, the loyal nanny.

"Mrs. Greenberger, back in May of 1982, when Dax was born, how were you supporting yourself?"

"I was selling cocaine."

"And could you explain what you mean when you say that you were selling cocaine?"

"I was actually brokering cocaine."

"What does a person who brokers cocaine do?"

"You get cocaine from one person and give it to another. You're like a middle person, a broker."

Her voice rising and falling, she spoke of meeting the mercurial Cuban drug baron, Milan

Bellechasses.* In the summer of that year, two
months after the birth of Dax, Milan and Laney
began brokering large cocaine deals. Together,
they bought an existing business from another
broker who had customers in California. The
purchase price was $300,000, which Laney and
Milan split fifty-fifty.

She detailed her sale of cocaine to Marc Fogel,
the Beverly Hills car dealer, his subsequent arrest by Los Angeles narcotics detectives, and her
decision to move to the cocaine capital of the
West Coast, Los Angeles. There, she testified, she
became the West Coast arm of Milan's growing
empire, an empire which began in Colombia,
where processed cocaine was prepared for boat
and airplane transit to south Florida. It would be
sent to Los Angeles from Miami in the trunk of a
car driven by Tally Rogers.

Laney was asked about her relationship with
Milan. "We had been friends and we just started
going out and became lovers . . . several months
after Dax was born. He was very good with Dax
and, of course, that made me happy."

"What was your relationship with Milan Bellechasses at the time you moved to California?"

"We were planning to be married."

In Los Angeles, Laney, Dax and Myriam moved
into a rental home; then, in the fall, she bought
the house on the cul de sac in Sherman Oaks. A
day or two before Thanksgiving, they moved in.

The following spring, she testified, after a
blissful six months in Los Angeles, Rogers stole
eleven kilos of cocaine from the vault in Laney's

---

* Bellechasses was convicted in July 1990 in Florida for conspiracy to import thirty kilos of cocaine into Florida. He has
appealed that conviction.

garage. Now, she said in her hushed voice, she began to fear the very man who had helped make her rich—Bellechasses.

What did Milan tell you after the rip-off? she was asked.

"He could have the Colombians sitting in my house," she testified.

In her testimony, Laney painted a dark portrait of Roy Radin, describing him as a ruthless bully bent on making "The Cotton Club" at all costs. He was a cokehead with a foul temper, a man used to pushing people around to get his way. She said she suspected Radin had mob ties back in New York, which frightened her. And she spoke at some length about her relationship with the handsome movie mogul, Robert Evans, with whom she became lovers not long after their first meeting, and who shared in her strong desire to be a full partner in the movie.

She insisted that Radin had promised her an equal share of the movie, and later, after the cocaine theft, that he had backed out of that deal and refused to share anything with her. She felt betrayed by Radin, but on the evening of May 13, 1983, the night she met him at his apartment at the Regency Hotel, events were out of her control.

"Did you talk to Mr. Radin at the hotel on the evening of May 13?"

". . . We talked about wanting . . . both of our desire to settle our differences over the Cotton Club and move things along. And also I told him that because of the theft of drugs and the money from my house . . . that I was under a lot of pressure from Mr. Bellechasses, that I had men who were with me all the time, that I was not in

control of anything. That I was very afraid and
not in control of anything . . ."

"When you left the hotel, did you leave with
Mr. Radin?"

"Yes, I did . . ."

"On the evening of May 13, did you have any
idea that your limousine was being followed by
anyone?"

"No . . . We pulled out of the Regency and
turned on Fairfax and went to Sunset. Mr. Radin
and I were talking about the movie, about the
company, about the negotiations with Mr. Evans.
He was in a very . . . belligerent mood. He was
telling me that he was going—that I should get
on his side, that he was going to take over the
company and Mr. Evans . . ."

"What else happened in the limousine?"

"When we were on Sunset a little ways, there
had been a bucket of champagne and a bucket of
ice in the limo that I had put there. And Mr. Radin was talking and he was moving around. He
was very animated. And he kicked over the
bucket of champagne and the ice and everything . . .

"I was in the process of leaning over trying to
pick up the champagne, the ice, and all of a sudden the limousine turned up a side street very
quickly . . . At the same time, almost simultane-
ously, when it turned the two back doors
opened."

"Did you see anybody on the right side of the
car when the door opened?"

"I saw Mr. Mentzer."

Laney testified that Mentzer ordered her into
another car, which she drove to her apartment in
Beverly Hills. There, she met Carl Plzak,
Mentzer's and Marti's friend, who was patiently

waiting for Lawson to show up. He was surprised to see Laney instead. For the next several hours, she and Plzak drove around suburban Los Angeles, trying to raise Mentzer on a walkie-talkie and through his answering service.

"I was trying to find out what was going on," she testified.

Later that evening, Laney drove to her friend Sol Besharat's apartment, and from there called Evans in New York, where it was nearly three-thirty in the morning.

"Why did you call Mr. Evans?"

". . . He knew I was going to meet with Roy Radin to talk about the Cotton Club and I had told him I would call him and let him know if everything had been ironed out . . . I told him what Mr. Radin had said—about taking Mr. Evans to the cleaners and taking over Paramount . . . And I told him that we had argued."

Early on the morning of Saturday, May 14, Laney arrived at Mentzer's apartment. There, Mentzer informed Laney that Radin had been armed in the limousine.

"Tell us to the best of your recollection exactly what Mr. Mentzer told you . . ."

"Just that Mr. Radin had been very angry, very upset. He had a gun and that he was shot. He was killed."

For the next few days on the stand, Laney spun a tale of deceit and mistrust, and of her own fear that Bellechasses would harm her because she had not repaid the value of the stolen cocaine. One of the reasons she was so insistent on being included in "The Cotton Club," she testified, was that she hoped to make enough money to pay back Bellechasses.

Then, she revealed that, a few days after the

murder, she and Mentzer flew to New York to meet Evans.

"Why did you meet with Mr. Evans?"

"I felt I should talk to him and tell him what had happened."

"How did he react?"

"Very upset . . ."

"Mrs. Greenberger, after Mr. Radin died was there anything that you did with respect to the project to finance the film?"

"No, nothing else."

Frightened of Radin's mob ties, Laney testified, she returned to Miami. After her return, she and Mentzer became lovers, and, to pay back Bellechasses for the stolen coke, she began making large payments to him.

From a hideout in the Florida Keys, Laney and Mentzer learned that Radin's body had been found in the remote canyon north of Los Angeles. After the discovery of Radin's fetid, dynamited remains, she testified, Bellechasses ordered Laney out of the country. Mentzer drove Laney, Dax and Miriam to the Miami airport, where they boarded a flight bound for Puerto Vallarta, Mexico. A driver met them in the seaside resort and drove them to a rented villa forty miles out of town on a dirt road.

After a three-week stay, a bored Laney asked a driver to take them to the airport. They flew to Tijuana, where Mentzer met them and drove them to Palm Springs. It was now the middle of July, two months after the murder, and, according to Laney's account, she was terrified that Bellechasses still might do her harm. Too nervous to stay in one place, she flew to Maui, then to Las Vegas, and, eventually, back to Miami.

* * *

After her extraordinary appearance on the stand, answering questions from her attorney, Laney's defense could be summed up this way:

(1) She did not kill Radin. Mentzer and Bellechasses did for reasons entirely connected to the drug theft. She wanted an equity interest in "The Cotton Club" for her own reasons. She went out to dinner with Radin on the night of May 13, 1983, hoping to work out their "Cotton Club" differences.

(2) She was told right after the murder that he had, in fact, been killed, but she did not tell police because she did not want them to discover her lucrative drug-dealing business.

(3) Evans knew nothing about a plot to kill his movie partner. He did, however, know of the drug rip-off—and thus that Laney was a large cocaine broker—and he did know Radin had been killed shortly after the fact. He also met Bellechasses. Evans supported Laney in her demands to be a partner in the movie; further, Evans offered her a job in a new production company.

(4) She was deathly afraid for her life and the life of her young son. She was so afraid that she behaved like a puppet, following every order, every whim, of Bellechasses, the puppet-master, and Mentzer, his surrogate.

(5) Even though she managed a thirty-kilo-a-year cocaine business, she was weak and easily manipulated by strong, determined men.

The other defense lawyers reacted quickly to Laney's story. Her argument that she was a mere puppet and not capable of violence herself sparked demands that the jury hear the incredible details of Larry Greenberger's murder, and Laney's preposterous story to Okeechobee police that he had killed himself.

Lowe's attorney, Mark Kaiserman, told the judge in a sidebar conference that he wanted the opportunity to show that Laney "was more than a passive observer" during the events surrounding Radin's death. What better way to do it than to tell the jury what had happened to her last husband?

"We would also like . . . to show the character of Mrs. Greenberger and we would request permission to try to show that she had an involvement in the death of Larry Greenberger . . .

"They [the defense] have attempted to portray her somewhat as a defenseless woman . . . and we feel we can show she had an active role in a crime involving the death of her husband. That would go to show that the defense that has been presented by Mrs. Greenberger is not to be believed."

Then Mentzer's lawyer, Charles Cervantes, dropped this bombshell to the judge.

"The basis for the cross-examination would be that we believe that prior to Mr. Greenberger's death, Laney Greenberger contacted Mr. Mentzer, suggested that she was having difficulties with her husband, and would ask Mr. Mentzer's assistance in essentially getting rid of him. Mr. Mentzer tried to avoid the subject, but Mrs. Greenberger persisted and wanted him out of the way."

Further, Cervantes went on, "after the death of Mr. Greenberger, that Mr. Mentzer was in Florida at the time of the funeral and that he had a conversation with Mrs. Greenberger and another individual who was identified to him as Terry Squillante . . . That a conversation was had at that point which led Mr. Mentzer to believe that Mr. Squillante and Mrs. Greenberger were in-

volved or responsible for the death of Mr. Greenberger."*

When his turn came, Conn attacked Laney in a
cross-examination that made her lawyers' decision to put her on the stand appear rather foolish.
Conn pressed her hard on her self-proclaimed
fear of Bellechasses.

"When did you become frightened of Milan?"

"When he told me the Colombians could be sitting at my house."

"Did you ever consider whether Milan might
tend to think it wiser for him to just let you pay
off the cocaine rather than cause some act of violence against you or your son?"

"Yes . . . He could try to keep me under his
thumb or he could just get rid of me and tell the
Colombians and that would be that. With the
Colombians, that would forgive the debt . . ."

"Did you feel that Milan could make good that
loss if he wanted to?"

"Yes."

"And did you ever ask him to make good that
loss?"

"No . . ."

"Did you ever say to him, Milan, the dope belonged to both of us and it is the responsibility of
both of us to make good for the loss?"

". . . I did ask him that."

"And how did he respond?"

"That it was in my hands . . ."

Then Conn pressed her if she had the funds to
repay part or most of the loss to Bellechasses. She
went step-by-step through her funds at the time
—$200,000 in cash, $100,000 in a trust account in

---

* As of July 1991, Florida authorities had made no arrest in
the Greenberger death.

Miami, plus property. "I didn't think I could afford to give him all the money I had," she testified.

In other words, Conn pointed out, she had the money to repay Bellechasses.

"Wasn't it worth the three hundred thousand dollars to protect your son?"

"Mr. Conn, I gave him eighty thousand dollars. A few days later, I gave him thirty thousand dollars. After that, I gave him fifty thousand dollars . . . If you gave it to him all at once he would have wanted more."

"My question to you, Mrs. Greenberger, is was it worth three hundred thousand dollars to save the life of your son?"

"I would have given my life for my son's life, Mr. Conn."

Later, Conn asked Laney about her and Evans' trip to Miami to see Bellechasses.

"Now the purpose, as I understand it, for you introducing Mr. Evans to Mr. Bellechasses was to assure him that you were in fact going to be receiving money in this film production deal and you could pay him off, is that correct?"

"Yes, to try and get him to give me time."

"Did you think you would be making so much money that you would be able to make a substantial dent in a drug rip-off involving hundreds of thousands of dollars?"

"I thought I would make enough money to support myself . . . and Mr. Bellechasses could have all the money from the drugs that he sold instead of giving me any of it."

In retelling the story of how Radin was trapped in the limousine, Laney was asked why she had jumped out.

"Because that's what I was told to do . . ." As if

she knew her answer did not make sense, she added, "Mr. Conn, I don't know why I did anything, but I did it."

"Now, did you believe at some point that Mr. Radin was in danger?"

"Just a possibility."

"Did you think that Mr. Radin had gone with them intentionally?"

"No."

"So, you knew he had been kidnapped at that point, is that correct?"

"I didn't think about it being kidnapped, but I knew he was in their company."

"You knew he had been taken somewhere against his will, is that correct?"

"Yes."

Conn took her through the events after May 13, after the point when she knew for certain that Radin had indeed been murdered, when she made calls to Lawson to tell him that Radin had gotten out of the limousine on his own and walked off into the night.

You lied, Conn told her.

Yes, she answered.

"You knew he had been killed."

"Yes."

On July 10, 1991, Superior Court Judge Curtis B. Rappe gave the jury his instructions, and sent them to deliberate. Nine months had passed since the trial had begun, and after all the testimony, Laney remained confident that she would be freed.

Her principal attorney, Edward Shohat, was confident, too.

"I believe we have answered the question of

who did the crime . . . I fully believe in this case. I will believe to my grave, if Laney goes to death row, she will have been wrongly sent there. She did not kill Roy Radin.

"I've come to know Laney as a woman with a street sense. She has a head on her shoulders. She was not charged with being a drug dealer. She was not charged with being a bad mother.

"She's named names. There is no turning back. She's burned every bridge. She goes forward from now on out."

The verdict was delivered to a packed and hushed courtroom on the morning of July 22. The jury had deliberated for a total of less than five days. Shohat knew the swiftness of the verdict was a horrible sign for his client, and he looked stunned and drained as he sat at the attorney's table. Next to him sat Laney Greenberger, emotionless, her back to the audience.

Then the verdicts were read.

Bill Mentzer and Alex Marti, the two shooters—first-degree murder and kidnapping with intent to murder. First-degree murder is a death penalty offense in California.

Robert Lowe, the portly limousine driver on the night of May 13, 1983—second-degree murder and kidnapping with intent to murder.

Laney Greenberger, the cocaine queen who longed for Hollywood respectability—second-degree murder and kidnapping with intent to murder. Hers and Lowe's conviction carried with it a sentence of life in prison without any possibility of parole. Her attempts to lay the murder on Bellechasses failed; he has never been charged with the crime.

All four immediately filed appeals.

The week before, Laney had told a bailiff she was going home. As she was taken from the courtroom, she knew the journey was over; this was as far as she could go.

HERE IS AN EXCERPT FROM *UNANSWERED CRIES* BY THOMAS FRENCH—A TRUE CRIME SHOCKER COMING IN MARCH FROM ST. MARTIN'S PAPERBACKS:

David Mackey was still at the conference in Rhode Island, and when he finished with the day's work he called Karen at home. There was no answer. He called again later, several times. Still no answer.

By midnight David was growing worried, so he called Anita Kilpatrick, Karen's roommate from the apartment on the beach. Anita said she hadn't seen Karen and suggested that maybe she'd gone to see her sister Kim, who lived in Dunedin, about twenty miles northwest of St. Petersburg. David called Kim's house, but Karen wasn't there, either.

The next morning—Thursday—David picked up the phone in his hotel room and tried again to reach Karen at the house. He called early, around 7:30, so he wouldn't miss her before she left for work. No answer. He tried again. No answer. Next he called Datacom. But Karen's boss said no one had seen or heard from her, either that day or the day before. He did not know where she was.

David called Anita Kilpatrick again. Both he and Anita were upset now. Clearly, something was wrong. Karen was not the type to skip work, especially a new job.

Anita started checking with police departments and hospitals to find out if there'd been an accident. But no one seemed to know anything about a Karen Gregory. Anita waited for David to call back. She was sitting on her couch when suddenly these pictures entered her mind. She saw Karen struggling with a man, shoving and fighting with a man who was taller than Karen. Then she saw Karen lying on the floor. Anita pushed the pictures out of her mind and told herself she was dreaming. She tried to read the paper but couldn't concentrate. She kept reading the same sentence over and over. She got up from the couch and started pacing.

Meanwhile, David was calling Amy Bressler, a neighbor who lived just up the street from his house. He asked Bressler to look out her living room window and see if Karen's Rabbit was parked in the driveway. Bressler looked over. Yes, she told him. Karen's car was there, along with David's.

Now David was sure something was wrong. He asked Bressler to go over and check on the house, saying he would stay on the line until she came back.

Bressler put down the phone. She walked over to the house and knocked on the nearest door, a side door. No answer. She walked around to the front door. It was closed, but she noticed that several of the jalousie window panes had been broken and that glass was scattered along the walkway. She knocked on the door. No answer. She walked around toward the back and saw that a bedroom window was open, the curtains moving in the breeze. She called out.

"Karen?"

No answer. With the curtains drawn, Bressler could not see inside the bedroom. But there was a slit, four or five inches wide, in the screen of the window—it had been there as long as David had owned the house—and so she put her hand through the opening and pushed back the curtains. An unmade bed was directly in front of her. She looked to the right, toward the bedroom door leading into the hallway, and saw a woman lying on the floor. The angle allowed her to see only the lower half of the body, but it was surrounded by blood.

"Karen?"

Bressler ran back to her house, where David was still waiting on the other end of the line. She was crying now. She was hysterical. She said she had to get the police.

"Something really horrible has happened," she told him. "I don't know what it is."

At 8:39 A.M., slightly more than thirty-one hours after the neighbors had heard the scream, Bressler called the Gulfport Police Department. Unsure whether the woman she'd seen on the floor was alive or dead, she reported what officially was recorded as a "nonresponsive person."

She was waiting in the street a few minutes later when Officer Cheryl Falkenstein drove up in a cruiser. Falkenstein got out,

alked past the broken glass on the sidewalk, and tried the
ront jalousie door. It was locked. She walked around the house
o the back bedroom window, pushed aside the curtains, and
aw the woman on the floor.

"Can you hear me?" the officer said. "Are you OK?"

No answer. By now a team of paramedics had arrived and
oined Falkenstein at the side of the house. They needed to get
nside quickly—for all they knew, the woman might still be
alive—yet the doors to the house were locked. So they decided
someone would have to go through the window. They removed
the screen and Falkenstein crawled inside head-first. She
walked toward the woman, saw that she was not breathing,
then quickly walked past her toward the front porch, where she
unlocked and opened the jalousie door for the others.

Falkenstein, a twenty-one-year-old rookie, was badly shaken.
She had been with the police department for only five months,
and in that time she'd never seen anything like what she was
seeing now.

All of the lights in the house were off. Inside the back bedroom, the one into which Falkenstein had crawled, a fan was
sitting on the floor, still blowing. On top of the bed, stained
with blood, was a blue flowered Hawaiian shirt. Next to the bed
were the faded green shorts Karen had worn to Neverne Cov-
ington's house two nights before. Karen's tennis shoes were
there too, with the laces still tied. Not far from the shoes was a
black umbrella and a stack of magazines. On top of the magazines was a phone, and as Falkenstein and the others looked
around, the phone began to ring. It kept ringing, even as the
minutes passed and no one answered. It would stop for a second and then start again. It just kept going.

A few feet away, on the carpet just past the bedroom door,
lay Karen. In the darkness of the hall, the paramedics had to
use their pen lights to see her. Even so, it was obvious that
there was no need to check her pulse. She was on her left side,
almost in a fetal position, with her face turned toward the wall.
She was still wearing the jewelry she'd had on that night at
Neverne's, and the same white T-shirt, too, but it had been
pulled up to just below her breasts. A black teddy was bunched
around her waist. She wore no other clothing.

It was difficult, there in the hall, to be sure exactly what had
happened to her. Her neck and head were covered with dried

blood, covered with so much of it that it was impossible to see the exact nature and number of all of her wounds. But it was clear that she had been stabbed repeatedly. On her lower back and one of her legs, marked in blood, were several handprints, placed at such an angle that they could not have been made by Karen. Scattered around her along the stretch of hallway carpet was a series of bloody bare footprints. Not far away, on the tile floor of the bathroom, was another bloody footprint—a partial one, about the size of a silver dollar.

Blood had been left all through the house. There was some on the sill and curtains of the window where Officer Falkenstein had crawled inside. There was more on the bed. Outside the bedroom, across the walls and floor of the hallway where Karen's body was still lying, there were large stains and smears. Out on the front porch, three drops had dried on the floor. On the door that led from the porch to the rest of the house—the door on which the visitor had knocked the evening before— there were smears below the doorknob. In the window panes of the front jalousie door there was a hole, and around the hole were some hairs that were the same shade of brown as Karen's. The broken glass from the door was strewn along the front walkway, all the way to the curb and out into the street. In the driveway, on the windshield of David Mackey's car, the visitor's note was waiting to be read.

Inside the house the phone was still ringing.

It was David, calling from his hotel room. He'd been pacing, staring at the walls, trying to imagine what could have happened. He'd waited several minutes, waited as long as his patience would let him, then repeatedly dialed the number at his house, letting it ring and ring until finally someone answered. It was a woman whose voice David did not recognize. An Officer Falkenstein.

"Is Karen there?"

"Yes."

"What's happened?"

The officer hesitated a moment.

"She's dead, sir."

UNANSWERED CRIES—COMING IN MARCH FROM ST. MARTIN'S PAPERBACKS